CINEMA AND CULTURAL MODERNITY

ISSUES in CULTURAL and MEDIA STUDIES

Series editor: Stuart Allan

Published titles

News Culture
Stuart Allan

Television, Globalization and Cultural Identities
Chris Barker

Cinema and Cultural Modernity
Gill Branston

Ethnic Minorities and the Media
Edited by Simon Cottle

Modernity and Postmodern Culture
Jim McGuigan

Sport, Culture and the Media
David Rowe

CINEMA AND CULTURAL MODERNITY

Gill Branston

OPEN UNIVERSITY PRESS
Buckingham · Philadelphia

Open University Press
Celtic Court
22 Ballmoor
Buckingham
MK18 1XW

email: enquiries@openup.co.uk
world wide web: www.openup.co.uk

and
325 Chestnut Street
Philadelphia, PA 19106, USA

First Published 2000

A catalogue record of this book is available from the British Library

ISBN 0 335 20076 1 (pb)   0 335 20077 X (hb)

Library of Congress Cataloging-in-Publication Data available

Typeset by Type Study, Scarborough
Printed in Great Britain by Biddles Limited, Guildford and Kings Lynn

For Lucy and Lauren, my top stars

CONTENTS

SERIES EDITOR'S FOREWORD

In seeking to open up new possibilities for thinking about cinema, Gill Branston's *Cinema and Cultural Modernity* recasts a number of familiar assumptions underlying current debates within film studies. At issue, she maintains, is the need to understand cinema within the broader formation of cultural modernity, an objective best realized through the careful elucidation of its histories, institutions, representations and, not least, audiences across time, space and place. Such an approach is thereby defined as much by its resistance to the lure of more traditional modes of critique as it is by its interrogation of the shifting boundaries demarcating the limits of cinema today. This is an exciting book, one which makes a host of intriguing observations about the 'mutating forms' of cinema while, at the same time, throwing into sharp relief an original basis for their examination.

The Issues in Cultural and Media Studies series aims to facilitate a diverse range of critical investigations into pressing questions considered to be central to current thinking and research. In light of the remarkable speed at which the conceptual agendas of cultural and media studies are changing, the authors are committed to contributing to what is an ongoing process of re-evaluation and critique. Each of the books is intended to provide a lively, innovative and comprehensive introduction to a specific topical issue from a fresh perspective. The reader is offered a thorough grounding in the most salient debates indicative of the book's subject, as well as important insights into how new modes of enquiry may be established for future explorations. Taken as a whole, then, the series is designed to cover the core components of cultural and media studies courses in an imaginatively distinctive and engaging manner.

Stuart Allan

ACKNOWLEDGEMENTS

Thanks to Stuart Allan for commenting on the final draft, and for his patience and encouragement through the writing; to Lauren Branston and Lucy Branston for stimulating talk, around this and much else; to Rod Brookes and Rob Seago for support and discussions through the stages of writing; to Ros Fane and Viv Cracknell at Open University Press for helpfulness in searching the illustrations permissions; to Rob Galvin for help in trying to research the ecological connections of blockbusters; to Christine Gledhill, especially for letting me see draft chapters of *Reinventing Film Studies*; to Val Hill, David Lusted, Andy Medhurst, Roy Stafford, Gillian Swanson, Tana Wollen and Lola Young for giving good phone and email; to Tessa Perkins for letting me see a draft of her chapter 'Who (and what) is it for?'; to Justin Vaughan at Open University Press for encouragement and patience throughout; to Christine Firth and Jonathan Ingoldby for scrupulous copy editing; and finally to my students, past and present, for their indispensable ideas and comments, even, or especially, where these were not what I expected.

Note
Open University Press has made every effort to trace copyright holders and to obtain permission to publish illustrated material. Any omissions brought to our attention will be remedied in future editions.

INTRODUCTION

For some film is dead, and film study with it. Even if we limit the term to moving, audio-visual, non-serial fictions, its boundaries have spread so far – to include ads, music videos, digital and TV forms – as to make the study of 'film' seem anachronistic. The January 2000 merger of AOL with Time-Warner, and then EMI, is seen as emblematic of the fate of the now dimly visible names of the big US film studios. (The deal was even discussed as 'television' or 'entertainment' merging with 'information' and Internet forms.) Within such conglomerate global holdings, the major film studios seem now no more than anchors for cross-industry marketing ('synergy') of toys, cars, music, computer games, fashions, fast food and so on.

If films are defined as existing on celluloid, they are a threatened species. They now circulate in mutating forms: celluloid, video and digitality, and forms that are a mix of all three (*Toy Story 2* was made without a camera, and screened without conventional projectors). This means that another one of their early and abiding fascinations, their status as a kind of 'trace' off the real, whether that be in giving documentary evidence or the sheen of a star's skin, is undermined. Films now are not necessarily made with real actors and settings: the illusioneering capacities of digital technologies proudly display their capacities to outstrip all the previous efforts of cinematic special effects (FX) (see Romney 1997).

If films are defined as seen, in complete form, on large cinema screens, in a space both public and private, then what of the fact that this is no longer the space where most films are viewed, or that zapping and other forms of pleasurably incomplete viewing, within home screenings, are now common? In other words, through all of the above, films' specific-ness as film, which has been traditionally handled in Film Studies, largely through textual work, seems to have been swallowed up by commercial and technological developments in other parts of huge conglomerates.

Cinema is not dead

This book argues that far from being 'dead', film and cinematic imagery are, and have been, central to high consumer cultures of the visual, in all their globally unequal spread. It is key to the convergence of screens in the twenty-first century. This is despite the greater importance of TV, for the circulation of certain kinds of cultural imaginings; despite the absorption of film into headings such as 'entertainment'; and despite the emphasis of distinguished film economists on the relatively small scale of 'Hollywood' compared to the turnover of, say, Microsoft or General Electric. Cinema spearheads conglomerate ownership of cutting-edge media industries.

Just as cinema could be argued to be the first truly mass medium, so Film Studies was the prototype for moving image media study. A book of this length can focus on only a few of the relevant issues. I have assumed that cinema is not so much dead as mutating, and in any case was always best understood through study attempting to hold together of all its constituting processes, rather than through the textual exclusivity sometimes implied by 'film study'. Some distinguished recent books (such as Stam and Miller 2000) collect writing on film with that on TV almost without comment as to their institutional and historical differences. While the overlap is now hard to disentangle, I shall assume that we can still talk of a cinema composed of 'films' which are mostly fiction narratives, overwhelmingly deploying the continuity, narrative and genre systems first developed in studio Hollywood. I do not include discussion of advertisements or music videos, though they can well be seen as tiny films, and have functioned materially as such in the careers of some of the biggest names in contemporary Hollywood. Nor is there space to treat documentary, though related issues around realism are briefly discussed.

Modernity

The book's ambition is to draw on and relate together recent positions in both film study and political debate, and to argue for the value of understanding cinema through an emphasis on its place in the formation of cultural modernity more broadly. There is an emerging sense that 'modernity' offers much for the materialist and critical understanding of media. The boom 1980s discourses of **postmodernism** (or 'pomo' as it's often called) seem unable to provide such a historical grasp, whatever the attractions of, by turns, Frankfurt gloomy or consumer-power-chirpy puns and rhetoric.

Modernity is far from a simple concept or periodization (see Morley 1996). It poses almost as many problems of definition as the notoriously slippery terms postmodernism and postmodernity. I have settled for a periodization which traces it back, through continuities from the nineteenth century, to the social, economic and cultural transformations emerging ultimately from the late eighteenth century political revolutions in France and the United States, and the industrial revolutions occurring initially in Europe. It is also associated with the accompanying rationalist ambitions of those intellectual movements that were known together, in all their contradictions (see McGuigan 1999: ch. 2) as 'the Enlightenment'. Very broadly, such changes, soon embodied in the emerging mass media, looked to a democratized future instead of to the deferences and stabilities of the feudal past. 'Modernity' can, more easily than 'postmodernity', with its highly textual and relativist emphases, be made to point towards egalitarian, redistributive political ideals. Although these are now understood as discursively constructed, nevertheless they will not go away and indeed often found the very identity politics which have so pleasurably fragmented the 'big' emancipatory politics of an earlier period. They, paradoxically perhaps, emerge from the Enlightenment's emphasis on the concepts of 'progress', 'productivity' and 'individualism', all so central to the dynamic needs of capitalism. The period needs to be located as capitalist, with all that has involved for transformations of power structures in the areas of gender, race, sexuality and class.

'The Enlightenment' and its political ambitions have been powerfully critiqued, from different directions – as no more than a 'grand narrative', yearning for history to have a shape and a happy ending; as Euro-centric; as proceeding via a rhetoric tellingly centred on 'Man' and his 'rights'; as oblivious to either the ways that discourses of 'Reason' and then science, can be operated instrumentally or oppressively, or have drives and goals of which they are unconscious. I do not want to operate a barricaded form of argument, but it seems, whatever the problems with these associated values, that 'modernity' can alert us to more satisfying projects than those fashionable approaches which announce that 'history is over' or that we are living in 'knowledge' or 'virtual' economies. These come close to celebrating only irrationality, meaninglessness and consumption, though this celebration is done often in a hip style, implying that some cool version of 'progress' is at work, which surely itself forms another, not new, 'grand narrative'?

Such debates have been replayed in the 'third way' politics of the British Labour government which, thankfully, replaced the part-feudal routines of the Tories on 1 May 1997. As Stuart Hall and others pointed out (Critical Politics conference, London, January 2000), because Thatcherism had represented itself as modernizing, in order to bring together an effective opposition (as well as to admit the strength of some of the arguments) it was felt necessary to mirror this thrusting rhetoric. In the process not only were certain forms of redistributive political emphases, as well as an interest in class inequality, lost (partly by being called 'Old Labour') but a sense of history, as well as of *different* possible modernities, was weakened. 'Thatcher's old friend TINA (There Is No Alternative) was revived' (Stuart Hall) especially around the supposedly inevitable capitalist logic of globalization.

In the late 1990s, in a move to connect the 'public' (male?) emphasis of 'Enlightenment rationality' to the more supposedly private (female?) pleasures of consumption, an emphasis was made on the fundamental modernity of 'cultures of consumption'. The realm of production, from Marxist approaches, has also been re-imagined. The 'rational, free-thinking individual' (read, 'man') set up by much Enlightenment thought perhaps

> learned some of these ways of being by being rational and individual in the experience of going to work and of materially constructing new forms of domesticity, in dressing as a fashionable urbanite and in going to newly commercialised leisure activities.
>
> (Slater 1997: 24)

– leisure activities such as the movies.

Hollywood, cinema studies and this book

This may sound a long way from Film Studies. Yet it opens up possibilities for thinking about cinema, its audiences held in fascinations and spaces conceptualized as both intensely public (classically, arrangements made to leave the home for the evening; movies watched with many unknown others) and private (the darkness ensured that responses were not overlooked by those others, the films made it possible to privately imagine the most 'deviant' ways of being).

My first excitement in the area was bound up with the political energies deriving from 1970s debates which drove to insist, first, that popular, denigrated media such as film should be celebrated and better understood. Though interested in form and the 'languages' of cinema, this was partly an egalitarian move, attempting to shift the terms of what was thought of as 'culture'. A second, associated move was to explore cinema for its possible connections to emancipatory politics, initially (and some would say disastrously) through the new structuralist-linguistic emphases then becoming available. Eagleton (1983) puts an extreme case for the opposition to the later moment of post-structuralism:

> Post-structuralism was a product of that blend of euphoria and disillusionment, liberation and dissipation, carnival and catastrophe, which was 1968. Unable to break the structures of state power, post-structuralism found it possible instead to subvert the structures of language. Nobody, at least, was likely to beat you over the head for doing so.
>
> (Eagleton 1983: 142)

Cinema study has since gone through processes which render complicated any nostalgic or simple recourse to realism, representation, or political economic determinism. Nevertheless, as several voices have suggested, the project of modernity in this area is not 'completed' but needs to be rethought. It involves 'within and against' moves: trying to think the aesthetic and formal lures of films in historical terms, and at the same time in relation to economics; trying to rethink terms which are devalued by overuse, but which will not go away, such as realism. I have had to select just a few emphases.

A book of this length has necessarily to focus on the histories, possibilities and problems of Hollywood cinema as providing most of the films which readers are likely to have seen and studied. Its imaginative power can be such that it often seems to connect with the dream depths of its audiences – and to disappoint on the same scale (though this is less often researched). So one part of the book's ambition is to summarize histories of Hollywood, trying to avoid several available models: a celebration of its global dominance as the victory of some magically natural talent for film storytelling around the 'global village' fireside; a mourning of the triumph of a simply imperializing force, or a desire to resist to the end the demonic guile of an ideological 'apparatus'. There is though, through all the chapters, material which draws on cinema-making outside, or at an angle to, those films thought of as Hollywood's prime products (the blockbuster and the 'quality' star vehicle). Also woven through, rather than occupying a separate chapter, are considerations of what audiences have been theorized as making of movies.

The book begins with three chapters which consider histories of Hollywood in their hybridity and complex material process through different historical periods. They try to emphasize the modernity of Hollywood, which is not best understood through the abstract and ruptural periodization of 'postmodernity', but may be better grasped through Miriam Hansen's bold, highly speculative reconceptualization of its 'public sphere'-like role (see Hansen 2000). Chapter 1, 'Hollywood histories', moves from the founding of cinema in Europe in the 1890s to the end of the studio system around 1948, seeking to understand this unusual industry by reference to influential terms such as 'standardization', 'classical Hollywood cinema' (CHC) and 'the culture industries'. The close connections to government as well as to advertising and consumption are explored as a key part of any chronicle of its commercial successes. An account of some of the violence, both physical and economic, deployed by Hollywood is also given, though this is held in a kind of tension with the undoubted commercial appeal of what Hansen calls its 'sensuous-aesthetic' innovations. Her ambitious suggestion that it can be rethought, as a kind of 'vernacular modernism', is briefly sketched and discussed.

Chapter 2, ' "New again" Hollywood', as its title suggests, emphasizes that Hollywood has repeatedly remade itself, and that aspects of the persistently 'old' as well as the innovative can be found, for example in the long history of tie-in products and other relationships with consumer culture, advertising and market research. At the same time such links clearly need to be reformulated for the qualitatively new 'high concept' or 'global event' blockbuster cinema, with its rather different formal operations, and its effects on the whole ecology of the industry.

Chapter 3, ' "Globally Popular" cinema?' tries to explore the differences made by multinational global financing and production to Hollywood 'films on screen', their narratives, their audio-visuality, their special effects as well as their different marketing emphases 'around' films. In particular, questions arise of what this implies for the 'American-ness' of global cinema, its relationship to other national and independent film-makers, including those in the USA, as well as the global–local ecology of blockbuster film-making in other people's 'local' environments. How, then, might we understand global audiences' engagement with products which are by turns as self-reflexive about and as intimately bound up with their own marketing as *Toy Story 2*? How does that challenging term 'popular' work for globally hyped and 'event' product?

Chapters 4 and 5, 'Authors and agency' and 'Stars, bodies, galaxies', explore theories around two key sets of workers given high status individuation, both in and outside film study: directors and stars. Debates around directorial authorship in cinema has formed a key part of Film Studies, especially in its formative 1960s years, anxious to assert equal status for cinema compared to other arts. This model of individual creativity is still alive and well – see the Tarantino godamongdirectors website – and often the result of successful discursive work by directors to establish their reputation. Hitchcock, in this as in much else a pioneer of contemporary Hollywood methods, is examined in a short case study discussing his skill in 'reputation management' within his own critical community, and the importance of understanding such discursive struggles for legitimacy in his now-secure establishment as a 'brand'. The chapter argues the case that approaches emphasizing other kinds of collectivity, process and situated agency in film-making remain valuable, and that out of them might be retrieved a sense of the politics of production as negotiated and collaborative rather than individual or heroically branded.

Theories of stardom are broached next, along with the place and emphasis given to stars' physical presence, especially their bodies, within digital cultures which now abound with other kinds of celebrity and (over)emphasis on constructedness. It is suggested that we need to move a little away from the emphasis on the infinite constructedness of stars' presence, so powerful as a critical tool when star studies were established within a very different cultural ecology. Star presence, and the actual agency of stars within their own career trajectories, might instead be emphasized (with political resonance) as embodying a sense of the reality of limits, such as place and time, playing on and through socially located bodies, and the possibility of negotiating successfully within these.

Chapter 6, 'Movies move audiences' attempts to explore both the ways that the 'textiness' of films has been thought, and the ways that cinema-goers, buried deep in such accounts, surface in terms such as 'identify' or 'escapism'. Many books now provide excellent examples of how to explore a piece of film textually. In the space available here, the focus instead is on the history of one of Film Studies' most famous theories, that of 'the look', including the contentious area of 'cine-psychoanalysis'. The heavily deterministic models of positioning emerging from this account and, oddly, from post-structuralism more generally, is argued to be hostile to exactly the emancipatory politics it often seems to be gesturing towards. As are two contradictory assumptions about audiences rendered visible in the terms *identification* (implying that audiences are helplessly 'sucked into' texts) and *escapism* (audiences use them to simply 'bliss out', with positive or negative 'effects'). Finally, the powerful sets of discourses and previewing or exhibition practices which prepare audiences to experience entertainment films ('texts' to us) are argued to be intricately involved in the pleasures or disappointments taken in them.

Chapter 7, 'Identifying a critical politics of representation', holds in tension some of the most tricky developments within recent Film and Cultural

Studies. It tries to explore some of the theoretical changes that have occurred since 1960s/1970s excitement at the usefulness of the term 'representation' for the kind of film study interested in cultural political change (which, of course, is not all film study, nor does it have to be). This now needs to include a sense of areas unmade, as well as gained, in the move to 'identity politics'. The title of the chapter, Tessa Perkins' (2000) phrase, argues for an incorporation of some of the theoretical achievements of the 1980s and 1990s, and a new commitment to 'a politics of representation . . . more thoroughly grounded within particular socio-cultural contexts' (Perkins 2000: 92). 'Politics', with its need for the shared, for solidarities and decisions, means rethinking the supreme emphasis on 'difference' of both structuralist and post-structuralist theory, and of some 'identity politics'. Issues such as realism and stereotyping are explored, as well as the need to remake or even rediscover the concept of 'class', now often only ritually invoked, usually to mean only 'working class', and rarely used for the divisions and inequalities within and across different cinemas (though see Munt 2000; Stam and Miller 2000).

One final note. While working, with Roy Stafford, on *The Media Student's Book*, I grew fond of the chance to incorporate other voices, through boxes in the text. I've kept the habit here, and hope it's helpful and fun, not an irritating distraction.

1 | HOLLYWOOD HISTORIES

There are precious few signs that the inhabitants of the late twentieth century have recently entered a new age, and that the doors opened up by the advent of modern societies have now closed behind them . . . What we need today is not a theory of a new age, but . . . a new theory of an age whose broad contours were laid down some time ago, and whose consequences we have yet fully to ascertain.

(John B. Thompson 1995: 9)

As I finish this book, Hollywood is once again pronounced to be in crisis. The chairman of Walt Disney Studios is reported to be joining the independent sector, saying that he would be happier free from corporate constraints. Two senior industry figures have complained that the studios are 'mere appendages of vast multinational corporations' staffed by 'a new breed of executive who would once have chosen to work on Wall Street but has come west to the film industry' (Campbell 2000). The French conglomerate Vivendi/Canal Plus has just announced a takeover bid for Universal (part of Seagram), drawing attention to the non-American ownership of parts of contemporary 'Hollywood'.

This chapter and the two that follow try to sketch the histories of Hollywood cinema, which seems to remake itself, or announce itself as remade, every few decades. This involves considering the major models for understanding or producing those histories, and for speculating about their effects. I want to argue that such histories are best understood not as fractured by dramatic breaks, let alone by some extreme postmodern 'rupture', but as part of a developing capitalist **modernity**. The remakings and repetitions of aspects of the studio system, as well as newness and differences, will be emphasized, as will its abiding nature as a major **capitalist** industry.

In focusing on Hollywood the global *majority* of 'other' film-making both outside and within the USA has had to be mostly excluded. However, Hollywood seems an obvious starting point, certainly for a book of this size, as the most *powerful* global form of cinema. Its economic impact (especially at the level of distribution) and its related, compelling 'sensuous-aesthetic' (Hansen 2000) attractions are inescapable at all levels of what are now tightly integrated audio-visual industries.

This chapter will try to explore the following topics:

- The ways that, for most its history, 'Hollywood' has never been one thing. Like other major capitalist industries, it has kept transforming itself, repeatedly entering new formal, industrial and technological phases and alliances, including those with government, which often overlapped or even contradicted each other.
- The importance of substituting for smooth announcements of epochal 'ruptures' such as **postmodernity**, some understanding of the survival of the 'old' as well as innovation, within historical moments which are always deeply uneven. The persistent objective of the American film industry, for example, has been, and remains, to make money by showing entertaining stories to paying audiences through the mass making, distributing, publicizing and exhibiting of films. From early on this enterprise was funded by East coast money and propelled by East coast decisions, and involved a close relationship to advertising and consumer cultures. Nevertheless, the contemporary forms that this logic takes are unprecedented.
- How we can understand the emergence of Hollywood's global dominance by the time of the early years of the **studio system**? Several models are available. Is it the result of supreme managerial savvy and business sense? Or of a mysterious universal appeal, whether benign – the eternal appeal of 'classical' form, the ability to make films that 'last' – or malign – the **ideological** guile of an 'apparatus' which dupes those who succumb to its lures. Or is it the absolute standardization of an entertainment product consumed by the mindless?

Early cinema histories

It is estimated that 'almost 75% of the films made before and just after the turn of the century no longer exist' (Kolker 1998: 13). Nevertheless evidence

> Lines have indeed to be drawn, to make any account possible, but it is always necessary to see ourselves as drawing them, and willing to redraw them.
>
> (Raymond Williams 1983: 10)

suggests that early cinema, first in Europe from 1895, and soon after in the USA, was a low budget form. Films were hardly publicized, ran for less than a minute, with no special effects, lighting, camera movement or even editing. They could be exhibited by anyone with a projector, a sheet, and perhaps some shelter for the audience.

This cinema of theatrical conjurors and fairground attractions or distractions was gradually replaced, first by bigger budgeted cinema in both Europe and the USA, but then mostly by the business success of US movies. This emerged from a concentrated film industry, producing in Los Angeles, funded from the late 1920s by Wall Street, distributing across the rest of the planet, and known as the studio system. From about the mid-1920s the industry operated monopolies and copyright power in the mass production, distribution, publicizing and exhibition of film. This process was accelerated, rather than totally transformed, by the development since the 1970s of 'blockbusters' and then ultra high budget global blockbusters.

> In 'Hollywood's greatest year', 1939, 33,687 people were employed in movie production. But the industry as a whole employed 177,420 people. For every actor, writer, electrician or carpenter, there were 5 distribution company salesmen, theatre managers, projectionists, ushers, and clerks staffing the 15,000 cinemas in the US.
>
> (Maltby and Craven 1995: 60)

Histories and archaeologies of cinema begin with accounts written by and for the film industry, by early inventors such as the camera operator W.K.L. Dickson, or the exhibitor Robert Grau (see Belton 1998a: 227–8), often, as Allen and Gomery (1985) have noted, working partly as history and partly as advertisement for the film industry itself. Then, up to the 1970s, film history generally used the methods of nineteenth century historiography: grounded in empiricist theories of knowledge, with evidence seen as unproblematic, as archaeologically retrievable 'facts', with events understood mostly as the consequences of the acts of individual agents, usually 'great men', rather than as processes involved in systems, **discourses** and their fluxes. Despite the post-1970s academicization of film history, widespread impressions of silent cinema are still likely to be formed from these fairly simple models of historical interpretation.

Many people seem to think of early cinema as simply 'primitive' films, of interest only in the ways they prefigure the 'mature' studio system, especially in its 'golden years' (see Figure 1.1). The surviving collections of rather damaged, black and white, short, silent films, depending on your taste, might show either a dodgy sense of humour, or a miraculously universal pre-literate appeal: a 'visual Esperanto' or universal language.

But what we now call early cinema is also persuasively readable in other ways. It emerges from 'a scatter of inventions' (R. Williams 1983: 14) as varied as Melies' use of one-reel films as an extension of conjuring, Lumière's

Figure 1.1 Early French production, pre-'Hollywood'
BFI Films: Stills, Posters and Designs

interest in recording events, documentary style, or Edison's desire, having invented the phonograph, to have films accompany it, as an ancillary to its sounds. By various means, these scattered commercial and cultural possibilities, across Europe and the USA, had by 1914 been centralized into 'the most widely distributed cultural form there had ever been' (R. Williams 1983: 14). As Miller (1999) summarizes:

> in 1914 most movies and much movie-making technology in North America was imported [and] Italy and France dominated exhibition in Latin America . . . [yet] by 1909 North American companies could rely on the local market to recoup costs and were tailoring export prices to meet other markets . . . from 1919 overseas receipts were factored into Hollywood budgets.
>
> (Miller 1999: 372)

The question unavoidably arises: *given that the earliest, successful pioneers of film were European, why did Hollywood have supremacy in 90 per cent of world markets by 1918?*

There is no single 'big bang' reason (see Grantham 2000). Nevertheless this does not justify a postmodern scepticism about *any* kind of historical explanation. Several major factors can be seen to interweave. First, the First World War (1914–18) was fought, despite its name, well outside the USA and had a devastating impact on competitor European film industries as well as on the links of German films to, for example, the huge British market (see Uricchio 1996).

Second, many early film producers moved to California from New York, to take advantage of an ideal climate for year-round film-making, plenty of sunlight, a huge variety of locations (mountains, sea, desert, cities), less expensive land for studio space and a cheap, non-unionized labour force (see Sklar 1975).

Third, there was the huge advantage of a massive 'domestic' market for US film-makers – that North American continent known as the USA, often taken to include Canada and, effectively, Latin America. Once the industry was established, this could virtually ensure profitability. Major costs were involved in producing the 'master copy' but thereafter prints were relatively cheap to make and distribute. Indeed it is often suggested that the relatively late entry of US films into world competition is due to the amount of profit which was still busily being made in the huge home market. Once that overseas entry was made, canny differential pricing adjustments for the consumer capacities of different markets enabled maximum overall profitability, along with the application of standardized business practices, especially in the field of production and distribution.

Such factors have to be understood in conjunction with the harsh methods often used to secure distribution and exhibition dominance. These cannot be wished away into a simple and circular celebration of market or managerial success. This would be to ignore the, often brutal, enforcements of advantage, and powerful alliances with government, at all levels of cinema-making. One major tension in historical accounts is between acknowledging the force of such methods and giving weight to the undeniable appeals of many of the films whose path they 'smooth'.

Chaplin's comedies, for example, are often argued to have the 'universal' charm of 'America's natural talent for entertainment'. But it is crucial that Hollywood's distribution and presentation machinery made such films universally *unignorable*, 'event' movies, as their equivalents remain today, rather than simply *available* ones. Edison's Motion Picture Patents Company (MPPC) trust pioneered brute force against those companies who challenged the copyright arrangements which he wanted to enforce for his own interests.

> The main purpose of [the MPPC], in Edison's view, was 'to limit the number of foreign brands allowed to circulate' in the US.
>
> (Grantham 2000: 44)

The French film-maker Lumière's successful operatives seem to have been squeezed out of the USA, by force, sudden cancellations and lawsuits, by 1914. It has been argued that French cinema (especially Pathé's Red Rooster films) dominated American screens in the nickelodeon era, but its success was partly stemmed by a smear campaign demonizing the films as dangerously alien, effete and immoral (Abel 1999). Economic force such as the purchase of local distributors in Brazil between 1915 and 1916, which almost wiped out Brazilian production (Shohat and Stam 1994: 28) has always been a structured part of the 'free market' glory of the US film industry, right down to the present-day struggles over quotas in global trade organizations such as GATT, MAI, Seattle and WTO (see Grantham 2000).

Issues such as these raise questions about other versions of Hollywood's past which overemphasize either its effortless or 'natural' superiority (usually via a focus on purely formal areas such as 'narrative'), or which celebrate its victory as one of managerial sophistication and creativity. Thus popular accounts of the early Edison MPPC violence against competitors are often either:

- subsumed into a celebration of a kind of Jack the Giant Killer victory of the independents over the MPPC, especially since this can be argued to coincide with the move to California in a way that melds temptingly with broader American ideologies of the frontier (see Sklar 1975: 67–8 for a rebuttal of such accounts of the move); or
- cited as though this was a once and for all victory of 'the little guys' on the issue of patents, whereas, as Gomery (1998a: 246) points out: 'it was to take flexibility of a different kind to gain long term control' of the kind Edison wanted.

A political economy approach to such histories could usefully emphasize that the success of Hollywood 'has been a co-ordinated, if sometimes conflictual and chaotic, attempt by capital and the state to establish and maintain a position of market and ideological dominance [and would find] governments every bit as crucial as audiences and firms' (Miller 1998: 372; 2000: 539–51).

However, it is also worth emphasizing that the 'US–Rest of the World' binary of cultural imperialism's accounts is forced to ignore the success of early US film, which Hansen (2000) argues is rather like the spread of a vernacular. Well ahead of the usual timings of the beginnings of **globalization** and **hybridity**, this 'universal language' was in fact made by turn of the century US film-makers and projectionists who not only were in close contact with rival European film-makers, but also were themselves often first generation European immigrants. (Even in the late 1920s, 'Two of every three Americans consciously claimed membership in an ethnic community, either as foreign born or their descendants' (Gomery 1992: 171).)

In England one is always running into people who are anti-American although they've never set foot in this country. And I always tell them, 'There are no Americans. America is full of foreigners.'
(Alfred Hitchcock, quoted in Grantham 2000: 1)

They have been further argued to possess mid-European Jewish taste and fantasies closely in touch with those of overseas audiences (see Gabler 1988) and operated almost from the beginning in small nickelodeons which gave them close contact with their, in turn, heterogeneous audiences. Far from being a sign of some, much later, postmodern break, the ethnic hybridity of US audiences, as well as broad forms of generic hybridity and

intertextuality with other popular forms such as pulp fiction or theatrical spectacle, have always operated in cinema. They served to aggregate audiences and enable popular work to take place both within and at the edge of existing traditions. As an example, the western, in its early years, melded the adventure story, the Wild West pageant, romance, US frontier rhetoric and landscape imagery from painting as well as cinema's superior capacity to film scenes of chase, spatial thrill and spectacular landscape (see Neale 1990b; 2000). A powerful argument has been made (Gledhill 1987) that early cinema incorporates the many and mixed attractions of theatrical melodrama, both in its 'male' swashbuckling adventure mode, and in its 'feminine' romance impulse. Such mixes were of course further differentiated by decisions to produce different versions of films for European and later world markets – the 'sad ending for the Russians' for example.

From 1920 onwards Hollywood 'could depend on at least 35% of its gross income arising from foreign sources' (Vasey 1996: 57). Key to such export successes was the continuing attention given to the nature of both the burgeoning US market and its many and intimate connections to Europe. Grantham (2000) comments on figures such as John Ford (born in Ireland), Charlie Chaplin (born in England) and Billy Wilder (born in Austria) as well as the huge number of studio heads from middle and Eastern Europe: 'The one Hollywood "major" . . . not founded by Europeans is the Walt Disney Company, whose . . . creator, against the Hollywood grain, was an American from Kansas City' (Grantham 2000: 29). Yet this popularity also includes the previously mentioned cosy relationships with government and often a static, conservative sense of 'what the market/public wants' which, while it may innovate, is often happy to go along with existing oppressive structures, such as those of racism in the USA and elsewhere, as long as they are maximally profitable. Market savvy, up until the passing of US civil rights legislation in 1964 was allowed to go along with racially segregated product and exhibition practices for the southern states (see Gomery 1992: chs 8 and 9).

Paul Warfield, the noted football player, recalled the first time he visited relatives in Tennessee in the early 1950s at age eleven: 'Inside a movie theatre, striding towards the front row center, [I] had [my] arms gently tugged by a cousin. We must go this way, I was told. Upstairs.'

(Gomery 1992: 155)

It can be convincingly argued that some of the diverse ethnic mix of the huge US domestic market as well as the first or second generation (generally white) immigrant early film-makers and then studio bosses, all enabled a more multicultural/multi-market (universal?) mode of storytelling than that of other early film-making cultures in separate, much smaller European states. This is very far from the 'natural talent for entertainment' for which many commentators credit Hollywood's commercial success. Nor is it exactly the result of the full democracy often suggested to be guaranteed as part of market choices in so many accounts of cinema and of 'the free market' more generally.

Movies as culture industries

Before proceeding further with discussions of consumer culture and cinema, let us consider one of the most influential approaches to media production: the arguments of the Frankfurt School on commodified 'mass culture' or 'the culture industries'.

The 'Frankfurt School' names a group of social theorists, most notably for our purposes Theodor Adorno, Max Horkheimer and Herbert Marcuse. They originally worked in Frankfurt in the Institute for Social Research, founded in 1923. In work which came to be called 'critical theory' they tried to understand the relationship between the economic and the textual in the modern industrial capitalist west, using a combination of Marx's approach to social analysis and Freud's sense of the relationship between the individual and the social whole. Fresh from their experience of Nazi Germany they experienced the Hollywood-dominated mass culture of the USA in ways that led them to argue that capitalism would be replaced by fascism, not socialism.

The culture industries are 'institutions in our society which employ the characteristic modes of production and organisation of industrial corporations to produce and disseminate symbols in the form of cultural goods and services, generally, though not exclusively, as commodities'.
(Nicholas Garnham 1987: 25, quoted in Miller 2000: 544)

A key term in their work was their coinage of 'the culture industries', now fairly familiar in policy documents and beyond, but then striking and sarcastic, since 'culture' and 'industry' were usually kept in separate and quarantined intellectual compounds. The issues they raised included:

- The levelling down to 'standardized' forms of both cultural product and audience response/expectation. One of their most famous pieces is entitled 'The culture industries as mass deception', and argues that the apparent consumer choices in the media are in fact 'the freedom to choose what is always the same' (Adorno and Horkheimer 1979[1944]: 167).
- Broader concerns at the oppressive and hierarchized nature of 'mass society' and the ideological role of the media in underpinning and reinforcing this.
- Debates on how to produce oppositional art within such commodity culture, and the degree to which it is even possible (see Bordwell 1989: ch 2; Hollows 1995).

In many ways, the attempts of the 'Frankfurters' to combine Marx and Freud resembled the approaches of the 1970s' 'apparatus theorists' associated with the journals *Cahiers du Cinema* and *Screen*. This later approach was to emphasize the idea of Hollywood as a somehow unified 'apparatus', working on the individual spectator at levels which integrated psychoanalytic with ideological lures and seductions. The Frankfurters were more interested in arguing that capitalist political-economic control of cultural production led to a highly **commodified** modern 'mass culture' (as opposed to culture supported by aristocratic individual patronage, as in the medieval period up to about 1750). Audiences were therefore best understood as simply a mass of consumers.

There are strong class and gender aspects to their writings at this point, in considering consumption within commodified culture. First, it is implied that whereas the 'folk' (in pre-capitalist social orders) had known their place, the 'masses' of the capitalist production line (no longer understood as having revolutionary potential) did not. They were therefore not satisfied with traditional high cultural forms which, it was asserted, would do them good. Culture is argued to have become subject to the industrial values of popularity and profitability *and therefore* to pander to 'the lowest common denominator'. The consequences for the films of the factory-like studio system were said to be that since mass produced culture involved assembly-line techniques, there followed, in a direct, Marxist connection of economic base and media 'superstructure', a standardization or homogenization at the level of both aesthetic and cultural-political values. The resulting films were always eyed as being formulaic, with 'tried and tested' ingredients and ideologically narcotic effects on their audiences.

Second, 'cinema's insatiable appetite, its appeal to the most promiscuous and undiscerning of tastes' have also been argued to show a contempt for

> Many people sacrifice themselves because they are too lazy to rebel; many tears are shed and they only flow because to cry is sometimes easier than to think . . . Clandestinely the little shop girls wipe their eyes and powder their noses before the lights come up.
>
> (Kracauer, German film theorist of the 1920s and 1930s, often associated with the Frankfurt School, quoted in Petro (2000: 582–3), from 'The Little Shopgirls Go to the Movies': 1927)

audiences, in metaphors typically used to construct femininity as 'passive', 'distracted', 'emotional', 'irrational' and so on (see Petro 2000: 582).

The only part of film-making argued to be 'free' was that of **avant-garde art** – experimental (and therefore non-formulaic) and individualist (non-assembly line, non-commercial), addressing small elite audiences. Its artists are seen as refusing to let their work be commodified and therefore as maintaining aesthetic and political 'freedom'. (See Chapter 4 for the implications of this 'outsider' notion of independence and authorship on thinking about the negotiation involved in all film-making).

The eloquence of much Frankfurt School analysis often seems won at the cost of both specific historical analyses and of a sense of the contradictory nature of modern capitalist cultural processes. Capitalist products have both an exchange value for their owners and shareholders, and a use value for their audiences, and sometimes the two can be fairly far apart (see Lovell 1980). Disney, for example, experienced audience liking (use value) for *Pulp Fiction* which as a result not only became highly profitable (exchange value) but also, to put it mildly, pulled against the 'family image' of the rest of the franchise and offended many big shareholders. In some ways the Frankfurt account resembles both the 'apparatus' theory of the 1970s, and also much postmodern pessimism about industrially produced culture (see especially the writings of Baudrillard, such as 1975, 1988). 'Real life is becoming indistinguishable from the movies', they complained, thirty years before Baudrillard, who echoes the sweeping analysis:

> Disneyland is presented as imaginary in order to make us believe that the real is real, whereas all of Los Angeles and the America that surrounds it are no longer real, but belong to the hyperreal order and to the order of simulation.
>
> (Baudrillard 1994[1981]: 12, cited in McGuigan 1999: 24)

It is worth mentioning, in the context of cinema, relatively recent interest in the theorist Ernst Bloch, a figure at the edge of the US Frankfurt circle

(Jameson 1990; Dyer 1993; Gaines 2000). Bloch's 1940s work suggested that a **utopian** impulse lay buried deep within popular art such as film, and that the 'double movement' of this resistant impulse and a conformity to dominant values is in fact necessary for commercial success. This position takes us to other theories of the liberatory potential of consumer products, such as those of the studio system.

Cultures of consumption

Recent theorists have argued that consumption should be rethought as a key part of the histories of capitalist modernity. This is a very different emphasis from previous ones on production, emphasizing questions such as who owns the means of production, the role of profit, the conditions under which workers produce goods – from Marx through to the Frankfurt School. Slater (1997: 9) provides a helpful guide to the ways postmodern discourse in the 1980s inflated consumerism to utopic or apocalyptic dimensions, depending on how you view it. Consumer culture is regarded, in many such accounts, to be fully formed *only* in the postmodern era. The 1980s, flushed with the apparent successes of Thatcherism and Reaganomics, saw 'postmodernism' as a new boom discourse, rediscovering consumer choice as the motor for economic advance, replacing an earlier Marxist emphasis on production, and the need to transform the power relations of its hierarchies of workers and bosses. Postmodernism's emphasis on consumption was aligned with ones on **post-Fordist** production methods. These are seen as marking an absolute break with earlier, less highly technologized forms of capitalist industry, and also as being unprecedentedly reliant on marketing (see Chapter 2). Yet, far from being a late consequence of industrial modernization, Slater (1997) argues that consumption is inextricably bound up with capitalist modernity as a whole and can be traced back, for example, to struggles over feudal 'sumptuary' laws, forbidding the wearing of certain fabrics by all but royalty (see Slater 1997: ch. 2).

   An interest in consumption for cinema study usually deals with post-1940s film-going or video watching. But early cinema's conditions, its urban and metropolitan contexts, are central to such study. An emphasis on the key role of New York *prior* to the move to Hollywood (then only an obscure suburb of the smallish city of Los Angeles) can make visible the urban conditions of consumption, as well as production, which fed the appetite for the wildfire spread of cinema – a spread which also encompassed 'Berlin, Paris, Moscow, Shanghai, Tokyo, Sao Paolo, Sydney, Bombay' (Hansen 2000: 337).

The repeated myths of silent cinema emphasize its unprecedented power *over* audiences: tales of spectators fainting, screaming, trying to escape the train or the splashing waves which seemed to come at them out of the screen (see for example Christie 1994). Perhaps however these function less as a proof of audiences' endlessly asserted gullibility (often feminized or exoticized), and more as proof of historians' desire for magic births or decisive turning points, or of journalists' desire to dramatize audiences' ways of relating to the new medium.

A press report of the first Lumiere show in Britain in 1896 reported that:

> In common with most of the people in the front row of the stalls, I shift uneasily in my seat and think of railway accidents.
>
> (Christie 1994: 15)

The audiences for early cinema in the USA have been persuasively argued to have been largely made up of low income urban workers. In both Europe and the USA, these people 'had won for themselves in the latter part of the nineteenth century a reduction of working hours, without a fall in real income, and consequently an increase in leisure hours and at least a minimal amount of money to spend on them' (Chanan 1996: 40). By about 1900, cinema's appeal for them was as 'part of the city landscape, as brief respite for the laborer on his way home, as release from household drudgery for women, and as cultural touchstone for immigrants' (Charney and Schwartz 1995: 5).

In addition to such pleasures in many of the new world cities, there was a *unique* concentration of several areas of media skill and resource in New York, itself at the communications centre of the huge continent known as the USA. Newspapers, music halls, records and music publishing provided not only a pool of entertainment and other cultural skills and forms but also cross-fertilization (multi-marketing?) at the level of publicity, popular journalism, feeding appetites for stories about filmed entertainment. As Hansen (2000) and others argued, along with the real destruction and loss of older forms in modernity: 'There also emerged new modes of organising vision and sensory perception, a new relationship with "things", different forms of mimetic experience and expression' (Hansen 2000: 333).

It is not just that the distribution and exhibition of films is unthinkable without electricity, modern forms of transport, accounting and communication. Others have argued that common experiences of people in the new

> Both motoring and the cinema offered the satisfaction of seeing the
> world 'whizz by': they suggest a detachment from means and conse-
> quence.
>
> (Christie 1994: 22)

cities of a rapidly globalizing modernity would have been powerfully homol-
ogous with cinema (see Figure 1.2). A few examples: seen from inside the
train, the speeding railway (and later car) journey habituates its users to a
cinema-like experience, where 'the person in a separate and quarantined seat

Figure 1.2 'A Quiet Sunday in London': one response to urban experience
Reproduced with permission of Punch Ltd

watched moving visuals through a frame that does not change position' (Charney and Schwartz 1995: 6). Or take the two poles of early cinema, seen by some to anticipate all that follows: travel 'actuality' films (with Lumière seen as the 'father of documentary') and trick films (such as those produced by Méliès and seen as the origin of fantasy in cinema). These have been argued as visualizing 'a modern experience of rapid alteration, whether by presenting foreign views from far-flung international locations or by creating through trick photography a succession of transformations which unmoored the stable identity of both objects and performers' (Gunning 1995: 16).

It is now speculated that such phenomena, and perhaps the endless glances of the new urban shopper (often gendered as female) and the cruising flâneur (usually imagined as a more leisurely, male stroller), stimulated by the sensual experience of the city's distractions, especially as imaged in the new shop windows, flowed into the 'vernacular' status (Hansen 2000) of Hollywood's analogous sensuous appeals. Early cinema, argue Charney and Schwartz (1995: 10), 'both epitomised and accidentally outpaced' other forms of modern life in the new metropolises, and this includes the much debated turn towards consumer forms, then seen as exclusively part of the feminine sphere. Rapidly emerging commodity-centred consumer cultures gave rise to experiences like the department store, with its culture of the spectacle of window dressing, its freezing of commodities in 'scenes' for quick appraisal against the rush of the street, or in its designed interior displays, resembling theatrical or film sets. Movie palaces themselves, in the big cities, have been described as being, like department stores, 'grand monuments to elaborate facades' (Ewen and Ewen 1982: 200, quoted in Gaines 2000), 'exquisite containers for opulence and excess' (Gaines 2000: 101).

Gunning (1990: 64) argues that the narratives of many early films (necessarily, given early cinema technology) are simply a string on which to hang the display of possibilities, fairground-like 'attractions' to shock, thrill or incite curiosity, displayed in the manner of a circus or fairground – or perhaps in the manner of the parade of commodities in the street. These devices, Gunning argues, did not disappear once narrative cinema established its hegemony, but went 'underground, both in to certain avant-garde practices and as a component of narrative films, more evident in some genres (e.g. the musical)' and now surfacing again in the carnival rollercoaster rides of the Spielberg-Lucas cinema of effects (Gunning 1990: 67). This is another argument for seeing Hollywood histories through transformed continuities rather than fundamental ruptures.

The studio system

But what kinds of work produced such profitable commodities? The capitalist industrial processes of 'Hollywood' in its 'classic' years, before the US state in 1948 finally separated exhibition from production, need to be seen as inseparable from their economic and institutional power.

By the 1920s Hollywood had begun the annual release to its cinemas of roughly 400 to 700 films per year (Schatz 1981: 6) by factories (usually given the more artistic name of 'studios') which functioned in many ways like the Ford Motor Company's production line. These were ranked into 'minor', studios (Columbia and Universal, plus even smaller outfits like Republic, Disney and Monogram, usually producing 'B' films) and the 'Big Five' or 'majors' (MGM, Paramount, RKO, Twentieth Century Fox and Warner Brothers).

> MGM resembled a Renaissance city state, its high walls built to prevent other studios from stealing their ideas, running its own medical and school system and police force.
>
> (British Film Institute Dossier no 1: 1980)

A key characteristic of this studio system for film-making was the organization of production into

- an oligopolistic (that is dominated by the small group of 'majors')
- **vertically integrated** (production, wholesale and retail activities controlled by the same company)
- factory-like and hierarchically organized flow.

> You had to punch the clock. They would walk round to see if everybody was typing. There'd be a lookout in the writers' building. When Warner or Cohen would be seen coming towards the building, somebody would say 'He's coming' and all the typewriters would start . . . He [Jack Warner] couldn't understand why people weren't always typing.
>
> (Gabler 1988: 324)

This monopolistic control of the industry was sanctioned by government on the grounds that two national crises, the 1930s Depression and later the Second World War, justified such a way of operating. Although the 'minors' had their own distribution arms, the majors were the only studios fully to 'integrate' production, distribution and exhibition, creating most of the high budget 'A' films with guaranteed access to their big first run metropolitan theatres. They also controlled vital inputs into such aspects of production as film processing, music publishing and sponsorship of Broadway plays.

The production process, from the 1920s onwards (see Maltby and Craven 1995: ch. 2), began with corporate (East coast, New York) decisions on the number and types of films sent from the studios (West Coast, Los Angeles) to cinemas for the next season. Motoring the system is this need to provide the cinema chain (owned by a major studio) with enough 'product' to ensure a smooth flow of both 'A' (90 minutes and a sizeable budget) and, later, 'B' (under 90 minutes, much smaller costs) features. Budgets were then allocated, involving a strict division of labour, along lines now called Taylorist or, more usually, Fordist. Workers were concentrated on specialist tasks (such as script-writing, direction or costume design), sometimes in a 'production unit' system, where a producer would work with the same director and crew over several films so as to utilize both capital equipment and contracted staff to the full. Bordwell *et al.* (1985) suggest that the introduction of the 'continuity script' in the late 1910s facilitated the 'scientific management' of cinema, allowing accurate forecasts of footage, schedules and budgets, ensuring that producers could check that directors were sticking to an agreed blueprint and so on, as well as allowing directors to devolve particular tasks well in advance of production.

> Selznick was particularly disturbed by Hitch's method of shooting just what was in the script and no more – no master shot of a whole scene, no variations of middle shots and close-ups which could be cut together in different ways and allow the film to be remade at the producer's whim in the cutting room.
>
> (John Russell Taylor 1978: 138)

'It was cheaper to pay a few workers to prepare scripts and solve continuity problems at that stage than . . . to let a whole crew of laborers work it out on the set or by retakes later' (Bordwell *et al.* 1985: 138). Thus emerged what is known as the **continuity system** for shooting and editing footage together quickly (therefore economically) and easily, its simple, unspoken rules avoiding the need to agonize over arrangements. The rules were always *both* formal and economic: a commercial aesthetic, as Maltby and Craven

(1995) call it. Kolker (1998) gives a good summary of the rules which most clearly embody the economic logic of the system:

> shoot whatever scenes are most economical to shoot at any given time (shoot out of sequence when necessary); cover any given sequence from as many angles as possible with multiple takes of each angle to give the producer and editors a lot of material to choose from.
>
> (Kolker 1998: 20)

The 'formal' rules of the system are designed for economic film-making, for the sake of a paying audience's enjoyment of an easily grasped narrative: always shoot one side of the 180-degree line of action; match on certain kinds of action cuts; always vary the angle from one shot to the next by more than 30 degrees; keep eyelines matched, that is maintain the direction a person is gazing in from one shot to the next, and create the illusion, through such matched gazes, that two actors are talking to each other. This, along with the shot reverse shot system for dialogue sequences, can produce the illusion of a conversation. Even if the expensive star actor in one of the series of shots has already finished the film and may be many miles away, he or she can be simply edited together with his or her respondent.

The broader rhythms of this risky industry drove studios to try to repeat successes, including the economical use and reuse wherever possible of human and other material – kinds of performance, of sets, costumes and even of film narratives, leading to the star-genre system, and the overall recognizability of different studios' product.

> Each studio had its own genre, its own set of emotions . . . its own photographic style – even its own musical sound. I could walk into a theatre lobby and tell which studio made the movie just by listening to the orchestration.
>
> (Gordon Willis, cinematographer, in Ettedgui 1998: 38)

This went along with various 'Dream Factory' political-economic strategies:

- the Hollywood oligopoly has been always protected by copyright (from Edison's MPPC to Disney's ferocious contemporary policing of copyright)
- the entry costs to membership of the 'majors' club demanded huge investment in distribution and exhibition as well as in ever changing and expensive, patented technologies
- economies of scale and cartel practices such as the Production Code, the

work of the Hays (later called Breen) Office, then the **MPPDA** (Motion Picture Producers and Distributors of America: founded 1922) and finally **MPAA** (Motion Picture Association of America: founded 1922). This code, set up by the industry itself, operated as self rather than state censorship, and was designed to facilitate the smooth flow of Hollywood product across the huge market spread of the home 'territory'. The Code ran, and sought to ensure maximum profitability, from rural southern states like Alabama where racism was common, to the more liberal areas such as New York.

In American movies before the 1960s, [the] Production Code dictated that characters got shot without bleeding, argued without swearing, and had babies without copulating.

(Linda Williams 1996: 490)

- export control eased the flow of US films across the rest of the globe, especially via the **MPEAA** (Motion Pictures Export Association of America), which referred to itself as 'the little State department' in the 1940s (Miller 1998: 372). Even today its role continues in countering attempted quota restrictions on film imports by states trying to protect their cinema industries (see Grantham 2000).
- the MPEAA later (from 1945) policed US film copyright abroad. It also 'eased' the flow of consumer products 'placed' in US films into export markets – and thereby the path of Hollywood into the hearts and minds of cinema-goers and key merchandisers alike. This was way before **synergy** became a buzz word for thinking tie-ins or product placements – or before postmodernism announced a 'new' world of intertextual commodification.

Hollywood exporters were aware as early as 1912 that where their films travelled, demand was created for other US goods. Will Hays told the J. Walter Thompson advertising agency in 1930 that 'every foot of American films sells $1.00 worth of manufactured goods some place in the world' (Hays 1931: 15) . . . a deputation of Argentinian businessmen . . . protested to the US Embassy about *It Happened One Night* (1934) because Gable was seen removing his shirt, revealing no singlet [vest] below and creating an inventory surplus [of vests] in their warehouse (King 1990: 32).

(Miller 1998: 373)

The function of tie-in and product placements in studio, not just contemporary cinema, is worth a moment here. It is often said that **product placement** and **tie-in** deals are now at unprecedented levels – the latest James Bond film at moments resembles a BMW car ad, *Star Wars* or *Toy Story 2* a computer games or toy ad. This is sometimes seen as part of a 'gloomy' postmodern position that we now swim through unprecedentedly commodified and intertextual confusion. But, here as elsewhere, there are continuities-with-difference to, rather than simple breaks from the studio system to be emphasized.

As early as 1910 filmed fashion shows were part of many entertainment programmes. In 1930 the relationship between Hollywood and the US fashion industry had been formalized with the founding of the Modern Merchandising Bureau, primed, with photos of fashions to be worn by stars in upcoming films, to devise styles like them (see Eckert 1991[1957]). By the 1930s merchandising was applied to every single studio release. Massive effort was put into coordination with local retailers. Studios would provide press books boasting of how well advertised an upcoming film would be by tie-in firms, especially fashion products for the largely female consumers of the 1930s. As Tom Dewe Mathews (1998) points out, drawing on an interview with Peter Kramer:

> Warners had million dollar contracts with General Electric and General Motors, MGM had a tie-into Bell telephones as well as to Coca-Cola, Paramount was with Westinghouse and all the studios had links to radio networks like CBS and NBC . . . directors in the twenties and thirties were encouraged to junk historical costume dramas and instead [make films] which could show off the latest Bell telephone, General Electric oven or Westinghouse refrigerator.
>
> (Mathews 1998)

Audiences in the 1950s slowly changed from being mostly composed of women to being dominated by young males. Though the studios hugely benefited from the publicity of tie-ins, and from government support and approval abroad for its role in export markets, they were recouping much smaller percentages from the tie-in agreements than from ticket sales. Gradually their merchandising arms withered away, until George Lucas reformulated the relation with his 1977 deal for 100 per cent control of the tie-in profits of *Star Wars*. (Disney had been there before him, licensing its own retail division, 'for comic books and toys even before they made *Snow White*, their first full-length feature in 1937' (Mathews 1998, quoting Kramer).)

The **block booking** and **blind booking** practices and other enforcements on exhibitors, both domestic and foreign, meant that they had to take 'blocks' of films chosen by the studio (instead of simply those they wanted), at times determined by the studio for maximum profitability of limited prints across 'first run' lucrative city sites ('clearance') (see Maltby and Craven 1995: ch. 2). Like the other cartel practices cited above, this was supported by various US governments (see Gomery 1998a; Miller 1998) until the 1940 consent decree in the anti-trust suit against the majors which began the 1948 **divorcement**.

---

for all its rhetoric of pure competition . . . the US film industry has been assisted by decades of tax credit schemes, film commissions, State and Commerce department representation, currency assistance.

(Miller 1998: 373)

In addition, the Second World War (1939–45), though not as emphasized as the First World War (1914–18) in the accounts of the demise of early Hollywood's rival industries, hugely enabled Hollywood's global consolidation in the 1940s. European cinemas were shut down, in the case of the Axis powers, or curtailed. A huge backlog of US films exported 'the American way of life'. They were literally speeded on their way by the developing US shipping industry (Miller 1998: 372) and by the associations of American products generally with GI soldiers, with freedom from war, and with the glamour of unfamiliar luxuries, whether they be nylon stockings, real coffee, chewing gum, Coca Cola or peanut butter.

---

the very local connections which Liverpool had with America . . . [as] a key trading port, occasionally offered these women fabrics, nylons, magazines, shoes from the States: Maria recalls giving relatives pictures of stars from magazines and asking them to bring back the fabrics shown.

(Lacey 1999: 57)

Classical or standardized?

The Frankfurt School was fascinated by the problems of standardized cultural production, but in the end often asserted that the factory production of automobiles was exactly like that of motion pictures. But a problem in thinking about the economic nature of the 'Dream Factory' is that though a product is manufactured, it is not the celluloid reels which are sold to audiences, but the possibility of pleasure in watching a competently screened film in agreeable surroundings, with all that involves. As Miller (1998: 371) points out, economics has had difficulty theorizing cinema. The studio system does strongly resemble other capitalist industries. The studio processes can be seen as the equivalent of factory production lines, with workers dedicated to specialized tasks, the distribution of film prints as the equivalent of wholesale arrangements, and exhibition of the product in cinemas as the final, 'retail' level. Yet each one of these leisure or luxury products, films, is different, unlike cars or deodorants which depend on as close a standardization as can be achieved on a 'run'. Bordwell *et al.* (1985) use the phrase 'serial manufacture' rather than 'mass production' of film in this context and quote Dore Schary, an executive producer working at both RKO and MGM:

> Efficiency experts trained in other industries are usually baffled when they try to fit the making of movies to their standard rules . . . a movie is essentially a hand-craft operation . . . but it must be made on a factory line basis, with production line economics, if we're to hold the price down within reach of most of the people.
>
> (Bordwell *et al.* 1985: 320)

Relatedly, in studio Hollywood, if investment is seen as made in individual films, then most investments, calculated on that as single product, are failures. Most studio films did not make their money back, but if enough were made, with accompanying control of distribution, publicity and exhibition, there would be some winners, and overall security of profit.

Bordwell *et al.* (1985) offer a refreshing revaluation of one part of this debate on standardized product, pointing to the crucial double meaning of 'standards': not only as 'sameness' but also as a kind of quality, that is to say as the *maintenance of* standards. They also argue that there is a tension in Hollywood's economic practices: between standardizing the product (for efficient, economical mass production) and differentiating films, as the studios bid competitively for a consumer's disposable income and time. Staiger (1986), for example, points to the way that cinema advertising discourses laid (and continue to lay) heavy emphasis on novelty, originality and uniqueness. Paradoxically this often involved the studio in the expensive cultivation of 'unique' personalities or stars or perhaps in a lavish kind of 'realism' and its means of production: massive sets and hundreds of people as in the realism of the Atlanta fire in *Gone with the Wind* (US 1939). All this highlights a real tension: between the imperatives of low cost and repetition, making for economies of scale (necessary for maximizing profits) and the ideologies of the high cost value of originality, displays, technological tours de force of cinema (also necessary for profitability).

A major competitor of the term 'standardized' in this context is 'classical', with its very different, more positive resonances. David Bordwell, Janet Staiger and Kristin Thompson are best known for their jointly authored book *The Classical Hollywood Cinema* (hereafter *CHC*), published in 1985. It makes a richly researched empirical and historical case, drawing on the huge (then newly opened) United Artists, pre-1948 Warners, RKO and Monogram archives, donated to the Wisconsin Centre for Film and Theatre research in 1969. Possession of this privileged cultural resource is key to the development of sophisticated accounts of Hollywood such as the work of Balio, Allen, Gomery, as well as the later writing of Bordwell, Staiger and Thompson. *CHC* (and what now seems like its successor volume, the much reprinted *Film Art*, first published in 1979) has become a canonical text in Film Studies, hugely influential on the expanding numbers of students wanting to study cinema in higher education from the 1980s in both the USA and the UK, who were and continue to be 'trained in its definitions' (Kaplan 1998: 273).

Its magisterial use of 'classical' was a contrast to earlier uses of the term 'classic', which tended to fall between two poles. First, there was, and still is, the use of 'classic' as a general term of approval, mostly at an aesthetic or very broadly systemic rather than industrial level, such as praise for Chaplin or John Ford having 'classic' styles. French uses of the term (see Hansen 2000: 335 for examples) culminate in Bazin's (1971) praise of certain westerns as exemplifying a classical quality, involving key terms such as 'maturity' and 'balance', which is not due to individual talent but to what he calls the genius of the system, the richness of its traditions, and its fertility when it comes into contact with new elements.

Second, such broadly aesthetic praise gives way, in the radical political climate of the 1960s and 1970s, to analysis of 'classic' Hollywood as a system, part of early attempts to think the ideological-psychoanalytic effects of such media forms. In such contexts *CHC* was first remarkable in rejecting established ways to approach Hollywood. Gone is Hollywood's image as simple popcorn 'Dream Factory', as are explicitly evaluative uses of the term 'classical', whether as critical of an ideological effect, or as celebratory of the maturity of 'the system'. Gone are oppositions between art and industry, with the latter as backdrop to a list of 'greats' – directors, stars, actors – celebrated as exceptions to its rules. Instead *CHC* attempts a hugely ambitious analysis of how the economic, the technological and the stylistic intertwine, via the norms of the system. To explore these norms the authors carefully examine, line by line, shot by shot, a statistically random sample of 100 of the 15,000 feature films produced by Hollywood between 1915 and 1960.

'Hollywood' is identified as a group style, rather like German Expressionism and Italian Neo-realism. However, these categories are used to describe what are actually rather different and heterogeneous product, such as, in the German example, low budget films of the Weimar period such as *The Cabinet of Dr Caligari* (Germany 1919) along with the vastly expensive and spectacular *Metropolis* (Germany 1926). Here is the first problem, since the sheer industrial clout of Hollywood's distribution and exhibition arms is downplayed in making such a comparison. German Expressionism, Italian Neo-realism and other national or group 'movements' are not players on a level field with Hollywood, but 'defensive formations shaped in competition with and resistance to Hollywood products' (Hansen 2000: 13).

For all the empirical richness and sophistication with which studio system practices are analysed, *CHC*'s account in some ways oddly resembles 1970s 'apparatus theory'. Since it is impossible to discuss 'texts' without hypothesizing their encounter with a viewer, the model of 'a' hypothetical 'viewer' is developed, along with the assumed processes this viewer would undergo in viewing a film. These processes are not derived from ideology or the unconscious, but from **cognitive psychology** and (less predictably) Russian neoformalist poetics (see Chapter 6) which attempted to defamiliarize the processes of narrative.

And despite the rich account of industrial practices and histories, the tone of *CHC* is that of an attempt at a 'value-free and scientifically valid account' which the term 'classical' does little to rescue (Hansen 2000: 340). For example, when dealing with the labour struggles and inequalities within the studios, it is the functionalist role of union structures which is emphasized (see Davis 1990; Neilsen 1990[1983]; Clark 1995; Miller 2000 for more work-centred emphases). The 'craftsman-labourer' is said to seek to 'achieve what the industry rewarded' in this account. The 'classed' or gendered nature of work in the studios, or the impact of the House UnAmerican Activities Committee (HUAC) receive little attention.

CHC emphasizes the past, tradition, a cool control, a concealing of artifice, the films' 'fundamental emotional appeal that transcends class and nation' (Bordwell *et al.* 1985: 3) which fits oddly with the following:

- The sense of Hollywood cinema, in the 1920s and 1930s, as the very essence of the turbulent 'modern'.
- The huge differences between films in the studio years. That unruly and sensational strain now theorized as **melodrama** and seen as spanning both

'male' and 'female' genres, and those genres which involve strong bodily response (such as pornography, comedy and horror) fit awkwardly into the 'classical' ideal (see L. Williams 1996).

- The role of exhibition and distribution practices, including such key components as the star-genre system and, more recently, armies of copyright lawyers.
- Hollywood's interrelations with audiences, and, slightly different, with reception theories (which Staiger did go on to research: Staiger 1992). *CHC* prefers the model of a 'sexless, genderless, classless, stateless "hypothetical entity"' (Nichols 1992: 64, quoted in Kaplan 1998: 276), 'biologically hard-wired' (Bordwell 1996: 23) to respond as programmed. This raises at least as many problems as have been explored for psychoanalytic accounts of films' workings (see Merck 1992).
- The relationship of Hollywood with consumer culture which, partly through product placements and tie-ins designed to stimulate desire for goods, motored the consolidation of early Hollywood, and remains at the heart of its formative inheritance from the early twentieth century capitalist metropolis (Kaplan 1998: 276–7).
- Questions of cultural-ideological influence with which the 1970s structuralist theories (often now collapsed together into 'Grand Theory' by writers such as Bordwell and Carroll 1996) had tried to grapple. To take one example, Smith (1998: 4) points out that *CHC* seems primarily interested in the 'compulsory norm' of the union of the (white) heterosexual couple at the end of most Hollywood films as an example of Hollywood's need for narrative closure, rather than as opening onto questions of gender, sexual politics and audience recognitions.

A speculation on modernity and modernism

Hansen (2000) suggests that the term 'vernacular modernism', rather than 'classical', best describes the global success of Hollywood films from their earliest years. 'Vernacular' has the sense of a 'lowly' form triumphant, as a kind of shared 'language' which can, however, be used for different purposes. Even Soviet montage cinema, she suggests, dedicated to the revolutionary overthrow of the capitalist system, was nevertheless deeply influenced by this 'vernacular'. Its typical combination of narrative causality, continuity editing, and construction of time–space coherence in the popular 'low' Hollywood genres (such as adventure serials, slapstick comedy) dominated Russian screens by 1915.

Such analysis avoids, or perhaps evades, the problems of

- applying 'popular' to all of Hollywood's products, and screening practices, across all periods – especially our own, which seems a very different moment
- weighing the evidence of audience disappointments as well as their varied enjoyments
- ignoring the often violent and always unequally distributed ways in which such popularity is enabled by industrial clout.

However, as opposed to 'classical', 'vernacular' does have a capacity to suggest how different Hollywood forms were appropriated and transformed in different global and national contexts. It also valuably avoids a collapse into myths of the 'universal language of cinema'.

Modernism raises different issues. It is a complex term, for which new definitions are emerging, partly as a response to the slipperiness of the term 'postmodernism' which, in one of its several meanings (see Morley 1996), suggests 'we' are now living in a period of democratizing break from the high status art forms called modernist. The term usually signifies a set of post-First World War art movements: the writings of Eliot, Woolf, Joyce, (perhaps) the montage film experiments of Eisenstein or the paintings of Picasso. These are often argued to be 'reflexive' works, revealing and updating the formal conventions of earlier classical or realist forms (such as the happy ending of the nineteenth century novel). Celebrated as high art, they are said to draw attention to the 'language' conventions they used in a way beyond the grasp of 'naïve' realist forms, often constructed as their defining 'other'. They are also argued to hybridize the cultural levels and geographical or historical sources of quotations: Picasso incorporates African art and cigarette packets into his paintings; T.S. Eliot quotes from European and Sanskrit languages as well as popular songs. Postmodernism now claims such hybridity and levelling for contemporary popular forms.

The timing and existence of 'modernism' in cinema has been hotly debated. As late as the 1960s and 1970s certain films (the work of Godard, Straub-Huillet and Antonioni) are cited as modernist for the ways they draw self-reflexive attention to the familiar editing or acting or realist codes of popular Hollywood cinema. In this model, Hollywood is seen as the 'classical' film equivalent of the nineteenth century novel and its happy endings, realism, 'transparent' language, and so on.

Hansen (1995, 2000), however, makes a slightly different move, drawing on the writings of the German theorist Kracauer, a figure on the fringes of the Frankfurt School. She suggests that cinematic modernity has always produced examples of cinema which is at one and the same time popular and reflexive, though she no longer defines 'reflexivity' in purely formal terms.

She suggests that popular films reflected on the historical experience of modernity right in the heart of Hollywood (and thereby also its export markets). She then argues that the reception of this popular-reflexive, rather than art cinema, can be seen as constituting an expanded **public sphere** or opportunity for 'publicness'. The term 'public sphere' comes from the writings of the German theorist Habermas (1989) arguing that modernity is partly characterized by public spaces for deliberative debate which emerged at the end of the eighteenth and beginning of the nineteenth century, along with industrialization and markets. Something called 'public opinion' began to form, in places like the coffee houses frequented by middle class men, and with it the promise of citizenship. These men could anticipate playing a role in what had been previously exclusive, still part feudal European states. The public sphere was theorized as informational, journalistic, 'official-political' public arenas or forms of those arenas, perhaps never actually existing but to be aimed at as an ideal, by public service broadcasting, for example. Cinema plays no part in Habermas's theory.

The line of argument was developed, by Habermas and others, that with the loss of such possibilities came the 'society of the spectacle' a 're-feudalization' of authority, reviving 'the courtly world of image management' (Silverstone 1999: 147) in which we are said to be living, as consumers, not citizens, and in which spectacular, image centred forms such as cinema are said to be central.

Such a public sphere is often seen as relic of a discredited 'Enlightenment', not worth reviving in its inevitably white, hyper-rationalist, male and masculinist forms (see Carter *et al.* 1998; Allan 1999; McGuigan 2000 for debates). Objections are made by both postmodernists and by those involved in the kinds of politics (around gender, race and sexuality) which were virtually excluded from what can sound like the gentleman's club of 'the public sphere'. Recent moves try to connect such public, masculinized images of an idealized 'Enlightenment' to the more feminized everyday experiences of the new cultures of consumption, which have been developing at the same time. One of the boldest strokes in this reconceptualization is Hansen's (2000) suggestion that the impulses of a democratizing modernism be understood not simply as high art forms, but as 'a whole range of cultural and artistic practices that register, respond to, and reflect upon processes of modernisation and the experience of modernity' (Hansen 2000: 16). Hollywood, as a key agent for the modernizing 'Americanism' inseparable from that consumer capitalism which swept the world from the end of the First World War onwards, promised and made specific images with which to grasp the sensuous allure of a fabulous consumer modernity. Bound up with this, Bloch (1990[1959]) (another figure on the fringes of the Frankfurt School) and others have suggested that such entertainment forms offered glimpses and fantasies of collectivity and gender equality, irrational yet connective dreams of new kinds of sensuous, comfort-ful and sexualized lives. Hansen (1991) gives two examples of early Hollywood circulating images which broke existing domains of 'public' and 'private' modes of conduct, and practices of visibility (especially of active looking) for women. The *Corbett-Fitzsimmons Flight* (1897) was a 100-minute long film of a heavyweight boxing bout, hugely popular with women, which offered them 'the forbidden sight of male bodies in semi-nudity engaged in intimate and intense physical action'. Hansen's other example involves the ways in which looking at Valentino's body, and the looks between him and the women characters in his films, also offered an alternative horizon of experience for women cinema-goers. She suggests (Hansen 2000) that this type of entertainment offered a space where the traumatic effects of modernity could be 'reflected, rejected or disavowed, transmuted or negotiated' (the silent injuries of class, perhaps, though less often those of race; the experiences of massified war).

Hollywood, often understood by film theory as trying to lure its viewers into a deceptive and ideologically poisonous 'illusion of reality', is here argued, at least in its early years, to constitute a kind of 'public sphere' (or 'publicness' as Donald and Donald 2000 suggest Habermas might be better translated). It is said to represent 'an emerging, heterogeneous mass public ignored and despised by dominant culture', conducting 'debates', albeit sensuously, around the changes which modernity, including cinema, wrought for gender and class divisions, appropriate behaviour in public, and so on. Hansen (2000) speculates on a certain fading of this capacity for cinema in the sound era (from the late 1920s onwards), and suggests that television has in some ways taken over the 'debating modernity' role which cinema may have had. Donald and Donald (2000) speculate that cinema may still have this function in totalitarian regimes. The question of the next chapter is what happens to the industry which arguably works with such dreams and sensuous debates as it undergoes global conglomcrate change, and as capitalist modernity enters its latest phases?

Further reading

Bordwell, D., Staiger, J. and Thompson, K. (1985) *The Classical Hollywood Cinema: Film Style and Mode of Production to 1960*. London and New York: Routledge & Kegan Paul.

Charney, L. and Schwartz, V.R. (eds) (1995) *Cinema and the Invention of Modern Life*. Berkeley, CA: University of California Press.

Gomery, D. (1998) Hollywood corporate business practice and periodizing contemporary film history, in S. Neale and M. Smith (eds) *Contemporary Hollywood Cinema*. London: Routledge.

Hansen, M.B. (2000) The mass production of the senses: classical cinema as vernacular modernism, in C. Gledhill and L. Williams (eds) *Reinventing Film Studies*. London and New York: Arnold.

2 | 'NEW AGAIN' HOLLYWOOD

> Shooting a bar scene recently, I noticed a huge Coca-Cola sign in the background. 'Get it out', I said, 'it doesn't belong in the shot.' The producer came up to me, saying 'that sign has contributed $200,000 to our budget.'
>
> (Haskell Wexler, quoted in Ettedgui 1998: 80)

> Crucially, information about international consumption [of films] is fragmentary and even contradictory because, despite the threats of the industry, dubbing and clandestine pirating abound . . . Bombay has 8,000 unauthorised cable systems using satellite dishes to grab whatever programming they can; . . . This is not a 'Third World' problem; Italy heads the international video piracy tables.
>
> (During 1997: 216–17)

The word 'blockbuster' originates from the city queues 'around the block' for a movie, sign of its success in the studio era. Though it is often used of the latest global hit movie, in fact films such as *Star Wars Episode One: Phantom Menace* (US 1999) are sometimes shown around the clock at multiplexes. Actual queues, rather than being a sign of commitment to a specific movie, are now few and far between, and often the place where a last-minute choice of film is made. Much contemporary 'cinema' involves neither cinemas nor their screens. Film viewing can involve illegal cabling of electricity and signal into a shanty town, or reception via the Internet or on a digital TV in a luxury car.

Such odd combinations make up contemporary 'Hollywood'. Films still exist as reels of celluloid, as they did at the start of cinema in the 1890s, and then as Hollywood's main product in the studio years. But more usually now they circulate as video cassette, digital, Internet and broadcast TV product. Blockbuster imagery extends off-screen to theme-park rides, computer game scenarios, toys, **IMAX** displays, simulator theatres and other entertainment forms.

By 'Hollywood', most people understand what is in fact only a part of its output, a few 'blockbuster' films each year, often costing as much as the gross national products of many poor countries. Financially crucial to the majors, and making up most people's experience of cinema-going, these films can no longer be thought of as single commodities. They are the anchors to huge franchises, lying at the centre of a network of commercial activities, hits which can be systematically reproduced, profitably fragmented and marketed across the parent company's other conglomerate holdings. Some of them (such as the James Bond films and Star Wars series) are now themselves referred to as 'franchises'. They are launched simultaneously on thousands of screens, with publicity campaigns almost as large as the production budgets themselves, and are re-experienced or even *pre-experienced* through endless tie-in merchandising, which both underwrites and links itself to the prestige of the mega-budget movie event or 'event movie'.

This chapter will explore

- the histories of the changes to, and continuities within the Hollywood studio system which have produced this stage
- key concepts which have been used to understand such processes, such as 'new Hollywood', 'high concept', 'post-studio', 'post-Fordist' and 'postmodern'
- some of the resulting characteristics of the blockbuster films 'on screen', which Chapter 3 will also discuss.

Post-studio histories

The gap between the film industry sketched above and that of the 'classic' studio years has provoked alluring debate in film studies. A number of terms try to describe the economic-production nature of contemporary Hollywood (see Smith 1998): **New Hollywood**, 'post-classical', 'post-studio',

> It's less scary to make a 50-million dollar film than a 10-million dollar film. For 50-million dollars you can afford big stars and special effects and you know you'll get some money back ... With a 10-million dollar film with no stars, you run the risk of losing it all.
>
> (Dag Bjorkegren, quoted in Barker and Brooks 1998: 18)

'post-Fordist', 'postmodern' and **high concept** Hollywood. Let us take the terms 'post-studio' and 'post-Fordist'. Studio system film production (see Smith 1998) is argued to have resembled other Fordist production-line methods (like those for the 1920s Ford car production that they are named after) involving

- economies of scale through standardization
- a precise division of labour within a mass production system
- some predictable standardization of the choices of consumers (summarized, for cars, in the slogan 'You can have any colour [of Ford car] as long as it's black').

These factory methods have mostly disappeared from a certain suburb of Los Angeles, as from many other areas of western manufacture. However, if you check the credits on recent big animation features, for example, there are sometimes visible traces of modes of labour rather different from the magical, 'postmodern', 'virtual economy' disappearance of 'Fordist' work celebrated in so many accounts of 'knowledge industries' like cinema and TV. South East Asian workers are part of a familiar story of 'outreach', non-unionized labour, the displacement of routine low paid work to abroad, and then a chasing of ever lower pay rates by the studio employers (see Webster 1999). Even electronic paint box systems are likely to operate this capitalist logic–Russia is already said to be offering lower wage rates than India for some kinds of routine computer work.

> a report issued last month showed that $2.8 bn worth of film and television money and 23,000 jobs had crossed the border to Canada last year ... to profit from production costs which are 25% less than Hollywood's. Salaries for technicians are lower over the border, and the Canadian government offers tax breaks.
>
> (Report of the collapse of plans for a new DreamWorks studio in Los Angeles, *Guardian*, 2 July 1999)

Nevertheless, dominant accounts of post-studio Hollywood are right to emphasize changes in the mode of production, though the term 'post-studio' tends to play down the persistence of the power of the majors within a still hierarchically organized and vertically integrated system. When the majors were forced to separate production and distribution from their monopolistic exhibition practices, at least in the USA, in 1948 they indeed lost the stable production routines which that structure enabled. But they remained major, with relatively few changes in membership of the elite club. Like other big firms, the studios or film factories began to operate in ways that have been characterized as post-Fordist. They co-financed more specialized and therefore risky package deals on individual films rather than operating standardized 'runs' of star-genre movies with a guaranteed take-up in cinemas.

This move to **package unit** assembled films, with the whole industry, potentially, as pool for a film's labour and talents, involved a growth of two kinds of 'independence'. **Independent** production companies (such as First National or United Artists) had existed during the studio system, usually defined as small firms with no corporate relationship to a distribution firm, that is a major; 'neither owned nor . . . owned by a distributing company' (Bordwell *et al.* 1985: 317). There 'were very few independent productions in the 1930s and only about 40 independent producers in 1945, but by 1958 some 58% of productions were "independent" ' (Hillier 1992: 7). While this remains a key definition, the role of truly 'independent' companies has diminished in Hollywood as connections to major studios for distribution have become ever more important, especially for the big budget blockbusters.

For the expensive packages represented by films such as *Terminator-2* (produced by the then-independent Carolco: see Balio 1998b), a second kind of independent company emerged, taking over the pre- to post-production work which had previously been divided and ruled by the studios. Talent agencies such as ICM (International Creative Management) and CAA (Creative Artists Agency) were founded in the mid-1970s. These specialized in putting movie deals together, assembling writers, stars and directors. A range of other firms sprang up, notably special effects houses such as George Lucas's Industrial Light and Magic, but also catering firms, make-up specialists, equipment hirers and others. Post-Fordist theorists call this process 'flexible specialization'. What were once points of a standardized production line, such as special FX, can, in this more specialized mode, be made to respond more flexibly to rapid changes in market needs, especially different 'niche markets' (Smith 1998: 7) but also fluctuating labour costs.

Some have objected that, given the varied nature of the studio system's output (more like 'serial manufacture' than 'mass production', as *CHC* argues), Hollywood between 1920 and 1960 is not an ideal candidate for 'Fordist' analysis. If this is so, then the break of 1948 was less traumatic for the majors than is usually assumed, and certainly less of a Jack and the Giant Killer victory for state regulation. (It is also pointed out that a few 'independent' production units, such as Selznick's or Goldwyn's, functioned during the studio system, and a few 'blockbusters' such as *Gone with the Wind* (US 1939) predate 1948.) 'Post-studio' along with a qualified version of post-Fordism, however, certainly seems a better term than the abstract term 'postmodern' in encouraging historically specific understandings of economics as they relate to cinema's commercial aesthetics. However, if it is used so as simply to stress the pastness of the studio system, it risks underplaying the still-presentness of the majors' dominance, certainly at the key levels of distribution, marketing and exhibition, and also in the still fiercely hierarchized and often economically violent organization of this capitalist business.

Several stages are usually listed as those through which Hollywood has arrived at its present condition, which we might call one of media conglomerate globalization. The moves away from the studio system, from the 1948 ruling to the mid-1970s (see the useful chronology in Maltby and Craven 1995: 466–82) have been heavily mythologized: melancholy imagery of major studios' deserted back-lots and vocabulary such as 'movie brats' to describe directors who are successful within the new conditions.

Key factors included changes in US demographics and media use after the Second World War, which involved a move to the suburbs and 'baby boom', hence less cinema-going, and the associated growth in the popularity of TV watching at home (1 million US homes had TV by 1949) rather than movie-going outside the home. This factor is heavily played on, and runs through Hollywood's, usually hostile, imagery of TV all the way down to *The Truman Show* (US 1998). Interestingly video, invented in the 1950s, and arguably equally influential, is not the target of such hostility, perhaps partly because of its obvious usefulness for the recirculation of Hollywood product.

The majors responded to TV partly by trying to differentiate their output from it, by such technological developments as 3-D, Todd-AO, Cinemascope and so on. But according to Gomery (1996b: 407–8) the decline in audiences began five years before TV became a viable alternative to cinema. In addition, far from being decimated by TV, the majors, from the start, were intrigued by its investment possibilities, just as they had been by sound technologies. They soon established a successful relationship with the TV companies, producing 'films for TV' and serials, and releasing TV rights to their backlog of films: the 'vaults' became 'libraries'. In 1960 the US networks started showing feature films in prime time, thus transforming, for the majors, the status of their collections of old movies. The results stretch right down to the AOL–Time-Warner merger in January 2000 and digital future markets. By 1961, 'Hollywood was turning out far more hours of TV programming than feature films, having reactivated their B-movie production processes to feed TV's voracious appetite for programming' (Schatz 1997: 79). As Gomery states:

> We should . . . recognise that for nearly half a century people have watched most films on TV . . . to Hollywood the coming of television has proved to be the most significant technical addition in industry history.
>
> (Gomery 1996b: 408)

Gomery also complicates the argument that this was Hollywood's first move into diversified operations, pointing out that from as early as the 1920s Hollywood companies had diversified by taking over the popular music business.

The US Justice Department brought a suit against the eight major studios in 1938, charging them with conspiracy to restrain and monopolize trade through the operation of restrictive practices in the distribution and exhibition of films. This action (sometimes called the Paramount decree) forced all the 'Big Five' majors to sell off their theatre chains, though only in the USA. Hidden in many accounts is the slow erosion of this 1948 anti-trust ruling during the 1980s Reagan years, the ruling being finally reversed in 1985. Now a few close knit duopolies control production and exhibition, again–UCI showing Universal Paramount films in the UK, and so on.

But the break was initially dramatic. The notorious blind and block booking system along with 'clearance', designed to help guaranteed steady cash flow, and thus a predictable demand from exhibitors which the studio production lines needed, vanished. The majors were forced to focus on financing and distribution (that supremely important source of power in the film business). They were shrewd operators in new postwar conditions of falling audiences and the first wave of corporate take-overs. The tectonic shifts began unevenly: Universal became Universal International in 1946, and concentrated on independent production; Howard Hughes sold RKO to General Telluride, a subsidiary of the General Tire and Rubber Company, in 1955. From the 1950s to the 1970s, the major studios were taken over in more rounds of big conglomerate buyouts – Paramount by Gulf and Western (1966), United Artists by Transamerica Corporation (1967), Warners by the Kinney Corporation (1969) and so on – making such cinema a minor strand of much larger global operations. Disney, by 1966, already had most of its wealth in theme parks and no longer in cartoons themselves (A. Smith 2000).

The majors also made shrewd accommodation to changing audiences and tastes, part of another periodization: 'New Hollywood' (see Kramer 1998a), a term which is applied to a spate of film-making between the late 1960s and the early 1970s (*Jaws* 1975 is often dated as the 'beginning of the end'). After the eroded audience figures of the late 1960s, when movie attendance had 'fallen to barely twenty million moviegoers per week (down from nearly one hundred million in the mid-1940s)' (Schatz 1997: 79), and a series of costly flops, the majors tried other kinds of experimentation. Film imports by then made up almost two-thirds of total US releases (Schatz 1997: 79). Since at least the 1940s – see the Italian Neo-realist *Paisa* (1946) for example – the studios had been involved in European production and finance, sometimes of innovative forms such as 'spaghetti westerns' (see Buscombe 1998).

it's his [Gordon's] insider look at how 'B' movies could be cranked out in the Europe of the '50s and '60s, when film production was becoming decentralised and significant profits could be made if costs were held down and host nations persuaded by creative producers to put up the soft money [which] is a terrific antidote to the veneer of glamour and genius so often applied to the industry.

(B. Ruby Rich 2000)

Newer 'hip' audiences were emerging, not only from that context and from the new wealth of movies on TV but also from the politically energized atmosphere of the Black Civil Rights movement, 1960s feminism and the anti-Vietnam War movement. 'New Hollywood' describes the emergence of often adventurous work by a group of male, white directors (Cassavetes, Coppola, Scorsese and others). They were mostly film-school trained, with experience of experimental film-making, whose work linked the traditions of classic Hollywood genre film-making with European art-cinema. Examples include films like *The Graduate*, *Bonnie and Clyde*, *Easy Rider*, *M*A*S*H* and *Midnight Cowboy* – all released in 1969.

The more commercially successful among the 'New' film-makers are now the grey eminences of film director or auteur-stardom: Francis Ford Coppola, Brian De Palma, George Lucas, John Milius, Martin Scorsese, Steven Spielberg. New Hollywood's film 'literacy' involved some impatience as well as fascination with 'old Hollywood movies', a new degree of allusiveness to both older Hollywood films and, cautiously, to European arthouse cinema. (*The Searchers* seems to have been an especially resonant text, possibly in part because of its indispensability as both 'classic' and 'revised' John Ford in the film courses which most of them had taken.)

> *Taxi Driver*'s jamming of styles: Fritz Lang expressionism, Bresson's distanced realism, and Corman's low budget . . . [it] is actually a *Tale of Two Cities*: the old Hollywood and the new Paris of Bresson-Rivette-Godard.
>
> (Paterson and Farber 1976, quoted in Rosenbaum 2000)

Along with this allusiveness went a loosening up of some of the conventions associated with the studio system: of its narrative expectations of an 'action' rather than 'character' driven narrative; of its endings often unambiguous and 'closed'; or of the professional norms of framing, editing and smooth camera work in the continuity system, geared towards efficient mass production. Additionally, this 'New Hollywood' often addressed themes that were perceived to be daring or controversial. It was interested in counter-cultural, even directly political subject matter, especially around the Vietnam War. It was also often explicit in its sexual imagery, though this was usually addressed to a presumed male, heterosexual viewer, and thus began to appropriate some of the appeal of European arthouse cinema. Along with the changes in US censorship practices, such as the demise of the formal Production Code around 1967 and liberal rulings on censorship, this 'knocked the bottom out of the European art film market', in Balio's (1998b) resonant phrase. Other, newer forms of realism also surfaced (especially in the work of John Cassavetes), such as the documentary 'hand-held' camera form called **ciné-vérité** (translated as 'cinema truth'), which was made possible by lightweight camera technology and shifting discourses around what now counted as 'realism', especially within TV. These factors enabled rather different kinds of lower budget film-making.

Yet though this 'New Hollywood' is often described as resulting from the impact of 'good' European artiness on young, film-educated US directors, a different strand suggests the resilience and contradictoriness of low budget work within the late stages of the studio system. Roger Corman of AIP (American International Pictures) and New World Films, made low budget 'exploitation' 'B' movies on tight time scales, such as *Attack of the Crab Monsters*, *Piranha* (yes, it does follow *Jaws*) and *The Wasp Woman* from 1953 onwards. In the very 'depths' of the Hollywood system this gave opportunities, sometimes for first work, for huge numbers of film workers, key directors, writers and actors for New Hollywood such as Bogdanovitch, Coppola, Dante, Demme, De Niro, Hopper, Sayles and Scorsese as well as women directors such as Amy Jones and Stephanie Rothman, who were employed partly to cut down on costs. Noel Carroll (1982) argues that

Corman can be credited with having established the 'two-tiered' film with 'special grace notes for insiders . . . for the cognoscenti, and soaring, action charged melody for the rest' (Carroll 1982: 74). The doubling of genres cited below by John Sayles, reminiscing about his time as scriptwriter with Corman, recalls, indeed seems to anticipate, one of the strategies of 'high concept' movie-making:

> On *Battle Beyond the Stars*, Corman said, 'If you can make *Seven Samurai* into a western, you can make it into a science fiction film'. He had another idea to make *Mutiny on the Bounty* in outer space.
>
> (Sayles interview, *Guardian*, 14 January 2000)

High concept and multi-marketed rollercoasters

Linda Williams, in one of the pieces which complicate easy periodizations, has argued that it is *Psycho* in 1960 which pioneered the 'roller coaster sensibility of repeated tension and release, assault and escape' in which 'narrative is not abandoned [but] often takes second place to a succession of visual and auditory shocks and thrills' (L. Williams 1994: 15). These textual shifts are fascinatingly accompanied by changes in exhibition practices, such as Hitchcock's insistence that nobody enter the cinema after the start of the film. This began the shift towards disciplined queuing, punctuality and also to the secret-keeping of audiences ready to be thrilled to death by their chosen movie. Reviewers' work now is almost defined by not giving away the ending of a movie, in contrast to the discussions of Film Studies, which need knowledge of the ending in relation to the rest of the film.

Jaws (US 1975) is usually cited as a watershed movie here, variously referred to as the first 'rollercoaster' or 'event' or 'summer blockbuster' movie. It was directed by Steven Spielberg and takes *Psycho*'s processes further, within the conglomerate industrial conditions of post-studio Hollywood. The 'package deal' system of post-studio film-making from which it emerged was new, but it involved one of the oldest aims of a volatile business: trying to avoid risk. This was offset by corporate franchise and marketing clout, as well as the traditional strategies (a degree of vertical integration with exhibitors) of the studio years. *Jaws* was pre-sold via a best-selling novel, with the movie rights purchased even before the novel was published. It was expensive ($3.5 million initially) by 1975 standards, and involved a huge promotional campaign with tie-in products such as mugs, posters, beach gear and TV advertising (see Schatz 1993). Its summer release, between late May and July, at a time when most films calculated to become hits were released at Christmas, is argued by Peter Kramer (1998a) to have pioneered a key exhibition strategy. Targeting mostly boys and young men, such a release can minimize bad 'word of mouth' by simultaneous hugely publicized release on hundreds or thousands of screens, followed by a long holiday playing opportunity, with the attractions of air-conditioned cinemas in the hot summer months of places such as the USA.

Distributors now widely publicize the enormous production budgets of blockbusters: typically three or four times that of a regular film, and usually at least equal to the production costs of large budget films such as one of the James Bond 'franchise'. These combined costs are presented as being synonymous with 'quality': 'size matters' in the words of the *Titanic* poster. They form part of a highly publicized intention to give the audience a spectacularly visceral experience, via both sound and image, which they will not easily forget. Theme parks promise a repeat of the cinematic thrill, and are now often built with the design talents of the same people making the movies. Douglas Trumbull's career, for example, goes from NASA (National Aeronautics and Space Administration) training films, through work on *2001*, *Close Encounters*, *Blade Runner*, to theme park, interactive entertainment and IMAX ride design. Franchised goods, especially toys, produce other webs of attachment to the 'hit' movie. All of this, along with corporate ownership of the press and TV channels eager for movie gossip and film clips, can help such movies become 'events', put discussion and speculation about it 'on the agenda' in a way that becomes culturally hard to avoid. The Internet quickly became part of these processes.

This mass of embedding publicity clout might suggest that such films cannot fail. In the long run, most high budget films, following the *Jaws* prototype deal, will eventually cover their costs through their after-life in TV, cable, video, rights to toys, books, music, theme parks, computer games and so on. The steady, studio-derived structures of distribution power across many different kinds of screen will tend to almost guarantee long-term profitability to any big film, even such a publicized flop as *Waterworld* (US 1995). I may zap across channels, recall I never paid to see *The Postman* (US 1997) and would now like to take a peek to know what kind of a turkey it is – but I have already contributed to its revenues via the 'blind booking' and 'block booking' deals of cable subscription.

Nevertheless, some would-be blockbusters can still be said to risk 'failure' as big earners. The crucial measurement is how fast the huge investments can be recouped in the crucial 'first weekend' takings, given the high costs of interest rates on loans, completion bonds and so on. Which brings us to 'high concept' and the renewed importance of marketing and test screening.

> The pursuit of money is the only reason to make movies.
> (Don Simpson, Paramount 'Corporate Philosophy Paper',
> quoted in Fleming 1998)

The term 'high concept' originated in the commercially funded US TV industries, and is often credited to Don Simpson. Wyatt (1994: 8) suggested that it is 'one central development within post-classical cinema, a style of film making modelled by economic and institutional forces'. Wyatt attributes it to two postwar factors: the rise of TV and the desire to appear responsible to Wall Street and the bankers – who have, since the 1920s, had a key role in financing Hollywood. Developed by Eisner (now head of Disney), Diller and Don Simpson in 1976, 'high concept' emphasizes three things:

- The successful pitching of a film at the pre-production stage, especially via market research processes and pre-sold marketability. For example the purchase of a book best-seller, as occurred with Peter Benchley's *Jaws*, begins a process culminating in the latest John Grisham or, rather differently, Shakespeare or Jane Austen adaptation.
- This puts an emphasis on the importance of being able to summarize the film, often a cross-over product, in a single sentence ('*Alien* is *Jaws* in a spaceship'), giving stars, genres and plot line, allied with a striking, unambiguous visual image, for example on a poster, as for *Jaws*. In summary, 'the look, the book, the hook' or, in Spielberg's words, which entered into industry wisdom, 'If a person can tell me the idea in 25 words or less, it's going to make a pretty good movie'.
- Successful saturation advertising, especially through TV, at the post-production, pre-first-weekend stages. The first weekend saturation distribution strategies depend for their success on such high awareness of the film *before* release. There is thus a huge reliance on TV for advertising, previewing and buzz around a film. The massive use of computerized audience feedback, making the 'first weekend' grossing box-office figures, is also new. Over-hasty verdicts, part of this process, are blamed by many film-makers for the failure to market certain films, which gain good reviews and word of mouth and which might well have otherwise gone on to become commercial successes. This works in tandem with the hasty adjustments to films made in the light of audience preview testing (attacked effectively by the ain't-it-cool-news.com website). Together they go some way to account for a certain homogenization of 'top level' product.

> Imagine a cross between Rambo and Dirty Harry, put him in outer space, and you have Todd (Kurt Russell) – an intergalactic warrior.
> (my cable company recent brochure)

'High concept' has been described as partly a reaction against the artistic status of the work of the early 1970s US auteurs. It certainly signals a new form of product dominant within Hollywood from around the mid-1980s though beginning with *Jaws* in 1975, and accentuated by the marketing tie-ins around *Star Wars* in 1977. As an example of what it involves aesthetically as well as economically, Wyatt (1994) contrasts *Grease* (US 1978) as an eminently 'high concept movie', with *All That Jazz* (US 1979) which, despite an emphasis on style, borrows from art cinema, tells a complicated story, has no marketing hooks and stars Roy Scheider, who at the time could not 'open' a film (that is, have his name ensure a big enough first weekend opening).

Though audience research was always important in the studio years (and some marketing research or MR had been used as early as 1915 to forecast market demand) there is now an unprecedentedly close integration of it with marketing and merchandising – as well as an unprecedented level of profitability in the films which succeed by such textual-marketing methods.

> Hollywood's ten top-grossing films have all been released since 1975 . . . even if one adjusts the figures to compensate for the dollar's reduced purchasing power – seven of the all-time blockbusters were still made between 1976 and 1985.
> (Cook and Bernink 1999: 102, quoting Hoberman)

By the early 1980s every major studio devoted a significant part of its marketing budget to MR. Wyatt (1994) makes the important point that its methodology of 'concept testing' on selected audience groups, gauging for example the connotations of particular film titles or trailers,

- cannot account for innovative film concepts
- overvalues strict adherence to the already familiar or the generic
- relies on hyperbole.

One ironic offshoot, he suggests, is that Medved (1993) and others who attack Hollywood as promoting anti-social, 'un-American' attitudes, are quite wrong, since its MR means it will seek out US *norms*, both aesthetic and social.

High concept films are often made by directors who began their careers

> The model works best predicting action and horror films . . . conse-
> quently, those films which should receive greater marketing help – in
> creating a coherent image of the film for the public – are pushed aside
> by the majors.
>
> (Wyatt 1994: 173)

making advertisements (such as Ridley and Tony Scott, Alan Parker, Adrian
Lyne, Hugh Hudson). It is not surprising then that their films are argued to
feature a series of visually arresting images (as in *Flashdance*, *Dirty Danc-
ing*, *American Gigolo*, for example) which often overwhelm their narrative
function. These may seem to resemble the 'stunts' or 'attractions' (Gunning
1990) of early cinema but have a very different origin and function: they can
be raided from the film to be used in advertising or music videos, and later
computer or DVD games around the film. Wyatt (1994) also explores the
strong match between image and music soundtracks, with a large part of
such films often effectively a music video.

The resulting 'texts' can be revealingly understood from this marketing
perspective, though the resulting films also work to offer different sets of
symbolic resources for several audiences. For 1970s audiences, *Jaws*' innovative use of hand-held camera for almost the whole of the sea sections (this
was before the invention of Steadicam), now usually unnoticed as an innovation, as well as the long speech given to Robert Shaw's character on the
delivery of the atom bomb, can be seen as part of Spielberg's 1960s experimental legacy, refreshing Hollywood while working skilfully within its
generic-industrial conventions. The film merges several genres so as to maxi-
mize potential audiences' recognitions and pleasures: the action adventure
genre; the 'coming of age' genre in Brody's conquest of his fear of the sea;
the horror-monster movie which traditionally appealed to 'young couple'
(and not simply young male) audiences; the buddy film. Studio films were
hardly ever 'pure' genre products. At the very least they usually contained a
romance sub-plot – in fact it is hard to imagine what such purity would be
like. Nevertheless, post-studio processes meant an accelerating awareness of
the need to multi-market and niche market films from the 1960s, along with
contradictions and tensions in the resulting films.

Jaws for example offers specific political pleasures such as the resonances
(for some of its original US audiences) of the traumatic shock of the 1972
Watergate conspiracy involving presidential corruption, which echoes in
the small town sleaze, media manipulation and greed which would open
the beaches for profit and whitewash their safety whatever the risk. Bound

in with this, the film handles the theme of what might constitute a more modernized masculinity in its focus on the three possible ways of being a man, working at a task with or without certain kinds of technology. These are embodied in Brody/Scheider (the regular guy, family man coming to terms with his demons), Hooper/Dreyfuss (the young techno-whizz kid) and Quint/Shaw (an older, pre-Second World War macho masculinity) along with the often comic, often tense, shifting father–son relationships between them. These are the traditional themes of male-oriented genres. That does not mean that female viewers cannot enjoy and involve themselves with the adventure, though they have to tolerate or disavow an expunging of the (traditional) 'feminine sphere' of the cluttered domestic setting which Brody seems glad to escape: the 'old man with breasts' on the beach, or the older woman who upbraids Brody for the death of her son (a resonance of Vietnam for many US audiences). All this has to be left behind so that the male adventurers can get away, thrillingly for all the audience, from that everyday world which contains women and their responsibilities and attachments.

Kramer (1998b) goes further. He argues that the summer release means that *Jaws* can be seen as self-reflexive, that is a text which openly states its own nature (a ploy previously argued as exclusive to more experimental modernist forms). The film is not simply a commercial entertainment machine, dumb and devouring as a great white shark. He suggests that the shark resembles the role of the film itself, appearing just before the Fourth of July holidays, something dangerous and unsettling, yet from which people can keep a safe distance; in fact that *Jaws* can be seen as 'about' the movie-going experience itself – its event status, the attractions it offers, and the intense responses it aims to evoke. The intensity and a degree of self-awareness, Kramer argues, go together, just as the adult accompanies the child to the movie (sometimes, of course, in the same body).

Such moves can be seen spread across Hollywood blockbusters, from the self-mockery at play in star images such as Schwarzenegger's, to the latest display of a broad kind of self-reflexivity in *Toy Story 2*'s narrative. This involves the collecting and marketing of different editions of toys, as well as the comment on the dolls which are most newly collected into the film's franchise tie-in, the Barbies, in the final complaint at the effort involved in such constant and compliant female smiling. The economic-democratic potential of such self-reflexivity of course goes only so far. One does not have to be arguing an all or nothing case for the downfall of corporate capitalism to feel that there is a bullying tone to the 'so what?' knowingness and *Titanic* ('size matters') corporate confidence around blockbusters, which Kramer sees as an attractive statement of corporate involvement in risk.

Yet, as Robert Allen (1998) puts it, such films 'retain the desire to enchant'. The commercially crucial tie-in products still need to evoke the original enchantment, experienced in the big theatrical viewing (as did the consumer products which were 'tied-in' to studio films). *Toy Story 2* may well rely economically on the huge toy franchises it anchors, but part of its charm is that it fictionalizes that very situation movingly and wittily. Along with the blockbuster's giganticism of budget, theme, spectacle and often length ('size matters' again) this also has to appeal to a 'child-adult' viewer. As Neale (1976) suggested in the mid-1970s, this was the way that Hollywood was 'relaunched'. Yet, paradoxically, he later (1990a) cites the line 'You've got to be fucking kidding!' from *The Thing* (US 1982) to explore the often violent self-consciousness of such high special FX films:

> aware that the Thing, and world it inhabits, are cinematic fabrications, the product . . . of an up to date regime of special effects; . . . that the powers of this regime have here been stretched to their limit; . . . it displays both these powers – and that awareness – to the full. It is a sign also of an awareness on the part of the spectator.
>
> (Neale 1990a: 161)

Again, how far does such self-reflexiveness go? Theorists of postmodernism such as Jameson (1991) suggest that the products of 'late capitalism' are incapable of parody, or of taking a position, but merely pastiche or rework in an uncritical, a-historical way, earlier forms and political positions. Hill (1998) specifies this distinction for cinema, suggesting, for example, that while Robert Altman's 'New Hollywood' product *The Long Goodbye* (US 1973) parodies some of the characteristics of the noir detective form, the more fully 1980s 'event' film *The Untouchables* uses the Odessa Steps sequence (from that piece of agitational Soviet cinema, *Battleship Potemkin*: USSR 1925) in a way that empties it of its original meaning without itself becoming a positioned parody of that meaning. It becomes simply an 'alibi for the film's ideological conservatism' (Hill 1998: 101). Contemporary Hollywood has arguably taken the practice a stage further, basing itself on endless pastiches of older genre movies, often winked at in the course of the film (such as *The Mummy*: US 1999), enjoyably mixing and playing with levels of the audience's generic knowledge while keeping in place quite regressive images, for example of Egyptians or of the true all-American hero. The casually stereotyped ethnic groups in the equally allusive *Star Wars: Phantom Menace* form another recent and controversial example of such limits.

Full global media conglomeracy

Though *Jaws* offers a kind of template of later product strategies, it was part of only the first wave of conglomeration. The second stage of tighter diversification involved more media focused corporations with 'deep pockets' (Schatz 1993: 83) and, recently, Internet technologies. The tiny number of companies dominating global film production through a few 'hits' each year are now relatively little changed in name and ancestry from the studio years, though the ownership of several of them is no longer a simple 'Americanism' (see Chapter 3).

- Twentieth Century Fox was taken over by the (then still) Australian Rupert Murdoch's News International in 1986.
- MCA/Universal was taken over by the Japanese corporation Matsushita in 1990 and the resulting company was swallowed by the Canadian drinks company Seagram in 1995. As this book was nearing completion in June 2000 a deal was announced for the French media company Vivendi to take over the resulting conglomerate, to be called Vivendi Universal, headquartered in Paris and worth $100 billion.
- Columbia by the Japanese Sony in 1989.
- Warner Brothers became Time-Warner, the world's largest media conglomerate in 1989, and in January 2000 entered history's largest merger, with the AOL (America Online) Internet company and with EMI music corporation.

> The merger of America Online and Time Warner creates the world's biggest online media company in a deal that is set to value the combined group at more than $350bn.
>
> (Jane Martinson, *Guardian*, 11 January 2000)

- A transformed Disney (formerly a 'minor') entered the new elite grouping from the late 1980s, indeed it is arguable that Warners and Disney now dominate the 'major league' (see Schatz 1997: 87–91; Wasko forthcoming on Disney).
- The other new name is the powerful DreamWorks Studio, founded by Spielberg, Geffen and Katzenberg though, astonishingly given its size, unable to finance the completion of its studio buildings in Los Angeles in 1999 revealing how difficult it often is to gain a foothold in that old club, the 'majors'.

> Eisner took the raw material – the classic movies and characters – and exploited them for all they were worth in the new home video market. Then came the expansion: the adult film division Touchstone, the new record-breaking animated movies (*Aladdin*, *The Little Mermaid*, *Beauty and the Beast*, *The Lion King*), the Disney Channel, the extra theme parks, the mighty Ducks ice hockey team, the stage musicals, the Infoseek Internet search engine, the cruise liners, the hotels, the buy outs of ABC and Miramax and the ESPN sports network. By 1987 Disney was top-ranked studio for the first time; by 1995 when it had landed ABC, Disney was . . . the world's biggest news and entertainment conglomerate.
>
> (Hattenstone 1999)

This further wave of corporate take-over of all of the majors by the mid-1990s announced their full positioning for 'the expected battle over the information and entertainment electronic super highway' (Gomery 1996b: 410). Though there is still fierce debate about the nature and role of 'cinema' within this global multimedia entertainment universe, it became clear that ownership of a film studio was cornerstone to a whole global media game. Movies (still defined as theatrical release, narrative films) fuelled much other entertainment success ('relayed' on video, cable, through franchises and so on) through their glamour, and form the staple of future product supply for video, cable, DVD and Internet link-ups.

The key status which their film studio holding represents for a conglomerate like Disney is not only such back catalogues of old movies, but also the capacity to produce new movies which their audiences can evoke and re-experience (or sometimes pre-experience) through games, toys, theme-park rides and videos long after the initial viewing is over, feeding the appetite and nostalgia for more.

Star Wars reissues and prequel/sequel episodes, for example, were partly marketed on the idea that parents (code for fathers, since taking children to the movies has traditionally been mothers' work: think about it) would be happy to take their children in order to re-experience their own childish pleasures. Box-office takings, a traditional part of 'cinema', crucial on the first weekend of a would-be blockbuster, are described by Gomery as now, more generally, having 'voting booth' function, their function being to give a rough indication of future revenues from other kinds of screening: 'In the United States today, the expected revenues from box office sales account for less than one-fifth of total revenues' (Gomery 1996b: 408). In such high risk and quick turnaround media industries, a reliable voting booth, involved with the most intimate fantasies and marketing connections of now global cultures, is a key resource.

Technological-industrial changes such as Sony's launch of the video cassette recorder (VCR) in 1975 and the decision of the cable station Home Box Office to go US wide in 1975, enabled by the launch of SATCOM 1, meant a huge increase in the opportunities for what Schatz (1997: 80) calls 'reiteration' of a movie's narrative and imagery through other media and commodity forms. Indeed Richard Allen (1998), arguing the 'end of Hollywood', points, for example, to the 'toyetic' demands made on stars, to allow their likenesses to be made into toys. In such a context, and following from disputes on the rights to star images for toy production related to *Titanic* (US 1997), Leonardo DiCaprio trademarked his name in August 1999. He was the first star to go quite that far, though he is part of a long tradition of litigation in the studio system (see Chapter 5; Gaines 1992a).

Further stages of technological-industrial change occur with the development of digitalization, beginning with the experimentation in Disney's *Tron* (US 1982) and accelerating in films like *The Abyss* and *Terminator-2* in the late 1980s, and the growth of the computer games industry. Huge changes to media conglomerates are promised for the twenty-first century. In September 1999 it was reported that Sony, having invested £666 million, had announced the launch of PlayStation 2 in Japan for March 2000 and in Europe for the autumn, reputedly involving a teaming up with George Lucas. The current *PlayStation* accounts for 40 per cent of Sony group's earnings. Matsushita is combining with Nintendo to rival it (*Guardian*, 14 September 1999).

> This year the games industry will top £5bn in turnover and for the first time exceed the takings of the world cinema industry. It is expected to continue to grow at 25% a year for the next five years as games consoles become more powerful and converge with other forms of media like the internet.
>
> (*Guardian*, 14 August 1999)

> Turkle's move away from psychoanalysis was promoted by a student who complained that a Freudian slip was no more than an 'information processing error'. She realised . . . computers were profoundly altering the ways people thought about themselves.
>
> (*Times Higher Educational Supplement*, 25 June 1999)

It may be that the importance of such games investment in films is producing new kinds of narrative. Not only does a film like *Star Wars: Phantom Menace* function, narratively, as a set of attractions which resemble an extended games or toy ad. It may also, in its 'prequel/sequel' narrative structure, play with and resemble the possibility of going back over previous ground which is enabled by computers. *Groundhog Day* (US 1993), in its play with the fascination of having a games-like control over the way your personal 'narrative' turns out, rerunning and rerunning it, seems a relatively early enactment of this 'second chance-ness' of the computer at the level of a film's narrative, as did *eXistenZ* (US 1999) with its movings between the reality levels of movies and games, or *Antz* (US 1999) with its mental landscape of a multilevel game or *Run Lola Run* (Germany 1999). Though other, older narrative fiction forms have played with such repeatability – see Charles Dickens' *A Christmas Carol*, Capra's *It's a Wonderful Life* (US 1947) or Powell and Pressburger's *A Matter of Life and Death* (UK 1946) – the impetus behind them seems religious, prompted by figures of death, quite unlike the orientation towards control promised by (over-)optimistic ideologies around new technologies and genetics. The deployment of digital special FX, at both visual and aural levels, helps determine, and its forms become determined by, the growing popularity of science fiction (SF) action movies from the 1980s. These allow for spectacularizable 'global' themes which involve both the display of digital special FX and the turning of a movie towards the status of computer games taster for its conglomerate owners: which scenes or moments can be anticipated by those (young) consumers with access to the technology, as part of an upcoming birthday or Christmas games purchase?

Since cinema continues to be a high risk investment, the majors' 'gatekeeper' power to distribute, exhibit and publicize blockbusters in ways that cannot be ignored remains key to major profitability. Even George Lucas, with the franchise rights and money to produce and finance *Star Wars: Phantom Menace*, had to pay Fox to distribute it. Their agenda is often the only one to choose from, whether in cinemas or on TV screens, a factor dramatized in the need to make or break the big film by assessing the first 36 hours' takings. Yet despite the identification of a single 'Hollywood' with such blockbusters, there are at least three main levels of Hollywood production (excluding its elusive connections with hard-core pornography, a huge video and Internet industry: see Kipnis 1998a).

Economically, the blockbuster is key, but the logic of the system also necessitates 'moderately priced hits' which

> serve to keep the industry machinery running, to develop new talent, and to maintain a steady supply of dependable mainstream product.

> Complementing these . . . are the low cost films from . . . outfits like
> Miramax and New Line Cinema.
>
> (Schatz 1993: 34)

Recent examples include *Thelma and Louise* (US 1990) and the surprise
Oscar winner in 2000, *Boys Don't Cry* (US 1999), distributed by Fox
Searchlight.

Related to this, Richard Allen (1998) and others have pointed to possible
changes to production from demographics, such as the growth in importance of the so-called 'echo boomer' audience, whom he argues have motored
the swift growth in VCR sales: by 1997 video was the most common way of
seeing a film.

1946–64 'baby boom' of births in USA

1965–80 'birth bust': US birthrate fell below 'replacement' levels

1977–95 'echo boomers', a demographic bulge as important as the
'baby boomers', forming 28 per cent of the US population and
according to Richard Allen (1998) a key influence on the films
made, and how they are circulated – by video for home viewing.

Blockbuster Video shops started in 1987; by 1990 they were sold to Viacom
for $8.6 billion. In 1996 theatrical (cinema) release formed only 23 per cent
of a studio's domestic income. Richard Allen (1998) suggests that this feeds
the move not only to children's products – see the huge success of Disney
films (*Home Alone*, *The Lion King*, *Tarzan*) – but also to more adult movies
for the large parent group, such as *L.A. Confidential* (US 1997), *Out of Sight*
(US 1999), *American Beauty* (US 2000) and *The Insider* (US 1999).

Lower budget production levels exist, in the USA and elsewhere, and can
be seen as a kind of cheap research and development for an industry both
ravenous and flexible. *The Blair Witch Project* (US 1999) is the most striking recent example. Made for $60,000, this had grossed $140 million by the
end of 1999 (Goodridge 1999) through a combination of astute use of Internet publicity and, crucially, but less emphasized, distribution by a well-
capitalized independent, Artisan Entertainment. Debate still rages about
how far its original 'cult' success in fact originated from fans (see *Sight and
Sound* Letters, January and February 2000).

Pulp Fiction (US 1994) is another example of a film which was either
declared to be the essence of the postmodern, as though it had emanated
mysteriously from the zeitgeist, or celebrated as the essence of cross-over
innovative arthouse, independent product – referencing Godard, making

unconventional use of narrative, following on from the *succès de scandale* of *Reservoir Dogs* (US 1992) and so on. In fact, impressive though it is in many ways, it relied hugely for its success on the Disney take-over of Miramax. This coincided with its release date, enabling saturation marketing, simultaneous release on 1300 cinema screens, effective lobbying at the Cannes Festival, tie-in products (T-shirts, posters, mugs and Uma Thurman's nail polish) and publicity for the soundtrack album. This was pre-sold and, innovatively, used extracts from the soundtrack dialogue as well as the skilfully chosen retro-music. Arguably, as audiences talked along to the familiar lines and felt themselves to be part of a controversial, 'pulp' or low status success (see Sconce 1995), this combination enabled the film to feel like, and even be acclaimed as, a 'cult' movie. This term is more properly applied to films which are initially commercially unsuccessful films and which *gradually* build up a following. *Pulp Fiction* with its huge Miramax-Disney release (and ensuing embarrassment for Disney's conservative shareholders as the first Disney film to feature anal rape and footage of drug injection) was able to achieve 'cult' labelling without having had to go through the hard 'earning' of such status via gradual word of mouth, as had happened with earlier cult films such as the *Rocky Horror Picture Show* (UK 1975).

The sets of circumstances, relating conglomerate and 'indie' forms, which made for this huge success, along with Tarantino's star-director image as ex-video store assistant (rather than film school graduate), hip drug-taker, festival circuit motormouth, fuelled a thousand hopes for other unknown young film-makers. Balio (1998b) citing the arm's-length take-over of foreign independent distributors by majors such as Disney and Turner Broadcasting, which took over Miramax and New Line respectively, suggests that one side-effect of studio investment in such companies is to deprive other national cinemas of major talent, without the studios incurring the expense of investing abroad (as they had to in the 1960s) (Balio 1998b: 68, 71).

> Miramax is described by *Variety* (4 January 2000) as 'niche pic juggernaut Miramax' and elsewhere as 'mini-major'.

It also suggests the old law of capitalist conglomeracy: that the big eat up the little (see the underwater scene from *Star Wars: Phantom Menace* – self-reflexive?) and the newly absorbed 'little' begins to behave a little differently in turn. *The Blair Witch* producers are rumoured to be already planning two spin-offs (*Variety*, 4 January 2000): one is reported to be costing $10 million. *The Beach* (US 2000) was seen by many to be bland 'white-bread' product (largely due to the economic and narrative imperatives which came with the involvement of a big star like DiCaprio) compared to *Trainspotting* (UK 1996), made by some of the same team.

Motivating such a spread of different levels of production is the industry knowledge that audience choices still cannot be predicted to an accountant's fifth decimal point. Indeed 'difference', up to the point where audience testing suggests it will be marketable, continues to be highly valued. Even in areas where 'repetition' is thought to hang out most obviously – the sequel, the second viewing – several kinds of difference are involved. The term currently invokes either the knowingness of the *Scream* series' play on conventions, or alternatively, authorial art discourses of difference, as in Peckinpah's *The Wild Bunch*. 'Hollywood now also plays a kind of cinematheque memorialising function when it re-releases films on their twentieth and twenty fifth anniversary' (Cook and Bernink 1999: 104), aided of course by nudges via TV 'seasons', inviting audiences to look for the differences accreted by the passage of time.

The majors have other strategies for minimizing financial risks. As in the studio years, they cooperate in the interests of trade and other lobbies, such as MPAA plans to counter European resistance to Hollywood's desire for further trading advantages in the 1993 GATT talks. As in the studio years, the majors rely as far as possible on tried-and-tested genres such as science fiction and action adventure films, on sequels, and on star images within those genres, though these are now designed for global consumption.

Each US film is allotted a hundred generic descriptions for individual use in specific markets. Kevin Costner's *Dances with Wolves* was sold to the 1990 French cinema-goer as a documentary-style dramatisation of Native American life, and *Malcolm X* (Spike Lee, 1992) was promoted there with posters of a burning Stars and Stripes

(Miller 1998: 377)

Such changes have led Gomery (1996b) to argue that we need a total transformation of how we understand and categorize economic performance, rather than simply working through ownership models. He points to the splitting of what seems like one industry into three kinds of business, depending on how income is gathered.

- Direct payment industries such as books, pay-per-view TV and movies shown in cinemas seem more 'transparent', perhaps even 'pure' kinds of purchase, because there is no direct advertising revenue involved so the 'polling booth' function for preferences expressed through buying a ticket can operate in a fairly direct way.

- Indirect payment refers to the capacity of advertisers to buy audience attention through commercial TV screenings of movies, which of course are not free, though they feel so, but funded by the purchase of the commodities whose advertising pays for the channel.
- Hybrids are mass media with a small initial charge (subscription cable, for example) which also rely on advertising fees.

Through the role of advertising in these two last models, as well as through tie-in products in films, Gomery argues that Hollywood, though relatively small itself, interacts with and promotes 'true big business in the United States' (Gomery 1996b: 417). Though ownership hardly vanishes in such an account, it does bring us to the closer integration between big budget publicity discourses and practices, and movies-on-screens since the mid-1980s, and its possible results 'on screen'. Let's now consider arguments that such films are globally popular, rather than simply hyped, and what their power might imply for the whole capitalist ecology of film-making.

Further reading

Cook, P. and Bernink, M. (eds) (1999) *The Cinema Book*, 2nd edn. London: British Film Institute.

Neale, S. and Smith, M. (eds) (1998) *Contemporary Hollywood Cinema*. London: Routledge.

Wyatt, J. (1994) *High Concept: Movies and Marketing in Hollywood*. Austin, TX: University of Texas Press.

3 'GLOBALLY POPULAR' CINEMA?

> Once upon a time it was a small gathering of people around a fire listening to the storyteller with his tales of magic and fantasy. And now it's the whole world ... It's not 'domination' by American cinema. It's just the magic of storytelling, and it unites the world.
> (Steven Spielberg, *Variety*, 7 December 1993: 62)

> the forces of globalisation, which most people outside the US, not without reason, view as uncontrolled elements, acting after the pattern of natural catastrophe.
> (Zygmunt Bauman, reviewing Fukuyama's *The Great Disruption: Human Nature and the Reconstitution of Social Order*, *Guardian*, 1998)

Writers and audiences still refer loosely to entertainment cinema as 'American' films, often saturated with American imagery and accents, peopled by stars, directors and other movie workers who have perhaps 'made it' from elsewhere but have usually relocated to California. Yet there have been radical changes since the 1960s to the ownership patterns, financing and forms of major films (now called 'event movies', meaning global events) which each year make up the bulk of industry profits, the commanding apex of a pyramid ecology. The very scale of the pre-production agreements needed, even for smaller budget films heading more quickly to TV, means thinking global and hybrid co-finance. Large parts of Hollywood are now both foreign owned and multi-market oriented.

Though all this is often celebrated as part of a fully democratic, 'postmodern' 'knowledge/information' world, or cited as part of an irresistible process of 'globalization', it also raises other questions:

- What differences do multinational global financing and production make to 'films on screens' as well as to their different kinds of marketing 'around' (rather than pre)-screen?
- What might this imply for the 'American-ness' of global cinema and its relationship to other national and art cinemas, as well as the locations in which it is often shot?
- How might we understand audiences' engagement with such products? How does that endlessly challenging term 'truly popular' work for globally hyped and unavoidable product?

Globalization, cultural imperialism and cinema

Though power structures and activities on a larger-than-national scale (including the Chinese and Roman Empires and Catholic Church) have existed for centuries, globalization can be seen as a distinctively modern development (see Branston and Stafford 1999: ch. 20). Analysis has emphasized the way that globalized activities

- are deliberately organized, rather than 'simply happening' on a global scale
- often involve some degree of interdependency
- are often instantaneous – and may, in the case of cinema's major release patterns, for example, be simultaneous.

The term **media imperialism** was previously used of the media industries' spread, usually in one direction. It points to the inequalities of a 'one-way flow' which initially followed the paths of nineteenth century western imperialists, and then worked in collaboration with US economic, political and military interests. US power is seen to replace that of nations such as Britain, Spain and France, whose languages and educational systems, however, have remained as powerful cultural networks across much of the globe. The use of this politically connective term 'imperialism' is understandable, given the intimate links between brute forms of imperialism and the associated spread of western media forms, both of information, advertising and entertainment (see Schiller 1997). However, the concept has come under revision for thinking about the contemporary world, which is now at some distance from the last imperialist wars and from the collapse of Soviet bloc 'anti-imperialist' counter-power.

The dominant emphasis of 'globalization theory' is now on the following factors:

- Kinds of global restructuring, both economic and political, which are said to have eroded the power of the USA.
- The condescending nature of images of a simple golden world of authentic, indigenous or 'quality' heritage, including films, enjoyed prior to the arrival of the US media.
- The perennial problem, especially for fiction forms such as cinema, of what exactly is the relationship between origin, especially economic origin, and product in the culture industries. Take *Starship Troopers* (US 1996), directed by the Dutch Paul Verhoeven, a violent, FX-led SF film which mildly parodies both military 'machines', and the blandness of some forms of US culture. In what sense can it be said to be (a) an American product or (b) inculcating American values in its audiences?
- The ways that audiences, and local needs and impulses partly appropriate and transform, for audiences, 'global entertainment product' (see J.T. Thompson 1995).

Such arguments, however, have often gone along with more widespread post-structuralist or postmodernist positions, especially with regard to:

- suspicions of *any* kinds of claims for general or 'good-enough' truths or explanations
- lack of interest in the material histories, especially of particular industries or their historical phases
- celebration of audiences'/consumers'/fans' capacity to endlessly transform popular media products by resistive or subcultural 'readings'.

This can be seen as part of postmodernism's rejection of Marxism, which grounded the imperialist model, setting up an interest in the unequal relations of production, understood as struggle and historical process. Celebratory accounts of audiences also tend to centre on the advanced industrial world, or PC-owning sectors within it for the study of Internet fandom, and ignore those cut off from advanced, or even basic, consumerhood.

Let us consider first, though, the advantages and strengths of American cultural forms, of which cinema still forms a linchpin. The enormously attractive energy, inventiveness and democratic address of many Hollywood films, throughout and beyond the studio years, are clearly key to its commercial success. Hansen's idea of 'vernacular modernism' speculates on this.

> You didn't think of America as a social place at all. You didn't think of
> it as having poor people or problems. It was just America, it was utopia.
> (Pauline, on movie-going in Liverpool in the 1950s, quoted in Lacey
> 1999: 62)

In Europe it can be vividly appreciated, from the role of US troops as characterized in a film like *Paisa* (1946) about the final stages of the liberation of
Italy from the Fascists, down to the ways (unfamiliar) US speech and accents
seemed classless to British working class audiences for American films of the
1930s and 1940s, certainly by contrast with elite, West End theatre-derived
clipped accents in many British films of the time (see Chapter 5).

Such success also emerges from the relationship between 'quantity' and
'quality' in Hollywood and other North American media. Mattelart *et al.*
(1984: chs 2 and 3) argue that economies of scale mean first that costs can be
largely recouped in the US domestic market (usually, arrogantly, taken to
include Canada, and often pre-1959 Cuba, as a test site or launch pad for
Latin American distribution patterns). Mattelart *et al.* point to what is paradoxically a huge advantage for low-cost experimentation within such mature
entertainment industries. They ensure a huge and constant flow of production, from endless TV pilots, to 'B' movies in the studio system and their
equivalents today (the films in the 'straight to video' category). Such flow is
not made adequately available to us in simple images of a factory-like production line, producing endless conformity. On the contrary, such a regular
flow enables risks to be taken and 'quality' to be produced. This in turn
allows a much less mystifying view of creativity than the pre-industrial, arti-
sanal emphases of much avant-garde writing. Talent can here be glimpsed not
as innate, but as having the capacity to be largely *learned* within such systems
(witness the frequent tributes to Roger Corman and his 'film factories' from
the many, now famous, directors, actors and writers involved in them).

But it also involves advantages at symbolic, signifying levels. There is a
powerful argument that the 'image bank' of global commodity culture
(including, now, song and music), tightly controlled via copyright and soft-
ware libraries, is saturated with US imagery. It extends through New York
skylines and yellow cabs, American accents, even the words 'L.A.', 'Miami',
'San Francisco' in popular music, through to baseball caps, Oscar cere-
monies and the Grand Canyon. To holiday in the USA is for many people to
feel as though they are on a movie set. This system of resonant symbolic
power is also to some extent self-proliferating, since intertextuality gives
huge richness from the relationship between repeated images, a 'process of

interaction and exchange [which] constantly nourishes the memory of the American image industry' (Mattelart *et al.* 1984: 95). New computer games, theme parks and toys 'blithely tap into and add to the density of this vast arsenal of images' (Mattelart *et al.* 1984: 96), even if Australian beaches are sometimes able to masquerade as Californian locations on screen.

Mattelart *et al.* (1984) further suggest, in a move attempting to link formal aspects of films to their economic nature, that the pace of the 'global hit' film, via its cutting speed, sets the speed of global product and makes slower paced movies more difficult to market. They relate this to the cutting rate for advertisements, which for many years has been faster (and the sound more distinct, seeming louder) than for films and the rest of TV. This linkage, of course, has produced many of the most celebrated 'high concept' directors (see Chapter 2), especially from British advertising.

The 'research and development' function of Hollywood's spread of production and the outlets where that can be tested is also enormously important. The majors ultimately both control and often enable huge amount of 'independent' product worldwide, even if at arm's length, through their deals with mini-major companies like Miramax and New Line. Such an economic functioning tends to deliver in contradictory ways. Successful non-US film-makers such as John Woo, or the *Trainspotting* team of Danny Boyle and John Hodge, will very rarely resist the pull to California, often for its pools of energy, possibility and talent as well as money. But they thereby impoverish their own originating industries in ways characteristic of conglomerate capitalism, always tending to absorb, to feed on the new, small, successful innovators. There is also an argument to be made that, whatever the fascination of Woo's *Face/Off* (US 1998) or Boyle and Hodge's *The Beach* respectively, there has been a certain homogenizing of their work since their move to Hollywood (see Chapter 2).

> There is an unfortunate history of American companies setting up in the UK – Warner Brothers being the latest – raising expectations and wages and then pulling out at the whim of management, often taking the most experienced and talented artists with them.
>
> (Ian Cook, *Guardian*, 8 July 1998)

Finally, speculatively, though the global clout of US-centred media industries through distribution and promotion practices is easy to demonstrate, it seems also the case that the entertainment model of engaging with capitalist modernity developed by Hollywood – through bright, energetic, abundant seeming, populist forms (see Dyer 1973) – is now spread globally. It saturates other cultural industries (much TV news, style journalism, advertising, computer games and music) and also permeates cultural spaces and practices such as media constructed sport, the style industries of gym, fashion and body culture, cars, food and interior design.

'To be global is to be American'?

A report on international responses to *Titanic* gives a glimpse of how diversely appropriated by some elite audiences are 'globally popular blockbusters' (Riding 1998). The phenomenal, 'global event' success of *Titanic* is received in Beijing, China by the Communist Party chief Jiang Zemin, thus:

> Let us not assume that we can't learn from capitalism. *Titanic* has a budget of $200 million. This is venture capitalism . . . I invite my comrades of the Politburo to see the movie – not to propagate capitalism but to better understand our opposition.

In Paris the philosopher Bruno Mattei sees the ship's fate as metaphor for an unjust word that may even have spotted its 'iceberg' but is none the less unable to avert catastrophe. Patrick Sakings, psychotherapist, is reported as saying that *Titanic* had challenged the belief that today's all powerful consumer society is 'unsinkable'. 'I think the film has awoken fear,' he said. DiCaprio is a teenage idol in Japan, yet even

> beyond [his] appeal, many of the characters in the film exhibited a great deal of what the Japanese call *gamen*, which can be loosely translated as having a stiff upper lip – or . . . perseverance in the face of extreme adversity.

(Riding 1998)

Simon During (1997) has explored, for the Reagan–Schwarzenegger 1980s, the tension between arguments for local diversity (of both production and reception) and Hollywood's hegemony in continuing to produce those few cinema hits each year which make up the vast majority of the industry's profits. He admits the catastrophic effects of this global dominance on national cinema production industries. But he wants to explore the possibility that these films are 'popular' rather than simply hyped. This leads him into a traditional route for cultural and films studies: fascinating textual speculations about the role of strong male bodies and special effects in the 'globally popular' films of the 1980s. Given the under-funded state of studies of overseas audiences (apart from the industry's own MR) for Hollywood movies, and the difficult methodological questions raised by these, this speculative, text-derived emphasis is inevitable, but worth noting.

Despite the emphasis of Cultural Studies on hybridity and difference,

During (1997) argues that since the 1980s some cultural products indeed seem to be globally popular in a universalized way: 'they are distributed and apparently enjoyed everywhere, at any rate wherever electricity is on line or generators and batteries can be transported and where they are not successfully banned' (During 1997: 211). Such mega-budget business is high risk. The relations between the components of such cultural production are constantly changing, especially at the four key levels of

- financing
- governmental regulations (outside the USA in the form of national-cultural import policies and censorship, which tend to be under almost constant negotiation)
- technology, 'which can change so quickly as to touch the actual plots of would be globally popular products – *Jurassic Park*'s plot, for example, was changed during production to accommodate technological innovations' (During 1997: 213)
- the market appeal of particular stars.

> It is just possible to take films that are globally popular and read from them a set of elements that are universal, in the weak sense that they are culturally translatable to the maximum degree.
>
> (During 1997)

Globalization inscribes itself into film-making most effectively at the moment of financing. The global-local logic of big budget blockbusters tends not to involve a globally equal spread of employment possibilities but films *shot* globally, across the world, often at some cost to local environments, but with the crucial, better paid decision-making and post-production industries localized mostly in California.

> With star salaries and production also escalating, studios were increasingly turning to independent and international financing sources . . . that . . . makes the top 20 production company chart somewhat problematic to correlate. Australia's Village Roadshow Pictures, which half financed *Analyze This*, *The Matrix*, *Deep Blue Sea*, *Three Kings*, and *Three to Tango* with Warner Bros should rank at number two on the chart . . . however the company is not listed as a production company on the films.
>
> (Goodridge 1999)

Key attempts at minimizing risks are:

- re-sales to foreign distributors, with different deals usually being made in each territory for separate film rental, video and broadcast TV distribution rights
- accounting procedures (such as cross-collateralization, in which the market performance of a movie in one territory can be discounted against its performance in another, and the purchase of insurance against the failure to complete, so-called completion bonds, whose sellers can have a substantial say in the making of a movie)
- major players in a production agreeing to take a share of its profits in lieu of up-front payments (see Chapter 2).

Although local distributors put up money only for films they believe will sell in their markets, certain power divisions, ethnic and national as well as economic, persist. As During (1997: 21) says: 'a star can only be established globally by Hollywood cinema, though some global product comes from elsewhere'. 'Lesser' players are often employed according to the familiar inequalities of capitalist global employment practices, with production decentralized into low wage economies, often Mexico, more recently Canada, or, for animation, South East Asia, while the (more expensive) highly trained parts of the workforce are still located in the USA, travelling to the cheaper sites from California (see Chapter 2).

> A recent *Screen International* survey (Goodridge 1998) showed that 'overseas grosses on major hit pictures now consistently dwarf the domestic grosses.'

The globalization of screen culture, then, means that certain Hollywood films are aimed simultaneously *at least* at two major markets: home and the rest of the world, with the latter category fragmenting into separate 'territories' (Japan and Germany dominated in the 1980s in terms of income flow). The James Bond films form a case study, over 30 years, of this kind of hybridization. It begins with the 'American pacing' overlay of an originally English/British set of stories (albeit already oddly hybridized by Sean Connery's Scottish accent) and extending to the niche marketing to different 'locals' and the shooting in different, but usually non-US and tourist-industry related locations. How significant, flexible and close to specific 'local' experience this kind of difference is, of course, raises many questions.

During uses an openly speculative, textual-cultural reading of the star-genre appeal of Arnold Schwarzenegger for the 1980s. He concentrates on the Schwarzenegger star vehicle *Total Recall* (US 1990), partly because it was directly controlled by Arnie, and also because of its global commercial success: it cost $60 million and grossed $300 million, of which $180 million came from non-US markets against a then industry average of 40:60 domestic:foreign revenues split.

World markets seem to welcome the roller-coaster intensities of what, following Tom Gunning's (1990) work on early cinema, has been called a cinema of 'action-attractions', 'exhibitionist cinema', which is 'less a way of telling stories than a way of presenting a series of views to an audience' (Gunning 1990: 56–62). He argues that 'cinema has reaffirmed its roots in stimulus and carnival rides' (Gunning 1990: 67). Contemporary 'globally popular' films are heavily dependent on bursts of special effects and stunts, particularly the presentation of highly stylized, acrobatic violence revolving around guns and hand-to-hand combat (requiring little subtitling) and often borrowing from non-western martial arts and associated movies (see the recent Hollywood success of John Woo, and, rather differently, of Jim Jarmusch's wonderful samurai-gangster film *Ghostdog: The Way of the Samurai*, US 2000). These attractions are partly demanded by 'high concept' marketing, for which such moments often overwhelm the film's narrative in exchange for highly glamorous images for the trailer, the music video, the computer game and so forth.

Given the lack of reliable information on consumption practices, During (1997) admits to falling back on textual interpretation and speculation – here around trained-to-extremes male bodies, such as those of Schwarzenegger, Stallone and Van Damme in the 1980s, in high concept, action centred special FX movies.

> These bodies are culturally specific: Schwarzenegger's body, despite his unprecedented mass, the definition of his cuts (to use bodybuilders' lingo) and his V shape (one that became popular in bodybuilding in the 1940s), is still modelled on a classical Greek ideal.
>
> (During 1997: 216)

But they nevertheless manage to 'travel' the globe profitably. Dyer (1997) similarly has suggested the multi-audience appeal and discursive traditions out of which such white, muscled bodies emerge and flourish. In the particular genre which Schwarzenegger made his own in the 1980s (though his star image has been retooled since), During suggests

> his body is a resource available when everything else – money, guns, status, power – runs out. It's the stuff of survival, there to be identified with by men whose clout is corporeal. Thus it grounds his appeal across

Figure 3.1 No comment: Jean-Claude Van Damme and gun in *Universal Soldier The Return (US 1999)*
Reproduced with permission of Columbia Pictures

the international division of labour . . . unlike most bodies formed in the . . . entanglement of heredity, lifeways, and work, Schwarzenegger's body is more alien than natural, the product of a rigorous regime of self-government as well as . . . steroids.

(During 1997: 218)

Such bodies are now joined, though very differently, by those of female 'musculinity' (Tasker 1998): globally distributed women action heroes such as Linda Hamilton in *Terminator-2*, Demi Moore in *G.I. Jane* and for TV and the Internet, Lucy Lawless as *Xena: Warrior Princess*. They offer a parallel to those athletes featured in media debates on the modification of gendered bodies in sport, or to computer games/TV/soon-to-be-film characters like Lara Croft, spaces where it is possible to sensuously speculate on the overlap and shifts between 'nature', 'artifice', genetics, gender and late modernity. During hints at how body training embodies relations which are embedded both in screen spectatorship and in the gyms and body culture of high-consumer societies, aiming to transform bodies, requiring constant self-inspection – touching, looking, imagining – centred on anxious or narcissistic reflections.

Tasker (1993) suggests that the public circulation of male body images such as those of Stallone and Schwarzenegger is split between two incommensurable discourses:

- a triumphant masculinization, a nostalgic harking back to earlier gendered displays of male muscle power from an era of manual labour and more secure gender divisions
- an insecurity about this image in 'post-industrial' cultures, a sense that the open display of such bodies is somehow feminized and less secure in its 'classed' masculinity than it appears. Hence the repeated martyrdom of Stallone characters (even in *Antz*) into masculinized 'sacrifice', and the turn of Schwarzenegger to comedy and/or roles involving self-reflexivity around a certain dumbness in the image (especially the voice) and a fantastical, cyborg quality of the body.

FX and global narratives

During (1997) suggests that the special effects in such movies, so often commented on as evidence of degraded audience taste, work in this genre to construct 'classed' characters, who can engage the world, not just outside the laws of physics, but outside of 'messy negotiations with the more powerful'.

More broadly, discussion of the possible role of special effects in contemporary global blockbusters has recently developed away from two previous approaches:

- those journalistic and academic discourses which see audiences as doubly poleaxed – duped by both the deceptive 'reality' effect of FX, and also by the visceral lures that cinema allows to be displayed
- some postmodernist writing which uses the terms 'simulation' and 'hyperreal' (from Baudrillard) quite loosely, to suggest audiences' helpless immersion in a confusion about what is and is not FX.

Barker and Brooks (1998) suggest that the appeal of films like *Judge Dredd* (US 1995), at least for Dredd **fans,** may on the contrary involve a kind of conscious submission to the spectacle:

> for those wishing to be 'done to', narrative is like a carrier-wave, similar to the role that rails play on a big dipper – necessary to carry you along, but not in themselves the point of the exercise . . . for those seeking spectacle, narrative is the means by which decisive moments of technology and effects can be reached appropriately. They frame those moments and help them intensify our experiences properly – but again, are only worth noticing in themselves when they intrude awkwardly.
>
> (Barker and Brooks 1998: 282)

Far from audiences being doubly victimized, these researchers argue that they enter into a kind of contract with such movies. They or we seem to show a kind of doubled attention and engagement at the 'special effects moment' (just as audiences have arguably always done at comic moments, where the involvement with plot is suspended for the sake of the laugh). Slater (1997) suggests another kind of 'doubleness', that 'two simultaneous senses of wonder are invoked: wonder at the experience of being transported to a fully realised unreal world; and wonder at the (incomprehensible, hidden) technology which makes it all possible' (cited in Barker and Brooks 1998: 283). Certainly there is a continuity between this and the 'overwhelming' of the narrative in high concept movie-making's valuation of highly visualized or spectacular moments which can be used to advertise and recirculate the film via TV trailers, music videos and so on. The FX moments of recent blockbusters have been argued to break through to moments of mute immersion in dazzling technologized spectacle, in ways which may link to, and mark a later stage of, the kaleidoscopic spectacles of early modern cinema. But another possible audience engagement is suggested by Pierson (1999), namely that of audiences whose relationship to computer generated special effects in movies has been altered by their everyday encounters with this technology, sometimes as producers and sometimes within a horizon of expectation or fantasy in which, for

> many young people, knowledge of special effects techniques now offers a kind of lure of stardom and power within the industry previously available only to screenwriters, stars, producers and directors.
>
> (La Valley, quoted in Pierson 1999: 162)

DVD (digital) special editions of films such as *The Matrix* (1999) spread further the array of conscious pleasures which audiences are invited to anticipate and replay for (a relatively few) big movies. Michael Allen (1998) indicates the complexity of

> the drive behind much of the technological development in cinema since 1950 [which] has been towards both a greater or heightened sense of 'realism' and a bigger, more breathtaking realisation of spectacle . . . The intention of all technological systems developed since the beginning of the 1950s has been towards reducing the spectators' sense of their 'real' world, and replacing it with a fully believable artificial one. In cases where a real life equivalent is clearly impossible, such as morphing effects in *T-2*, the pictorial quality of the effect must be sophisticated and 'photo-realistic' enough to persuade the audience that if, for example, a tiled floor transformed into a human figure in real life, it would look exactly like its screen depiction does.
>
> (M. Allen 1998: 127)

It will be fascinating to see how computer generated imagery (CGI) develops in the next few years. Will audiences 'demand' ever accelerating kinds of newness in CGI FX? Will this continue to fuel the animation boom? Will it lead to more of the kinds of narrative problems in *Terminator-2*, where the sensationally morphed villainous cyborg was, when you stop to think about it, too powerful to believably run out of breath running after a car? Or is Jonathan Romney (1997) right when he suggests that there will be a kind of backlash as the 'weightlessness' of CGI effects leads to audience appetite for 'evidence' of the bodily real onscreen?

Pigs have yet to fly on screen; cows already have, carried aloft by the computer generated tornado in *Twister*.

(Romney 1997: 205)

During (1997) suggests that a global movie like *Total Recall* consists of more than such 'attractions' alone. However important the immersion in dazzling spectacle and reminders of off-screen theme-park rides or computer game scenarios, narrative continues to be necessary to 'string the beads together', and still constitutes one of the defining parameters of cinema (films, unlike much TV, are still mostly designed to be watched, as narratives, at one sitting). The overall plot needs to perform a balancing act. It has to simultaneously secure both the metropolitan and the non metropolitan or even overseas audiences which have been pre-traded in the initial package deal. The story of *Total Recall*, for example, fictively exaggerates contemporary neo-colonialist relations, including 'blonde unsympathetic wife' and 'marriage to dark local woman', familiar from old colonial romances, who 'plays second fiddle to Quaid but is, like him, violent, strong and effective'.

Total Recall and global products like it, During (1997) suggests, are enabled to succeed in various world markets not just by playing narratively with desires for anti-First World insurgency but by setting up the assumption in advance that its audiences live inside an emphatically global culture.

> The images of a futuristic city under late, late capitalism allow *Bladerunner* to be read as a social critique. The opening images of the industrial city's flaring smoke stacks and hazy pollution signify a world of total industrialisation ... the mixture of signs from Japanese, European and US capitalism points to a future society where trilateral capitalism has achieved its dream of a world economic system.
>
> (Kellner *et al.* 1984)

In this it is helped by the generic, planetary assumptions of science fiction which has in recent decades explored global themes such as ecological finitude, surveillance, the effects of global culture, genetic engineering, simulation and so on. During argues further that *Total Recall*, like *Jurassic Park*:

> breaks through the horizon of species-being ... because minds can be surgically implanted and mutants can form communities, the species' internal divisions into cultural, national or ethnic communities seem peripheral.
>
> (During 1997: 221)

Yet he points to ideological samenesses in such films, a repetition of limits in the very interests of multi-marketability. *Total Recall* expresses no anti-colonialist revolutionary dream. The exploited Martian miners require a white, North American secret agent ('Arnie') to win their (barely articulated) freedom for them and are portrayed as dehumanized mutants; it also turns out that Quaid/Schwarzenegger's whole adventure might be implanted, and therefore the entire story of Mars's liberation a simulation.

It has been argued elsewhere (Jeffords 1994; Sartelle 1996) that the era of the modern blockbuster, from *Star Wars* (1977) to the present, can be seen as one with an unusually close convergence between US popular culture and US official political culture. This was dramatically true during the presidency of ex-film star Ronald Reagan (1980–8), who used lines from blockbusters to promote his national policy initiatives: 'go on, make my day'; 'the force is with us'; 'where we're going, we don't need roads'; the so-called 'Star Wars' Defense Project. Like much cultural criticism at this level, such writing has difficulty connecting the levels of US government policies and 'films on screen'. It has, as a result, to argue speculatively that there are deeply compensatory fantasies at play in these movies, mostly around the ways that the 'aliens' are constructed so as to allow enactment of anxieties around the USA's recent history, especially the traumatic defeat in Vietnam. Colin Mac-Cabe (1999) has, in similar vein, suggested in this context, referring to *Saving Private Ryan* (US 1998) and *The Thin Red Line* (US 1999) that:

> Ideological readings of films are usually both predictable and uninteresting . . . But these two films . . . demand ideological analysis . . . [they] make crystal clear that the greatest military power the world has ever known will not now allow even one of its soldiers to die in any foreseeable military conflict. For if Tom Hanks can die senselessly then anybody can and nobody will.
>
> (MacCabe 1999)

Sartelle (1996) suggests a kind of playing out of anxieties around feminism in the fate of the blonde but demanding wife in *Total Recall* ('consider this a divorce'), a familiar 'getting shot of the awkward woman'. It may also be part of the reassuring success of the, still typically white, male hero and his capacity to have belief in himself, a very Reaganite and American desire to validate the ideology of human beings controlling their own destinies and, indeed, of the free enterprise system itself. Sartelle (1996) argues this is also present in Sarah Connell's slogan of 'No Fate' in *Terminator-2*. I would add that this is the stuff of Schwarzenegger's global star image, the immigrant who still bears his 'unwieldy' surname (no studio in the classic years would have allowed him to keep such an un-American name), has not smoothed out the ethnic markers of his Austrian accent, is ever ready to emphasize what America has done for him, even as his presence speaks hybridity.

Exhibiting global/local inequalities

Distribution and exhibition do not simply 'deliver' a commodity unaffected by their delivery routes, especially the previewing and the exhibition practices needed to ensure money back on global blockbusters. A film has to make two and a half times production costs to go into profit. A print costs around £1000 to make. So to open at 204 cinemas around £204,000 is spent on prints. If it has 'opened big' in the USA, there are already over 1000 prints available. Hence the importance of reviewing/ publicity processes, especially in the distinction between *marketability* (how interested an audience initially is in attending the film and in contributing to the crucial first-weekend figures) and *playability* (how much the audience seems to enjoy the film, evidenced via word of mouth and so on).

> It makes you wonder sometimes if critics think independent film-makers live in a vacuum, that they can just make another movie whenever they feel like it. Are critics unaware . . . that a bad review hurts 'Hoop Dreams' in ways that it could never hurt 'Dumb and Dumber'? For an independent film, every moviegoer turned away by a dismissive review is disastrous.
>
> (Tom DiCillo 1995: 15)

Crucial TV and press reviews are heavily dependent on studio clips – from the electronic press kits (EPKs) of the big PR companies – and on photos with which to make programmes ratings worthy and print material eye-catching. The use of film clips outside this relationship otherwise poses copyright and permissions research costs, plus the fact that some stars are asking, and getting, separate approval on their use. All this impacts not only on populist reviewing programmes but also on those, increasingly few, film review or serious documentary programmes, certainly on British TV. (In 1993 it cost, on average, for a minute or part thereof of film, £500 for British and £2750 for US films, whether 1 second or 60 seconds were used.)

The discourse of reviewing programmes is now, with few exceptions, insistently ratings driven, with the implication that this is the best guide to the viewer's own choices as consumer.

> To ask a film critic which film is worth going to is 'as inappropriate as asking a geographer or geologist why they don't tell you where to go on holiday: my job . . . isn't to provide a brochure of favourite beauty spots but to map out the ground and to try to understand its construction.'
> (Judith Williamson, 1993: 15, a now very unusual view of the role of film criticism)

TV audiences, for example, are made highly aware not only of the domestic sales rankings of films in whichever 'territory' they happen to be watching, but usually also of their sales rankings from 1 to 10 in the US market. Additionally, such rankings now routinely often include video and DVD sales, and even exist as free-floating inserts on several cable channels. In the UK, television programmes such as Channel 5's *Moviewatch* are sponsored by firms like Blockbuster Video, and though a modicum of critical reviewing takes place, one cannot help wondering about what might be the impact on the supply of information and clips of consistently probing or non industry-oriented reviews. The way that such discourses conceal their blandly uncritical role is often by using a mode of address like that of the music press: avoiding seriousness, often laddish (or laddette-ish), and with lashings of postmodern irony. As with other audiences, little is done to explore whether disappointments are felt by viewers at the ways they have been addressed by these programmes. They form a growing genre, corresponding to a more knowing audience (at least as far as Hollywood genres go) for both cinema itself (*Scream 2*, the sequel to *Scream*, for example, features a scene of a university discussion of sequels) and for TV review programmes (see Sconce 1995). The audience is often assumed to be younger, hipper and drunker than that for Barry Norman on Sky-TV or *Late Review* on the 'minority' BBC2 channel, with its evocation of a high powered dinner party and the pleasures of polite disagreements.

Press reviews are also structured to dovetail with the major studios' product, with the complication, of course, that many newspapers are now owned by the same conglomerate as the films they are reviewing. You do not have to be arguing a crude economic determinist model of media influence to see that this may, over the long term, have some influence on their stance towards certain kinds of films.

The fact that reviewers have a tiny toe in a glamorous pool, and love to have their phrases used on posters, might also determine some of the hyperbole of certain reviews: even if hostile, they may still work to publicize a

> *The Independent* pointed out, 15 October 1999: 'The *Sun* thought *Waking Ned* was "the most charming, funny and loveable comedy of all time".' It was made by Twentieth Century Fox, proprietor Murdoch, who also owns the *Sun*.

film. The hip, postmodern avoidance of value also surfaces in those review columns, and also Internet sites, which routinely now imply: 'see it: it's so bad it's good' – but usually about a big studio product which is so unavoidable it is likely to be profitable.

Mall viewing pleasures include the experience of safe, clean, comfortable and well-equipped cinemas – with plenty of 'kiddie-adult' foods on sale. The largest screens for such 'universal' product (not available in the majority of small towns let alone rural areas or parts of the world still without even running water) are more like other cathedrals of consumption (large banks, hotels, hypermarkets, major stores) than simply 'mall cinemas'. Smaller screens within the multiplex (between two and sixteen screens) and megaplex (more than sixteen screens) are often less scrupulously assembled and staffed, both in terms of soundproofing, projection and the length of the projected 'throw' of the image. But for the large screens, high levels of expenditure are needed, including the advanced digital sound systems promoted by visually spectacular advertisements. These can showcase the hit-driven soundtrack, possibly already enjoyed on CD by the audience, or the digital special effects within both the visual and aural 'soundscape' (see Sergi 1998) sections of the film, also available for enjoyment on the Net, or as computer game, theme-park ride, DVD version and so on.

Comparatively few audiences have easy geographical access to, or the **cultural capital** (see Chapter 7) which would enable them to enjoy, alternative kinds of cinema, films occasionally shown in a small multiplex screen, but more often in 'art cinemas' or regional film theatres (as they are off-puttingly termed in Britain, managing to imply 'not-London' and theatre-related 'artiness'). Not everyone can afford or has access to cable, or to video shops with a good selection of products, for comparable domestically screened films.

During (1997) suggests an important gender dimension connection between the viewing contexts of 'globally popular' films and certain genres, a suggestion which undermines to some extent the claims for a transparent 'polling booth' testing of 'popularity' through global receipts which Gomery (1996) suggests (see Chapter 2). The power to make choices in various local viewing situations is usually unequally divided between genders. Outside the core economies, video is mainly viewed not on privately owned VCRs but in video cafés and, as in rural Papua New Guinea, in mobile video trucks that travel from village to village. During cites Vasudevan on the case of Indian video cafés, arguing that masculinist violence on screen is attractive in part because it helps exclude women from public space – an argument that might well be extendable to other contexts (Schlesinger *et al.* 1992: ch. 6; During 1997: 217–18). He comments on the strange fact that although romances, including telenovelas, are popular in many cultures where women dominate domestic viewing space, and in literary novels, there is not yet a centralized, globally popular women's cinema based on romance. *Titanic* is a suggestive success in this context, using its FX in the service of a romance. However, it has not yet been followed up by a second, full-on blockbuster FX romance. Indeed, it seems that to some extent that there was a re-masculinization of production in the 1990s, via the prevalence of Tarantino-style gangster/action movies.

To complete this sketch of niche marketed, multi-ethnic global products, we could cite the increased importance of the kinds of racially non-specified facial features which animation has always had the potential to offer, and which make up one of the advantages of contemporary big budget globally marketed animation. The creatures in *Antz* (US 1999) or *A Bug's Life* (US 1999); the young dark be-wigged Queen, in a series of Japanese style costumes, make-up styles and hairdos in *Star Wars Episode One: Phantom Menace* (US 1999) for example, suggest an awareness of major global audiences as well as a flattening of local difference. (Though it is striking that in this most global of products, at least in the English language edition, the latest *Star Wars* movies, the voices seem to have been constructed with a much more casual ear to ethnic caricatures.)

> the works of Disney, almost alone among the products of the moving image industry, never became obsolete; by marshalling a meticulous and merciless army of copyright lawyers the company is able to continue milking its product, releasing and re-releasing the Mouse, the Duck and Snow White as fresh experiences for every new child and every new adult in the world.
>
> (Anthony Smith 2000)

Jonathan Rosenbaum (1999) makes some interesting points on Verhoeven's more recent multinational films, suggesting an answer to my earlier questions (see Chapter 2) on *Starship Troopers*:

When did American action blockbusters stop being American? Some-time . . . between the genocidal adventures of George Lucas's *Star Wars* and those of Paul Verhoeven's *Starship Troopers* . . . [even though] *Starship Troopers* . . . boasts an 'all-American' cast that could have sprung fully blown from a camp classic of Aryan physiognomy like Howard Hawks's *Red Line 7000* . . . *Star Wars* was made at a time when American popular cinema still belonged mainly to Americans; now it belongs mainly to global markets and overseas investors, and because so-called American cinema is the brand that sells best in international markets, that's what it says on the label . . . Maybe that's why loss of identity was the very theme of *Face/Off* – another recent multinational action special, and one whose success perhaps marked the end of John Woo's career as a director of Hong Kong action films.

(Rosenbaum 1999, on *Chicago Times* website)

He discusses Verhoeven's comments in the press book for *Starship Troopers*, saying that as a Dutch director 'I felt that initially I wouldn't know enough about American culture to make movies that accurately reflected American society . . . [thus] I felt I could make science fiction films'. This transplantation of the local talent of other countries' film-making surely has implications for the ways that the USA is able to symbolize and imagine its 'own', 'local' experiences. Certainly, even the slight but recognizable, though coded, references to the Watergate political scandal or echoes of Vietnam and Hiroshima, in *Jaws*, at a much earlier stage of globalization, seem an intensely local inflection, compared to some of the SF globality of much contemporary blockbuster films ostensibly set in America.

Film makers and advertisers were exploiting the absence of a maximum noise limit to pump up volume [in cinemas] past the 85 decibel danger level, causing serious and lasting hearing damage, said [the British Standards Institution] yesterday.

(*Guardian*, 12 August 1999)

As well as often resulting in pleasurable 'product', the technological clout of such films can operate oppressively (occasionally to the long-term physical detriment of audience hearing). It works within the 'heights' of the film industry, as an insistent technological determinant: 'fill up the soundsurround'; 'use the expensive equipment: it cost us'. As ever, high tech product and expertise limits access to the elite club of blockbuster makers by raising the entry costs sky high.

> manufacturers want to develop multi-channel mikes and go to, for example, Glacier Bay where the icebergs are breaking up to capture that.
> (Randy Thom, Hollywood sound designer, School of Sound, 1999)

> As soon as you involve a studio the spend goes up 100 times. After I sold *El Mariachi* to Columbia I had to make a stereo sound mix for the movie run . . . [we] could have done it at a [tiny] studio where *Reservoir Dogs* was done. But no, I had to mix it on the Sony lot, in the $5,000 a day studio . . . It just robs people of power if they think they have to start spending money.
> (R. Rodrigues, director of *El Mariachi*: US 1994)

'Size matters': aside from the ecology of Hollywood's steeply hierarchized levels of production, and its intimate links with consumer economies, film studies has hardly begun to explore ecological questions around big budget film-making's deployment of a certain scale of resources, and its attitude to the shared global environment – or rather other people's local environments.

Few globally powerful film companies seem to have the 'Values and Principles' section in annual reports in which other companies lay out at least the rhetoric of responsible ecological policies. This was dramatized in 1999 by the furore and legal action around the remaking of the beautiful Maya Bay location in Thailand, used for Fox's *The Beach* (US 2000: budget $40 million; slogan 'Innocence never lasts forever': self-reflexivity?). This was a National Park in which local people said the Thai government should never have given permission for filming. There are at least two levels of 'local' there (see the Thai students' website, www.thaistudents.com/thebeach/press.html) and such tensions have existed for much longer. The story of the making of *Apocalypse Now* (US 1979), told in Eleanor Coppola's film *Hearts of Darkness*, is partly one of huge damage wrought to the Phillipines environment (permission given and parts of the local airforce lent by General Marcos) in order to simulate US saturation bombing of Vietnam. Like *Burden of Dreams* (1982) about the German director Werner Herzog's filming of *Fitzcarraldo* (1980–1), which involved the actual deaths of several Amazonian indigenous people, it was read as celebration of the grand if bizarre heroics of (male, white, western) auteurist film-making. The making of *Passage to India* (UK 1984), to take another non-US example, is said to have involved

dynamiting sacred caves in India for filming. Is it conceivable that global–
local power structures would ever work in the other direction, to enable an
Indian film-maker to 'alter' Stonehenge or Mount Rushmore? Some of the
paradoxes of such inequalities are sketched by Salman Rushdie, writing on
'Attenborough's *Gandhi*':

> an incredibly expensive movie about a man who was dedicated to the
> small scale and to asceticism. The form of the film, opulent, lavish,
> overpowers and finally crushes the man at its centre . . . It is as if
> Gandhi, years after his death, has found in Attenborough the last of his
> series of billionaire patrons.
>
> (Rushdie 1992[1983]: 106–7)

The agenda, and access to evidence, does not yet exist, in study of cinema,
to think through such possible 'global–local' connections. These might contribute to a growing ecological politics of sustainable size. They would need
to explore the relations between the huge budgets, obscenely hierarchized,
of certain blockbusters, exhibiting carnivals of destruction, consumerhood,
while, in parallel, celebrating the small, the uncommodified and undiscov-
ered. The two poles are perceived as too distant to argue together, and will
continue to be unless media globalization is 'named' as an advanced capitalist form, currently operating in and for conditions of unparalleled
inequality between rich and poor, and successfully argued against as not
inevitably having to take this form. But of course it sounds much more
friendly to keep talking as though we all inhabit a 'global village' as equals,
listening to stories around the fire.

Clearly cultural globalization cannot be thought about simply as local culture's enemy. Any close examination of, for example, the US–French quota
wars over the years reveals an immense sedimenting down of complex
myths, hostilities, suspicions and hybridities (see Grantham 2000). Questions about the fate of other people's local environment in the hands of some
film-makers are not the same as nostalgic evocations of some lost innocence
or quality guarantee inevitably possessed by films from 'national cinemas' or
'art cinema'. These ignore not only the European ethnic hybridity of early
Hollywood and the necessarily hybrid form of its pre-production deals now,
but also such aspects as

> The dual address of every so-called 'national' cinema: a fictional unity
> imposed at home at the cost of cultural and regional differences in order
> to be successfully promoted abroad as a distinctive 'national' com-
> modity.
>
> (Kinder 1996: 596)

The names for 'other' films from those produced by 'Hollywood' now range through the terms art, independent/indie; alternative, opposi- tional, minority, arthouse, niche, speciality, to (at Cannes Film Festi- val 1999) 'boutique'.

Much recent work has been interested in the ways that 'Hollywood' needs a variety of levels of product for its 'niche' markets, and will voraciously pick up independent or other national 'talent', especially since the resources swal- lowed up by blockbuster production can easily leave the rest of the exhi- bition slate empty. This, however, can be a contradictory process.

- It sometimes means that the first smallish budget feature film by many indie directors (and often, by extension, the work of new novelists who wish to write film scripts) seem often designed, particularly in their dis- play of expertise in violent action sequences, to function as 'calling card' for entry to Hollywood high budget, therefore action adventure produc- tion. All of this tends to marginalize more slow paced films.
- Balio (1998b: 68, 71), citing the arm's-length take-over of foreign inde- pendent distributors by the majors (also including US outfits such as Miramax by Disney or New Line by Turner Broadcasting) suggests that a side-effect of studio investment in such companies is to deprive other national cinemas of major talent, without the studios incurring the expense of investing abroad (as they had to in the 1960s, partly enabling the innovations of 'spaghetti westerns', for example).
- It also embodies the old law of capitalist conglomeracy: that the big eat up the little and in the process the little who survive sometimes comes to resemble the big. It is rather like much contemporary tourism, thematized most recently in *The Beach*, which, in seeking difference, often goes a long way to destroy it.

Recent theory, especially around Internet fandom, has emphasized audi- ences' creativity in appropriating meanings and pleasures, reading in ways called 'resistant', sometimes called 'producerly'. But it is still the case that for an audience 'reading' to be resistant, there needs to be a sense that what is being offered does have a preferred meaning which is being resisted (Perkins 2000). Sometimes the resisters would like to 'win', to be the producers of more than semiological naughtiness. This does not necessarily involve only the very expensive process of actually making films. The marketing research methods outlined in Wyatt's (1994) 'high concept' model are, as he suggests, not designed to enable different kinds of film-making to be asked for, let alone surveyed by the pollsters. Nor are they sensitive to audience disappointments and complaints, such as those voiced by Nowell-Smith:

> the vast majority [of Hollywood's films] are . . . liberal . . . in their deployment of bad language, sex and violence. This can no longer be interpreted as a move towards realism; . . . it constitutes a new rhetoric by which films affirm their characters as . . . above all different from TV. Nor does this apparently transgressive rhetoric have a power to shock, since what seems like excess has become a routine selling element.
>
> (Nowell-Smith 1996: 765)

In the case of globally distributed Hollywood product, the films cannot be argued to offer such preferred meanings, but are unignorable in distribution terms: there is often very little else to see in the multiplexes, however much Hollywood needs other levels of production, especially for TV. This of course has implications for the USA itself, and therefore for the rest of us. John B. Thompson (1995) has argued that images of other ways of life constitute a resource for individuals to think critically about their own lives and life conditions (cited in Branston and Stafford 1999: 254). Though such arguments have been persuasively deployed in relation to news stories, as a cultural reservoir for opposition to fundamentalist regimes, they can also be applied to cinema. Yet the problems of foreign films' distribution in the USA are formidable.

> According to French film-maker Bertrand Tavernier, a mere two per cent of all screen time in the United States is allotted to foreign films. 'We are kept on reservations like the Cherokee or the Navajo' . . . 'Our films are shown only in a few places – New York City, Los Angeles, a few other big cities.'
>
> (Balio 1998b: 63)

Balio (1998b) explains the (hugely localized) reliance on New York as launch pad, containing much of what national press exists, and also a large part of the audience for **art films** (defined as foreign language, or English language films from outside the USA) audience:

> Advertising costs are exorbitant and, although good reviews can propel a film to a successful nationwide release, a bad review or an unfavourable notice by the *New York Times* can kill it. Outside New

York, a picture without a famous director or recognisable stars has little chance of garnering any media attention.

(Balio 1998b: 65)

As Peter Wollen (1998) speculates:

The problem with the American dominance of global cinema . . . is not that it prevents Britain (and other countries) from developing cultural identities for themselves but . . . it also threatens to deprive America itself of views of America from the outside. American dominance simply reinforces America's own powerful, yet provincial cinematic myths about itself, . . . structured around terrifying misrecognitions and appallingly narcissistic fantasies . . . harmful not simply to everyone else in the global market but also, above all, to America itself.

(Wollen 1998: 134)

Further reading

Barker, M and Brooks, K. (1998) *Knowing Audiences: Judge Dredd, Its Friends, Fans and Foes*. Luton: University of Luton Press.

Grantham, B. (2000) *'Some Big Bourgeois Brothel': Contexts for France's Culture Wars with Hollywood*. Luton: University of Luton Press.

Nowell-Smith, G. and Ricci, S. (eds) (1998) *Hollywood and Europe: Economics, Culture, National Identity 1945–1995*. London: British Film Institute.

Wyatt, J. (1994) *High Concept: Movies and Marketing in Hollywood*. Austin, TX: University of Texas Press.

4 | AUTHORS AND AGENCY

> We must not only think of society or the group acting on unique individuals but also of many unique individuals, through a process of communication, creating and where necessarily extending the organisations by which they will continue to be shaped.
>
> (Raymond Williams 1965: 117)

The idea of 'authorship' and the creativity of the director as being key to the value of a film has been crucial to the establishment of Film and Cinema Studies. Associated terms such as 'independence', 'maverick', imaging a 'creative' space 'outside' something called 'the mainstream', as though it were one, irresistible flow – these also continue to be powerful ways of thinking about how films get produced, and how individuals act within those processes. They have played a huge role, for example, in forming the celebrity of Quentin Tarantino, as well as in stabilizing the output of 'art cinema', which otherwise is classified by much broader labels like 'movements' of 'national cinema'.

'Mainstream' practices themselves are structured by this discourse: top ten film polls and other canons; the ways that film production information is classified on the Internet; the 'branding' of big Hollywood films by the name of the director or the Oscar awards attached to it. Emblematically however, the Oscars reward only a tiny proportion of film industry labour. The categories of celebration are still fiercely hierarchized: 'art' ('individually authored') at the top (in categories such as best director, best actor), 'craft' (collaborative, practice determined) nearer the bottom (beginning with the term 'supporting' actors). Rarely are the conditions of copyright ownership in relation to the status of different makers discussed: for example the implications of the fact that the studio is legal 'author' of US films, but the 'authorship' of the director is established by law in France (see Grantham 2000).

This chapter will explore:

- the development of, and challenges to, theories of individual authorship as they have developed for directors in cinema
- the commercial importance of directors' own attempts to legitimize their reputation via the discourses of authorship, and how this worked in the case of Hitchcock
- the ways we might now think of both collective production processes and individual **agency** and negotiation, within cinema's industrial processes.

Theories of authorship and cinema

The notion of authorship can be traced back to humanist, early modern, Romantic notions of the individual, and back beyond that to medieval western ideas of God-given inspiration, literally of 'giftedness' for certain individuals. Though the modernizing moments of the Enlightenment and nineteenth century industrial processes challenged the source of such 'gifts' in God, high valuations continued to be given to the idea of the individual (usually male, white, of an educated class). This was partly necessary for Enlightened belief in human (rather than God-centred) progress through the agency of individuals who can be appealed to rationally rather than religiously. This individual rationality and agency are seen as starting point for all knowledge, action and value, in later authorship approaches to art (see McGuigan 1999: 37).

Much later, with the challenges of 1960s and 1970s **structuralist** and **post-structuralist** debates, this confident assertion of individuals trying to understand and act on a world outside themselves was shaken by, for example:

- Theories of the key role of language structures (including those of filmed images) in shaping, not simply reflecting reality and meaning itself (the so-called 'linguistic turn'). For film this meant, in time, a fruitful focus on the importance of determining structures, such as editing conventions, or genre, or even the role of the cultural formation of directors or films. All these shape what a director can 'say' in ways which are often outside his or her conscious control.

- Related emphases on the impact of unconscious processes on the 'rationality' which is so valued in models of historical and scientific progress. These also fundamentally shake the 'intention of the author' so confidently asserted in much interpretation ('what David Lynch is trying to say here is . . .').

At the same time, rather different positions, which developed out of the 1960s feminist and US Civil Rights movements, were questioning the evidence that proclamations derived from Enlightenment values – such as 'Liberty, equality, fraternity' – actually spoke for them. They drew attention to the ways such proclamations usually excluded their specific oppressions, experiences – and also their contributions to work which was often celebrated as simply made by gifted, individual, white men.

These challenges had a knock-on effect for emphases on individual authorship which film criticism had operated since the 1910s and which took the now familiar form of asserting the central significance of individual creativity within cinema's industrial practices, usually locating this in the director, or sometimes the scriptwriter. Studio Hollywood, while it could market the major studios as reliable 'brands' through their genre-star commodities, had relatively little use for strong claims to directorial authorship (certainly as compared to its later promotions of Lucas, Tarantino, Spielberg, Scorsese and others).

Though discourses of authorship, focused on the director, were crucial to the emergence and even survival of European and other kinds of art/'national' cinemas well before the 1950s, any attempt to establish the serious study of popular (that is Hollywood) film had to overcome a long insecurity about its artistic status. This was focused by some of the 1930s to 1960s mass culture positions of the Frankfurt School (see Chapter 1). They argued that 'good' cinema, like all good art, is the product of individual genius or authoring; that it is necessarily watched by a small audience, a community of individuals able to understand its aesthetic codes and conventions – in fact, is art cinema. Within this model the cultivated audience was said to choose to watch films on the basis of *directors*/auteurs whose individuality was taken for granted. The mass audience, by contrast, was said to choose on the basis of *stars*, negatively characterized as manufactured and standardized personalities offering only the simplest kinds of (illusory) identification for their fans. Such attitudes are present in the treatment of one of the most important moments for rethinking authorship in film studies.

The 1950s French *politique des auteurs* (best, though clumsily, translated as 'the political or polemical position of being for authors') and the accompanying 'New Wave' cinema, were crucial in helping to shift perceptions of authorship. Interestingly they are indivisible from the renewed commercial and distribution triumph of Hollywood films in Europe after the Second World War. There were several determinants on this 'moment', which actually lasted several years (see Lovell 1980, summarized in Cook and Bernink 1999: 81–2; and Grantham 2000). One crucial factor was the end of the Allies' blockade of Vichy France in 1945. The consequent sudden influx was made up not only of GI soldiers and American dollars, as part of the Marshall Aid plan for the postwar reconstruction of European capitalism, but also, once more, of American movies. These had been held up by the blockade and were seen by many as a key part of liberation.

> the demand for American films was enormous, covering all strata of society, and all political tendencies. To be able to watch American films was seen as a sign that the country was free again.
>
> (Jean-Pierre Jeancolas 1998: 48)

Studio movies began to be interpreted, at least by the cinephiles around journals such as *Cahiers du Cinema* or *Positif*, as having different patternings, including those attributed to the director, than might have been visible in the original, more delayed order of their release timings for US audiences.

> The Americans want to treat us like they treated the Indians! If we are good, they will give us a reservation, they will give us the Dakota hills. And if we stay quiet, they will give us another hill.
>
> (Tavernier, quoted by Jeancolas 1998: 59)

Ironically too, there were encouragements to film-makers from the new Gaullist French government, hostile to American cultural imperialism and keen to help foster the French industry by subsidies. Thus the young, mostly male writers and film-makers of the 'New Wave' (usually dated as beginning in 1959) such as Truffaut, Godard, Rivette and Rohmer were involved both in debates on films, and in actually making them. This was a powerful combination at a moment when Film Studies was just beginning to legitimize itself in colleges, schools and universities via debates on authorship. In addition, the economic shakiness of the postwar French film industry made space for the development of lightweight equipment and cheaper film stock, meaning that it was easier to make low budget films with a looser, freer take on the norms of editing and scripting. The 'New Wave' of film-making which resulted was not confined to France but extended to comparable white male artists and critics in postwar 1950s Britain (the 'Angry Young Men'), and the Beat generation in the USA.

One very successful 1950s French film offers a slightly different 'take' on this. The 1956 success of *And God Created Woman* – 'Roger Vadim's low budget Bardot vehicle' – is a precursor of other possibilities for French filmmaking in the 1950s. But not so easily slotted into the emphases of male director-centred, 'art' related authorship is the extraordinary presence of the 22-year-old Brigitte Bardot. This was the first major, and wildly successful, role to express her powerful star image as 'both traditional sex object *and* agent of her own sexuality . . . unlike the more "reactive" Monroe she takes pleasure in her body and expresses her own desires' (Vincendeau 1998: 496). Though the questions raised by Bardot for sexual politics were taken up by the philosopher Simone de Beauvoir in her 1960 book on the star, it was only later that such feminist discourses, or even a higher evaluation of stars and performance, were to enter film study.

> In the late 1950s [Bardot] allegedly earned France more foreign currency than the Renault car factory.
>
> (Vincendeau 1998: 496)

The 1950s New Wave cinema and authorship theories emphasized however not star presence, performance, or the gendering of these, nor even the unofficial status of art cinema as a place where female nudity and 'daring' sex could be seen in the 1950s and 1960s (until Hollywood, in response, loosened its Production Code). The 1950s theorists, often steeped in literary approaches and a suspicion of the 'merely' physical lure of actors and stars, made a very different case. French cinema of the time, against which Truffaut, Rohmer and the rest were reacting, was often identified with kinds of 'quality' literary adaptations or costume films, which the French still specialize in, and now trade globally. It was seen above all in a negative contrast to American popular cinema. Especially celebrated, from the newly discovered 1940s Hollywood output, were the darker, angst-ridden male-centred manifestations in film noir and the gangster/detective movie. These could be aligned with French existentialist postwar discourses. But they also sat well with celebrations of the American male 'vision' and 'energy' of the first directors (such as Ray, Fuller, Hawks and Ford) to be chosen for the most extreme position on the director as author. This went further than the assertion that the writer-director could be called an 'author'. It argued that even directors who did not write their own scripts could be discovered, 'beneath' the apparent repetitions of genre films and Hollywood production lines, true authors taken over by their vision and by implication battling away, always *against* 'the system'.

A note on *mise-en-scène*

An important part of such French 1950s intervention in theories of film was the amount of close textual analysis which it opened up in order to argue its case. This involved attention to the work and effects involved in *staging the events of film for the camera*, or *mise-en-scène* as it was known, a term from French theatre. This was used in two ways:

- by André Bazin in his polemics on realism in cinemas. He argued for the superiority of directors such as Welles and Renoir who used long takes and the eloquence of sets, lighting and so on (which he called, together, *mise-en-scène*) as opposed to directors (such as Eisenstein) relying on the connections made by editing
- by critics such as Andrew Sarris, trying to make a distinction between 'true' fully creative 'auteurs' and 'mere' *metteurs-en-scène*, who 'simply' staged events for the camera, 'obediently' following the script.

Such detailed discussions usefully drew attention away from what were then the most valued aspects of film analysis, the script and editing. They insisted instead, via the inclusion of cinematography and set design, both on other visual aspects of cinema, and the difference of cinema from theatrical performance. This insistence on the specifics of cinematic practice was important.

Nevertheless, now that these modernizing positions have entered into not only mainstream film study but also wider kinds of journalism, it is possible to argue that in *mise-en-scène* we have been left with an overused and misleading term (see Lovell and Kramer 2000: 2). It collapses together an unwieldy collection of processes, from set and costume design, lighting, actors' performance, and often camera actions. Confusingly, the major Film Studies textbooks retain the slipperiness of what is included under this heading, sometimes designating *mise-en-scène* as a practice which includes cinematography and production design, then listing those activities *alongside* it, as though separate. Sometimes it is referred to at the level of the shot, sometimes the frame, and occasionally as a more abstract category of spatial expressivity (see Maltby and Craven 1995: ch. 5).

Given the huge expansion of empirical knowledges about the specifics of set design, costume, performance and cinematography since the 1950s, and their proliferation into journalism, advertising and publicity discourses, we are now well beyond the stage at which the director-directed focus of this term

> After *The Godfather* I got a lot of phone calls from people wanting to know what I did to get the brassy, slightly yellow feeling to the photography . . . the truth is, that colour effect wouldn't have worked without the lighting structure of that film, and *the* lighting wouldn't have worked without Dean Tavoularis' wonderful set designs and Anne Hill Johnstone's costumes.
>
> (Gordon Willis, cinematographer, quoted in Ettedgui 1998: 125)

remains useful. Indeed it may have delayed recognition of the collaborative dynamics of production processes, and the valuation of production histories within film study, let alone interest in the sound aspects of what is best called film's audio-visuality, which *mise-en-scène* leaves out of the frame.

Cultural politics, agency, authorship

The huge dilemmas of authorship positions have been well documented (see Crofts 1998). They centre on the ways in which a modern, industrialized, expensive popular art such as cinema, heavily dependent on performance, was validated as 'art'. Paradoxically, this was achieved by recourse to pre-industrial Romantic notions ('authorship') of the single, non-performance artist (such as writers or painters, often subsisting on patronage) as sole source of meaning in a text.

Theoretical approaches were, and continue to be, strongly male centred. Take, for example, the highly gendered way that validation of the German émigré director Douglas Sirk took place via authorship, especially since he worked, unlike Ray or Ford or Hawks, in the key 'female' genre of melodrama or 'woman's film'. The influential theorist writers Elsaesser (1972) and Willemen (1971) for example praised his work predominantly for precisely its critical distance from this genre, attributing this to the political and aesthetic legacies from his origins in Expressionist and Brechtian theatre debates in the Nazi Germany which he fled for the USA in 1937 (see Gledhill 1987: 43–79). Feminist research was later able to

- excavate audiences' involvement with 'melodrama', and thus to question why the production of such a cool distance from the operations of melodrama was assumed to be necessary and desirable
- argue for other, patriarchal 'patternings' invisible to the early male auteurists (see Cook and Bernink 1999: 157–71 for the lines of debate)
- make visible the 'hot', polarized melodramatic enactments of even strongly male genres, such as the western.

The proportion of women directors in the Director's Guild of America, though only 10%, still represents an improvement over the 1985 level of 4%.

(Lesley Felperin, editorial 'Chick flicks', *Sight and Sound*, October 1999)

Within production approaches, it took determined feminist archaeology in the 1970s to make visible the work of such directors as Dorothy Arzner, Ida Lupino, Germaine Dulac or Maya Deren (Figure 4.1) – not surprising given

Figure 4.1 Avant-garde, low budget film-maker Maya Deren in her own first film, *Meshes of the Afternoon, 1943*
MoMA/Film Stills Archive

the very few women employed as directors or even cinematographers in studio (and later) Hollywood. Women cinematographers are rare, perhaps because of the usual kinds of discrimination against women entering and being given responsibility in a highly technological, 'macho' industry. Editing, usually a post-production process, away from the male dominated order of the set, is an area in which there are some distinguished women workers, such as Verna Fields, Spielberg's editor on *Jaws*, or Thelma Schoonmaker, Scorsese's editor on *Raging Bull* and many other films.

> the directors of this decade [the 1980s] were not unusual in their self absorption, ruthlessness or cruelty . . . Interestingly, female players are few and far between in this book, unless you count the catalogue of discarded wives, battered partners . . . and abused actresses.
> (Sean O'Hagen, reviewing and quoting Biskind, *Guardian*, 31 October 1998)

The classificatory discourse of 'the artist' as 'romantic outcast', social misfit (at worst insecure, boastful, devious) is also key for understanding how the hierarchies of gender work in cinematic authorship. How difficult it is to imagine a female equivalent of the title 'The Master', used of Hitchcock and Kubrick, or to imagine films like *Burden of Dreams* or *Hearts of Darkness* (see Chapter 3) being made to celebrate the chaotic and megalomaniac processes of a woman director on a mega budget film. How invisible, mostly, has been Demi Moore's role as highly successful producer in her own company, Moving Pictures, compared to her visibility as a star body (see Tasker 1998: 8). As Linda Grant (1998) puts it, 'artists are above the rules and women are . . . in charge of socialisation'. In such contexts a director like Kathryn Bigelow has been celebrated, not only because she has been 'media friendly' or 'post-feminist' in not presenting herself as a woman battling against the odds (see Tasker 1999), but also perhaps because her work is fascinated by areas which have been traditionally designated male: violence, sexualized voyeuristic practices, and big budget action set pieces. Within the power of the same kinds of gendering discourses, Felperin (see above) suggests a double edge to the fact that there are now many more women producers, agents and publicists: is it perhaps because women are seen as better at 'people management'?

Authorship emphases have also contributed to undervaluation of the explicitly political affiliations and intelligence of chosen film workers. This involves a blindness to the sheer slog, the routine negotiations as well as more heroic conflicts necessarily involved in politics – and in making films (see Cook and Lovell 1981). Rosenbaum (cited in Crofts 1998: 314) suggests that Andrew Sarris, the influential US auteur critic, tended to leave out of account some of the directors and screenwriters blacklisted in the HUAC anti-Communist witchhunts. Ignored thus were huge gaps in the careers of directors such as Edward Dmytryk, Herbert Biberman, Carl Foreman, Joseph Losey, Abraham Polonsky, writers like Lillian Hellman, actors such as Paul Robeson and John Garfield, and the fact that Gene Kelly, actor and director, like many others, was driven into exile by McCarthyism.

> Kelly . . . was one of the generation of film artists who were formed politically within the Popular Front, and went on to revitalise Hollywood in the 40s and 50s (among them Orson Welles, Elia Kazan, Nicholas Ray and Joseph Losey: their European counterparts were Renoir and Rossellini) . . . he was forced to leave the US for Europe before *Singin' in the Rain* was released and did not return until an acceptable deal had been worked out with the witchhunters.
> (Peter Wollen, editorial, *Sight and Sound*, March 1996)

Ironically, some of the 'fertilizing flow ' of European film in the 1960s was worked on by US exiles from the blacklist (see Gordon 1999; Rich 2000). Such controversies were dramatized in the protests, at the 1999 Oscar ceremony, over the award of a Lifetime Achievement Oscar to Elia Kazan, the most prominent director to turn friendly witness to the witch-hunters.

Relatedly, when such accounts construct an apolitical and ahistorical notion of individual 'genius' they often obscure, to take one example, Orson Welles' involvement with left politics, or the anti-Semitic, Red scare campaign waged against *Citizen Kane* for its treatment of the conglomerate newspaper boss William R. Hearst (see the television documentary *The Battle for Citizen Kane* 1995 WGBH) let alone the political charge of that film. Such histories form very different images of the talented director from those of Hitchcock, who pioneers so many strategies used in recent cinema.

Branding authors: the case of Hitchcock

It is summer 1999, and hard to miss the Hitchcock centenary, following the bizarre 1998 author/director-centred project of Gus Van Sant's scene for

> In Hitchcock's 1939 contract with Selznick he was forbidden the right of final cut. Yet interviews, and even Selznick's publicity machines, stressed Hitchcock's authorship of his films.
>
> (John Russell Taylor 1978: 120)

scene reconstruction of *Psycho*. I do not want to enter here into evaluation of Hitchcock's talent as a director. For the purposes of thinking about the different historical valuations of the work of directing, however, I want to suggest, following Kapsis (1992), that Hitchcock's career is a prototype of the way that some studio system directors have actively worked to construct and classify their images. They function now even more like brands (as perhaps stars have always done) in the technical sense that a 'brand attempts to persuade consumers of a product's quality prior to purchase or experience, usually by the reputation or image of the producing company' (Branston and Stafford 1999: 434). The struggle for critical reputation and therefore access to cultural capital and associated power, for directors as well as stars (see Chapter 5), needs to be seen as part of discourses around authorship, agency and collective production.

Though Hitchcock was seen, even in the 1930s, as a 'master craftsman', it was only around 1965 that he was awarded the crucially different status of 'artist', in response partly to his own publicity, but also to interest from French auteurist film critics, and adulatory books by Peter Bogdanovitch and later François Truffaut. He can now be seen as assiduous crafter of his own image, creating it rather in the manner of a successful commercial brand, a process which has been hugely built on since his death. To take one example, the 1997 Cinemania CD-ROM mobilizes classic (meaning Romantic) authorship emphases through 'well known' stories about 'The Master'. For example, he memorized the lines of his films; had no need to look through the lens; did all his own storyboards; and by the time he came on set was bored, having 'done it all'. Such anecdotes clearly signify 'genius' in the most pre-modern ways possible: the transcendent vision of the all knowing, all 'mastering' artist, even to his slight boredom with the processes of performance, 'tamed' by his storyboarding control. Next follows his father's cruel act of putting young Hitchcock in a jail cell: the 'birth of the author-director' with its origins in Romantic-Oedipal individual trauma and obsession. Then comes an invitation to consider our relationship to his films as audience. 'I play them like an organ', 'The Master' is reported as saying, an invitation for us to enter the pleasures of a masochistic position (see L. Williams 2000) which is now part of the routine marketing of blockbuster rollercoasters, even if we are now also invited to occupy the position of expert or knowing audience by the trailers, magazine articles, interviews and so on around such films. Finally, Cinemania discusses his nicknames and cameo roles, jokier than a painter's, but still unique 'signatures' of 'the author'.

Kapsis (1992) argues that Hitchcock's reputation rests, not so much on the films themselves or his successful struggles with others in the production process (especially producers such as Selznick, script writers and actors), but with key negotiations over reception and reputation. Drawing on Becker's (1982) work on artists and their 'artworld', Kapsis emphasizes the importance of how critics or distributors (gallery, publishing or cinema) respond to artwork decisions. If the author can successfully claim status by building critical consensus within the relevant 'artworld', this can bring such advantages as some immunity from censorship, bigger budgets, perhaps the right of final edit.

Hitchcock was always active in making his own reputation, and in bolstering high, as well as jokier, more populist estimates of authorship more generally. As early as the 1920s he promoted the idea of the director as the prime force in film-making, through articles, British Film Society discussions and so on. His first cameo appearance was in *The Lodger* (1927) and by December 1927 he had developed the first sketch of his famous profile, sent as a Christmas jigsaw to friends and colleagues. From the 1930s onwards he accelerated his promotional activities, for example wearing clothing which accentuated his obesity when meeting reporters, and using publicity about his 'Falstaffian' size to attract the US press when considering the move to the USA in the late 1930s. He sensitized critics to key sequences in his films by discussing them beforehand, something which prefigures contemporary reviewing and publicity practices. In this he was simply practising, writ large, a process described well by his cynical follower Claude Chabrol:

> I need a degree of critical support for my films to succeed: without that they can fall flat on their faces . . . So . . . I give [critics] some little things to grasp at. In *Le Boucher* I stuck Balzac in the middle and they threw themselves on it like poverty upon the world . . . 'This film is definitely Balzacian.' And there you are; after that they can go on to say whatever they want.
>
> (Chabrol, quoted in Bordwell 1989: 210–11)

Hitchcock also gained control of the release dates of five of his films, taking them out of circulation in the early 1970s, partly because he believed that this would increase their commercial value. This indeed happened when the guardians of his estate released the 'lost films' beginning in 1983, partly, suggests Kapsis (1992: 119–21), to undercut the effect of Donald Spoto's controversial biography *The Dark Side of Genius: The Life of Alfred Hitchcock*, a book which circulated severe criticisms of Hitchcock, albeit from a half-admiring position. The withholding of the films from circulation 'as a legacy for his wife, Alma and his daughter, Patricia' (Kapsis 1992: 119) also seems to have increased, in particular, the artistic valuation of *Vertigo*. This film now seems to be unassailably estimated as 'art', and is recirculated in mutually accruing movements of intertextuality, involving the deployment of Hitchcockian imagery by photographers and gallery artists like Victor Burgin and Douglas Gordon.

Within all these negotiations over certain films' classification as 'art', Kapsis (1992) emphasizes the key area of genre. He argues this, not, as in French 1960s positions, as a formulaic constraint which the 'gifted' director struggles against, but as intimately tied to the success or failure of claims about whether serious work can be done in particular genres. Prior to the 1960s, most American film critics did not take Hitchcock seriously because the thriller was not perceived as a significant genre. His ability to build his reputation then helped to render the form respectable (along with auteurist celebrations of film noir and action-thriller directors like Hawks and Ray: see p. 92).This in turn has meant that directors like De Palma, Lynch and Bigelow can work in the thriller genre and expect to be taken seriously. Then, as with any successful brand, the fact that the thriller, 'his' genre, was validated artistically only further augmented his reputation – as pioneer of such seriousness. He became the 'gold standard' by which other thriller directors are judged – as 'Hitchcockian' or not. Thus his name recirculates to add to its accumulated cultural resonance. Kathryn Bigelow, for example, defending herself against charges of offensively voyeuristic and erotic content in *Strange Days* (US 1995), reaches for the Hitchcock comparison (Tasker 1999).

Even feminist film theory, not perhaps the most obvious candidate to celebrate Hitchcock's work, has added to his reputation in academia. Because he is now canonized as 'The Master' of a certain kind of, often misogynistic, suspense thriller, feminist critics have felt the need to 'take this on', as happens to any group faced with a sufficiently provocative canonical text.

Hitch put his thumbs into the director's frame shape and said [of the marital rape scene in *Marnie*] 'when he sticks it into her I want the camera on her face'. I split from him then as scriptwriter.

(Ed McBain, BBC Radio 4, 23 October 1998)

A key test-bed for the developing theory of 'the look' is 'obviously' Hitchcock (see Modleski 1988). Yet in the 1999 celebrations the focus has rarely been on feminist positions: at most the contribution of his wife, Alma, to his work was occasionally noted. There were no articles by women critics in for example, the *Sight and Sound* August 1999 Hitchcock special supplement, and only one answer from a woman director out of the fifty-six answers to questions such as 'what is the importance of Hitchcock to you personally?'

Finally it is relevant in such contexts of reception that one of his lifelong friends was Sidney Bernstein, who even in the 1920s was seriously interested in audiences. 'He . . . organis[ed] the first systematic national surveys of picturegoing habits [in Britain]' (J.R. Taylor 1978: 51). Hitchcock's alertness to both the importance of orchestrating the expectations not only of critics but also of the rest of the audience well illustrates the modernity of his exhibition practices, exemplified through *Psycho* (US 1960). This has been seen as textually *the* groundbreakingly post-studio/post-classical film, with audiences subjected to unaccustomed and disorientating shock in the areas of narrative, editing and use of the star; the horror genre taken into new directions, dislocating feminine and masculine, normal and psychotic, the safe family and the 'outside'. Only relatively recently explored is Hitchcock's agency or authorship in shaping the film's exhibition: no one allowed into the cinema after the beginning; critics required to watch it with audiences; exhibitors shown a short training film on how to exhibit the movie; Hitchcock asking for permission to remix the sound after hearing audiences' response; audiences made to line up, in ways prefiguring theme parks and, later, blockbusters, in order to take pleasure in 'losing the kind of control they had been trained to enjoy' (L. Williams 1994: 17).

In such ways Hitchcock forms a bridge from studio to post-studio practices, especially the shaping of directors as auteurs-stars: as showmen, as brands, even as franchises, their names sometimes as commercially important for the films they make as those of their stars, their work moving across cinema and TV and advertising (Figure 4.2). Jostling now, for employment, on a film-by-film basis in the 'package unit' post-studio system, they, rather like stars, display their huge salaries and trademark styling. This may involve narrative, or the 'look' of a film, or thematic preoccupation – David Lynch as (at least until *The Straight Story*, 1999) purveyor of darkly visual and surreal narratives, Cronenberg promising a particular set of arthouse-horror-futuristic preoccupations, and so on.

Collective production and agency

It should now, given the proliferation of journalism and TV programmes about the making of movies, be easier to make critical materialist accounts

Figure 4.2 Hitchcock: the author goes on, and on
Associated Press (AP)

emphasizing the collective dynamics of film production, analysing the creative input of producers and even marketing staff. These factors, along with theoretical critiques of the idea of 'individuals' as authoring their own lives, go some way to dissolve notions of the individual artist in the autonomous realm of cinema or TV or literature.

Yet post-studio publicity systems, whether for 'ultra-modern' cable or special edition video and DVD issues, only occasionally extend their openness about the working practices of cinema beyond celebrations of a narrow and fairly traditional range of workers: director, chief actors and stars, special effects 'wizards' or certain selected pieces of storyboarding and script on some DVD editions. Rarely do industry documentaries for cable or other publicity forms invite interest into other activities and structures of film labour. The ideological contexts are often myths of the free floating and utopic 'knowledge economy' (into which high tech film-making and the young hero special effects person fits so neatly) or of the traditional division into art, authors and 'mere' technicians or extras.

The beginning of the 'late modern' Hollywood period, around the decline of the studio system from 1948, coincided with the beginnings of a theoretical erosion, at least within film studies, of a sense of the power of individual (male, white) author-directors, radiant as stars with possibilities for controlling their own movies via 'magic', genius or inspiration. Yet, as noted earlier, some strands within 'auteur structuralism' of the 1960s and 1970s now seems to have sharpened other political contradictions in authorship approaches to cinema without taking any further the democratizing of authorship models which it seemed to promise. Its modernizing project was to seek to apply Marxist, psychoanalytic and 'scientific' structuralism to what was, however, often a ranking of individual cinema authors based in Romantic paradigms of creativity. The furthest step in the anti-humanist direction of such positions came in the work of Roland Barthes, and then of Michel Foucault. Barthes' piece 'The death of the author' (1968) emphasized the semiotic process of signification or meaning-making as emerging from both sides of the text, via audience and signifiers, independent of the intention or control of the author.

The importance of such semiotic approaches, focusing on socially sanctioned codes of meaning rather than God-given truths, is now firmly part of academic textual approaches to moving images. But it is worth emphasizing how Barthes both downgraded the intentions and agency of the author and at the same time made abstract the ways in which readers' activities could be celebrated and explored. His model dissolves away two important emphases which deserve to be re-emphasized and need to be historicized.

First is needed a sense of the film worker, whether director, star, actor, editor and so on, as having agency, as potentially 'making a difference', for which intentions are needed, though always as part of the give-and-take of negotiations with others in cultural-political structures. This would go all the way from nuances of film stock decisions by Tim Burton, to the histories of struggles such as those by Olivia de Havilland and others against the seven-year star contracts of the studio system, or of the actors, directors and script writers who stood up against the witch-hunting of the HUAC.

> Continental cultural theory has obsessively theorised the element of constraint in action, while marginalising and in some cases explicitly negating the element of freedom . . . This is a liability for any theory which wants to explain – and even advance the cause of social and individual freedom.
>
> (Murray Smith 1995: 44–6)

Second, the historical specifics of different audiences' interactions with movies and their knowledge of various 'authoring' contributions need to be explored in relation to distribution and exhibition practices. An example of how a more activist cultural politics around authorship might work is Medhurst's (1991) intervention on the side of conceiving both author and audience as agents. Writing on *Brief Encounter* (UK 1945) he argued the need to have the homosexuality of the director (author) Noel Coward acknowledged not only as an incidental biographical 'auteurist' detail (which post-structuralism would assign it), but also as a fully significant influence on the screenplay, into which it is codedly written:

> the furtiveness and fear of discovery that end Laura's and Alec's relationship comprise a set of emotions that [Noel] Coward would have felt with particular force and poignancy, and which gay men have responded to with recognition and admiration.
>
> (Medhurst 1991: 198)

To argue this, Medhurst goes against structuralist and post-structuralist approaches, which would simply ignore moves to incorporate the biographical and the intentional into textual interpretation. Medhurst sees this as both effacing the cultural politics of such a text, and also as destroying one of its pleasures, the 'special thrill' of such a film for gay audiences, actively engaging with that aspect of the 'hidden' within the film on screen.

Foucault's insistence that authors are constituted through discourses and institutions 'drew attention to the protocols of reading needing to be in place in order to "find" an author' (Cook and Bernink 1999: 311). We are already conditioned, by powerful commercial discourses, seeking to dramatize the author/director's self, to look for all the identifying moments which are, for some, a 'Jane Campion' or a 'John Sayles' film. Indeed, as Corrigan (1991) argues, such commercial auteurism does not now have to involve the viewing of a film. We do not so much 'find' the author as construct his or her authoring signature, or character, through all the snippets, trailers, gossip and interviews which are routinely circulated around a film especially, now, through the Internet.

The preparation of such identifying discourses is increasingly central to the marketing of movies by the name of the director. As King and Miller (1999: 312) point out, there is a huge difference between the long list of credits on most films now – a union achievement, forcing some credit for those who have worked on the movie – and their marketing as, for example, 'a Steven Spielberg movie'. In Spielberg's case his contribution may only have been as producer, and in the case of many such 15-minute-credit movies, the director's name is certainly not used to celebrate the important work of orchestrating so many diverse talents. Corrigan argues that it is now possible 'to already know . . . the meaning of the film in a totalising image that precedes the movie in the public images of its creator' (Corrigan 1991: 106), whether this be Sam Mendes' interviews for *American Beauty* (US 2000) as the product of a British theatrical sensibility, or John Lasseter's centring a more collaborative image for *Toy Story 2* (US 2000).

As Andrew Tudor (1999: 63) has pointed out, of the 'linguistic turn' which language based structuralism wrought in so many subject areas, Saussure's notion of 'langue' as a verbal language's structure, and 'parole' as the individual ways in which it is deployed, *does* distinguish between system and agency. Audiences, including post-structuralist academics in their outings to the cinema or even in their free trips to the Internet, do not passively float in a sea of intertextuality. Judgements are made, within the 'intertextual' chain, about the ways a film (often meaning a director) has replayed a particular genre, or a reference has been deployed or a group represented. Intertextuality exists in many specific forms. 'Legitimate' references exist along a spectrum of differentiation – as parody, or pastiche, or deliberate allusion, homage, even as accidental. And of course there exist 'illegitimate' forms of intertextuality: we may not plagiarize in the academy, or 'pirate' and break copyright in cinema, video and Internet forms. While any trawl through a Tarantino fansite reveals the extraordinary persistence of a belief in the authoring intent of the director ('QT will be able to tell us what is in the suitcase') and an immersion in the world of certain fictions, it is also the case that some borrowings are judged plagiaristic or not worth doing. Dis-appointment is voiced, for example, in the anti-Tarantino website (www.impossiblefunky.com/qt/RD1.htm) about the extent to which *Pulp Fiction* draws on *City on Fire* (Canada 1979), the author of the page further disap-pointed that copyright or gatekeeping powers did not allow him to show his film detailing the extent of Tarantino's borrowing.

We need to make such differentiations, as well as retrieve and rethink ideas of individual agency and choice for both directors and audience members within the collective processes, structures (and sometimes chaos) of film production and publicity practices. The 'fool's paradise' of an older exag-gerated faith in the individual and 'his' utopian vision, power and so on need not be replaced by the 'fool's hell' of totalized structuring, with no one able to be said to act at all. As elsewhere, people make and watch movies but not in conditions of their own choosing. Catherine Grant (2000), for example, argues that new uses of the circuits of director-authorship now operate. She cites the ways that such discourses have bolstered marginalized 'Third' cinema in Latin America. This often tried, in the 1960s and 1970s, to oper-ate collective and non commercial production and distribution methods. It also gained some access to world cinema markets through the 'name recog-nition' of a few of their 'directors'. From the mid-1980s onwards, directors such as Alea, Solanas and Birri have financed their film-making by 'working in tandem with producers and distributors, who have ceaselessly capitalised on those names . . . fronting the marketing of their movies, allowing them-selves repeatedly to be interviewed and profiled in the international media, and thus securing co-production and other international funding'. If agency never quite went away, in a sense of structures as not totally structuring, then this does not have to mean collapsing 'independence' into a wishfully innocent notion of individual vision outside all structures, whether for makers or consumers of global film and author images. Though a sense of complex and dynamic play between elements is far from being widespread as an approach, Robert Stam (2000) summarizes well what is now available for a modernized authorship study at its fullest:

> Auteur studies now tend to see a director's work not as expression of individual genius but . . . as site of an encounter of a biography, an inter-text, an institutional context, and a historical moment . . . the director orchestrates pre-existing voices ideologies and discourses, without losing an overall shaping role . . . work can be both personal and mediated . . . artists are creative . . . [they] orchestrate pre-existing voices, ideologies, and discourses, without losing an overall shaping role.
>
> (Stam 2000: 6)

Further reading

Caughie, J. (ed.) (1981) *Theories of Authorship*. London: Routledge.

Cook, P. and Bernink, M. (eds) (1999) *The Cinema Book*, 2nd edn. London: British Film Institute.

Corrigan, T. (1991) *A Cinema without Walls: Movies and Culture after Vietnam*. New York: Routledge.

Kapsis, R.E. (1992) *Hitchcock: The Making of a Reputation*. London and Chicago: University of Chicago Press.

Vincendeau, G. (ed.) (1995) *Encyclopaedia of European Cinema*. London: Cassell.

Wyatt, J. (1996) Economic constraints/economic opportunities: Robert Altman as *auteur*, *Velvet Light Trap*, 38: 51–67.

5 | STARS, BODIES, GALAXIES

> Economically stardom is a patent on a unique set of human charac-
> teristics . . . [which] include purely physical aspects.
>
> (Wyatt 1994)

> a **star** is a performer in a particular medium whose figure enters into
> subsidiary forms of circulation and then feeds back into future per-
> formances.
>
> (Ellis 1982: 1)

Do you go to see 'the new Johnny Depp' film or 'the new Tim Burton'? Commercial dramatizations of the figures of both directors and star actors are
now often equally privileged in studio publicity discourses. The range of
entertainment forms for the commercial construction of fame, as well as the
ways in which contemporary cinema delivers that fame, mean that the ways
in which we define film stardom need to be reconsidered yet again (see
Geraghty 2000).

   To begin with earlier approaches. The relatively late interest in stars by Film
Studies, and then, interestingly, the fact that key work has often been done by
gay writers, may be partly accounted for by the literary or art school training
of largely male, film scholars from the 1940s to the 1960s. They were attuned
to the literary and thematic qualities of films, and then perhaps editing. They

were not used to appreciate, let alone celebrate or explore the fascinations of the play of performing bodies and faces, of both sexes, made-up, lit, framed, fragmented, sound designed and edited into the narrative motion which is a film. Indeed for most of us, to express adequately what our favourite stars mean for us remains an intimate challenge.

In the 1970s and 1980s academic study of stars explored

- the labour involved in the construction of stars' presence on screens
- the key *parallel narratives* of their lives, partly constructed and circulated by studios, and intended to make up a perpetual 'invitation to cinema' (Ellis 1982: 1)
- what might be the cultural-ideological effects of such constructed presences on and off screens.

It tended initially to operate a mixture of semiotic and sociological methodologies, along with the psychoanalytic discourse so central to Mulvey's (1975/1989) 1973–5 early essay on 'the look' on the fascination of gazing at (female) stars. Stars were thought of as personalizing key social meanings and ideologies (such as those of gender, sexuality, class, race and consumption) and thereby making them natural. Any critical politics seeks to denaturalize such fascinations. Star images were therefore explored as 'sites of cultural politics' (Gledhill 1991: xiii). Monroe is an example in relation to models of femininity and occasionally to race, in the insistently white nature of 'peroxide blonde' glamour on which her image draws.

More recently this emphasis has been muted and to some extent replaced by interest in the power of audiences, especially fans, and, within that group, especially 'subcultural fans' to reformulate and appropriate the terms on which the studios circulate star images. Film Studies' early suspicion of sociological approaches to cinema has here, as elsewhere, been partly replaced by an interest in ethnographically oriented fan studies, theoretically informed by semiotic approaches (see Stacey 1994; Lacey 1999; Jenkins 2000 [1992]), and, more problematically, Internet research. Questions of **representation** and the power of dominant values, which were raised by earlier approaches, have sometimes been too quickly written off as 'old hat' in the face of audiences' asserted power (see Chapter 7).

This chapter seeks to:

- explore further the histories and practices of cinema via the operations of star systems
- consider cinematic stardom in relation to other visual-cultural systems, especially celebrity and 'body cultures' such as those of media constructed sports, or 'the gym'

- explore how far the emphasis on a fully modernized politics of representation might be still relevant to discussion of stars and their various performances (see also Chapter 7).

Stars in studio histories

Pre-Internet, traditional film history can be divided into two areas:

- books surveying various fields such as cinema technologies, industries, the role of the state and so on in broadly social, historical ways
- biographies, usually of stars, usually addressed to fans, deploying highly individualized accounts of screen history. These often celebrate stars' agency, even, or especially, in struggles with powerful institutions, such as the important battles over stars' seven-year contracts by Olivia de Havilland, James Cagney and others which is part of the break-up of the studio system, or the struggles of stars like Bette Davis to control the roles they performed.

The studios at first ignored 'stars' – actors in whose off-screen lifestyles and personalities audiences demonstrate a particular interest, which seems to translate into measurable box-office revenue. Recent historical work suggests the 'star phenomenon' began in theatrical advertising of certain actors' names in the 1820s. But it was not immediately, directly transferred to Hollywood, or the many other film industries across the globe which developed in parallel, along the same lines, such as Indian cinema (see Gandhy and Thomas 1991: 108). This was partly because of the costs involved, particularly in higher salaries for stars, until around 1909–14 (see Gaines

---

Moving Story Magazine (founded in 1911 by J. Stuart Blackton as a publicity tool for the Motion Picture Patents Company) encouraged readers to write in about their viewing. But rather than suggesting new endings and ideas for stories, fans wrote with questions about the players.

(Gaines 1992a: 38)

1992a: 36–9; Belton 1998b: 344–5 for debates). It was used by the early studios to bid for control of exhibition and distribution markets, and to help 'standardize' and 'differentiate' their film product, along with emerging specializations in different genres, kinds of spectacle and editing norms. As Gaines (1992a) suggests, the star system can be understood as a dynamic in which the monopoly strategies of the studios were/are fought by monopoly strategies employed by stars. These seek to control stars' own image, and, importantly, revenues from it, but in ways modelled on the industry itself. Gaines summarizes:

> De Cordova made a distinction between the 'picture personality', which appeared around 1909, and the 'star' . . . which did not emerge until 1914 . . . the strictly professional aspect of the 'picture personality' merges with a new dimension – a private life – to produce the 'star' . . . around 1914 . . . the star's life became available as a narrative paralleling and (at the same time) reinforcing the on-screen image. Stories about an actor's idealised family life, for example, actually bolstered the ideology of blood relation worked out in the domestic melodramas so popular in this period.
>
> (Gaines 1992a: 37)

This system is still in play, for example in stories and rumours around Catherine Zeta Jones's relationship with Michael Douglas and Sean Connery at the time of the release of *Entrapment* (US 1999), a film partly circulating via discourses around 'older men and young women'.

The economic status of stars in Hollywood is complex, fitting easily neither as labour, commodity nor capital, though with aspects of all three. But for the studios, as Schatz (1981) wrote:

> the key commodity . . . was the routine star-genre formulation – Each studio's stable of contract stars were product lines unto themselves and thus the basis for each company's distinctive 'house style' . . . trade mark star genre formulas [were a] means of stabilising marketing and sales.
>
> (Schatz 1981: 77)

Stars became a way of organizing the market for a film, indeed were inextricable from genre pleasures: a 'John Wayne western', a 'Bette Davis weepie'. They could even be cast 'against type' so, for example, *The Great Lie* (1941) could be trailed: 'contrary to former Davis pattern Bette Davis's new film does not find her killing anyone or acting nasty'. The reputation of the producer-institution, including this star-genre promise, was meant to guarantee audiences predictable pleasures on screen, including a certain level of expenditure or production values.

The term 'bankable' is still used as a shorthand for stars' success, though the relationship between domestic (meaning US) and overseas grosses is now a complicated one. Goodridge (1998) for example, in a *Screen International* survey of stars' status via relative international and US earnings, uses the combined measure of the international total, the US total and the US opening weekend total. Others define a major star exactly as a 'brand' which is defin-able as an image which persuades consumers of a product's quality prior to purchase or experience. This translates for cinema into 'a performer who can open a film on the strength of their name alone'.

Common-sense perceptions of 'successful stars' turn out to be quite tricky to define more closely. Economists (and of course Hollywood accountants) have tried to assess the exact amount of profit which stars bring to films. Wallace *et al.* (1993) for example, made complex calculations of factors affecting profitability which they argued included the ways that parental sanctions determine viewing, the popularity of different genres and the cost of hiring certain stars. As a result they calculated that stars appear to account for approximately 22 per cent of the rental value of popular films (Wallace *et al.* 1993: 22–4, 11, 16, 21, cited in Stam and Miller 2000: 600).

More commonly, perhaps, stars have been argued to function as a key part of Hollywood's relationship to the broader economic structures of US capitalism. In the 1930s, for example, over-production of manufactured goods had reached crisis point in North America and the large banks fund-ing Hollywood sought coordination of businesses in order to shift goods from warehouses to consumers.

> Two adjacent changes occurred throughout the mid-1930s: Hollywood stars showcasing make-up, clothing and other items of dress-up sensi-bility; and direct tie-ins between screen texts and particular products . . . By the Depression, Hollywood stars were the third biggest source of news in the United States.
>
> (Miller 2000: 599)

Two recent instances illustrate the changes as well as the continuities at play in this area. Leonardo DiCaprio refused to allow a doll in his likeness to be made as a *Titanic* tie-in product, and later trademarked his name. Tom Hanks's voice (only) was used for Woody's character in *Toy Story 2*. He refused to let the toy be made in his visual likeness (which was not used in the film) but gave interviews, for press as well as radio, using his whole star image as well as his voice to publicize the film. Such post-studio struggles around the marketing of toys from blockbuster movies and the use of stars' voices illustrate both the spread of marketing and the extension of the sig-nifiers of 'the star's body' in contemporary culture.

Stars and cultural politics

Such economic histories are now unlikely to be understood as separate from the most central and fascinating aspect of star study: the exact nature of the symbolic commodity which is being traded, within an institution, cinema, which sells the possibility of various kinds of pleasure. What fantasies and cultural positions might stars' performing bodies, on and off screen, circulate, confirm or subvert?

Dyer's (1979) pioneering work on stardom sought to move debate away from celebrations of stars' individual 'magic' towards more cultural-political ways of viewing them. He argued for their constructedness, in two ways:

- sociological, such as studio economic histories or the labour which goes into constructing a star's presence
- **semiotic**-structuralist, looking at the codes of understanding at work in the fascination of the significations at play in particular faces, bodies, star life stories, especially as these are structured into oppositions. These Dyer then tries to relate to dominant values or ideologies especially around gender, sexuality, class and ethnicity.

Dyer (1979) sometimes came close to implying that the whole image is always available for all audiences. Nevertheless his work was crucial in denaturalizing stars' presence (though you might check out endless Internet sites for evidence of how natural seeming the idea of stars' authenticity still is). One of his key moves was to argue that the star 'image' was in fact composed of several related but different fields of meaning, in various relationships to the producing studio:

- **Performance** in films, some of them 'star vehicles', argued to be particularly shaped around a star's image outside it, and to the star's importance within its narrative.

> What matters in such a role (Harry Lime in *The Third Man*) is how much the other characters talk about you. Such a star vehicle really is a vehicle. All you have to do is ride.
>
> (Orson Welles, in interview with Peter Bogdanovich)

- Promotion, by which Dyer (1979) means deliberate, often studio originated publicity.
- Publicity, which he defines as closer to 'what the press finds out' than promotion. Though the overlap, and even the original distinction, is a tricky one, there are instances where it is clearly still operative. Hugh Grant's arrest for 'lewd behaviour' with a prostitute in Los Angeles was clearly not promotional, though it is now an unmistakable part of his star image, and is involved in that of his partner, Liz Hurley, via speculations on the nature of their relationship, forgiveness and so on.

- Criticism, reviews and commentary, including writing about the star after their death, which for figures such as Marilyn Monroe and James Dean was soon more substantial than that during their lives.

Further, Dyer (1979) argued that such images related to dominant values, and instabilities in those values. Stars have a capacity to 'heal' ideological contradictions from their surrounding culture which are often at play within their images. Marilyn Monroe, for example, played and embodied a highly sexualized yet non-threatening, childlike woman in role after role on screen, as well as in publicity about her private life. This was perhaps a reassuring and alluring figure for many men at a historical 'moment' of masculinity confronted by emerging feminism in the 1950s.

The ideological relationship between stars and their embedding social contexts operates differently for different cultural and national moments. Carter (1998), for example, suggests that in 1930s Nazi Germany, stars' images came under pressure from the Propaganda Ministry. This emphasized the biological-racial essence of character, which 'should' correspond to external appearance via cinematic realism, and it stressed differences between the German film industry and Hollywood. Within its films, the Nazi regime emphasized the importance of public rather than private lives, in roles designated as 'Self Sacrificing Mother' or 'Heroic Leader' for example. In such a context the star image of Marlene Dietrich, seeming to float playfully free from her 'soul', bound up with masquerade and stylistic excess – and certainly free from roles as Self-Sacrificing Woman, let alone Mother – posed particular problems, partly accounting for her emigration to the USA.

Broadly, an interest in the cultural politics of stardom has sustained much work in the area until recently. It now seems to have been partly replaced by an emphasis on the following:

- 'Performance', a complex term, much used partly because it has resonances not only, obviously, from acting, but also from contemporary linguistic, philosophical and even work theory ('performance related pay'). In these broader contexts it often emphasizes visible evidence of a process working in practice.
- The activities of fans (often used to stand in for audiences in general) to produce an infinite number of possibilities for the *use* of star images. This is sometimes played so as to relegate any kind of textual or industrial discussion to the dustbin of history.
- A sense that the 1970s battles over representation, the cultural politics through which stars were debated, have been won; there is no need, such

voices insist, to keep banging on about gender, or race or those other tire-some categories of oppression.

It may be that post-studio system star images, constructed across many more 'sites' than previously (theatre, TV, music videos, websites, DVD editions, as many interviews as they can manage) and appropriated in the wildest, most creative ways by fans on the Internet and elsewhere (see Jenkins 2000), now have absolute global 'travel' and multi-meaning. They often seem less close to Dyer's model of meaning (which ultimately draws on structuralist 'binaries' of definition) and more related to diffuse global celebrity systems.

Yet even though sports stars, TV stars and music (video) stars compete for symbolic weight in global cultures, it seems to be the case that, as Gledhill (1991: xiii) suggested, 'cinema still provides the ultimate confirmation of stardom'. Dyer's more recent work (1991, 1998a) suggests that star images, explored textually, still operate a kind of contradictoriness in their film performances, one which is heavily tied to dominant values, hence their fascination and resonance for most audiences. In 1991 Dyer explored the star image of Julia Roberts, the 'first female star for 20 years whose name alone could sell a movie'. He suggests that her obvious cinematic strengths (conventional beauty, some acting ability) are nevertheless not enough to explain her phenomenal success (which has accelerated since 1991: she is one of the very few female stars whose name alone can bankroll a major movie). Subsidiary forms of circulation of her image (Internet sites, fan magazines, gossip columns, fashion magazine and news-paper articles) and her performances coalesce, as so often, around the dis-course or theme of authenticity, understood in highly gendered ways: the sudden burst of 'the smile'; the way her often troubled personal relation-ships are told and referred to in films, plus a relationship to post-feminism, especially in the identity-try-on pleasures of shopping in *Pretty Woman* (see Brunsdon 1997). The roles she plays have had a powerful mix of strength and vulnerability, all the way from *Pretty Woman* (US 1990) to *Notting Hill* (US 1999) and especially the 'confessional' dinner speech on stardom in that film. In the 1980s she was 'in the right place at the right time', a common-sense phrase which Dyer prises open, for Roberts' case, to suggest a key contradiction at the heart of western commercial culture's relation to feminism:

> Roberts embraces feminism insofar as it is no longer creditable to be a bimbo or a housewife for the female audience. At the same time, she doesn't suppress the bimbo or housewife so far that she fails to appeal to male audience . . . She's no victim, yet there are some disturbing

implications of female desirability – she's vulnerable, that is to say eminently hurtable.

(Dyer 1991)

Yet in contemporary conditions of celebrity, as Geraghty (2000: 188) points out, 'the emphasis on the polysemic film star as a site of resistance can no longer . . . account for the variety of ways in which film stars function'. With the long period needed to make films (as compared with other mechanisms for fame creation), stars need access to other publicity systems to keep the image current, either as a 'professional' or as a celebrity constructed through stories of their 'private life'. Moreover, Geraghty argues that a stable, rather than a contradictory, image is needed for those stars who trade on a certain kind of professionalism, for example, Van Damme as a displayer of acrobatic masculine prowess; Jim Carrey as a manic comedian; Sylvester Stallone as an underdog muscleman, and so on. The uniqueness of cinematic stars, she suggests, is claimed by those who display, and are discussed in terms of, performance skills.

Perhaps the resistance model around stardom is better played around other sites of 'representation', such as the numbers of black actors and executives in Hollywood (see Screen Actors' Guild website).

As the black director Reginald Hudlin says: 'Hollywood's power circle has levels of segregation that would not be accepted in IBM or American Express'.

(Goodwin 1998)

The present success of the black actor Will Smith, for example, masks other, continuing inequalities. He is able to command $15 million a movie, to 'cross over' from the affections of the 25 per cent of US audiences made up of African Americans, and to outrank even Tom Cruise in recent *Variety* star box-office surveys. Yet only two black actors have received even Oscar nominations since the late 1980s in the most important categories, as actors, screenwriters or directors. 'Denzil Washington is seen as "bankable" when he is teamed with a white star such as Meg Ryan in *Courage under Fire*, which was a big hit, [but is] perceived as not being able to carry a "black" film like *Devil in a Blue Dress* . . . which took just $16m, despite terrific reviews' (Goodwin 1998). At such points the institutional makes up a kind of Catch-22 loop: the perception of what will constitute a 'big hit' and therefore the self-fulfilling prophecy efforts of marketing, the numbers of cinemas booked for the opening weekend come to help determine the perception of which stars will be bankable in what kinds of combinations, and therefore what will be marketed as though it were a potential big hit. 'Crossing over' is not a step that can be taken solely by actors, outside of the support systems and structures of marketing.

> Barry Norman (January 1993, BBC1) quoted the troubling statistic that roles for female characters over forty make up only 9% of roles in feature films.
>
> (Stacey 1994: 263)

> She made *The River Wild* . . . [partly] to provide a role model for her daughters . . . 'The fact that, after fifty, women disappear from films except as grotesques tells our children something. It sends a message that older women are not valuable, are not interesting.'
>
> (Meryl Streep, *Guardian*, 27 November 1998)

Age (like expectations on actors to go nude in films) still operates in wildly unequal ways for men and women – compare the recent romantic roles of Sean Connery, Michael Douglas, Clint Eastwood (who usually have casting approval of their co-stars) and those of Susan Sarandon and Meryl Streep. The degree of sheer dislike of older women at play in even such highly praised British films as *Little Voice* should be dismaying for any woman who hopes to live beyond 25. It is perhaps one of the achievements of cultural politics, as well as the proliferation of entertainment led journalism, eager for copy, that such disparities now enter popular and journalistic discourse. The casting of, for example, a 24-year-old Grace Kelly with the 52-year-old Clark Gable in *Mogambo* (US 1953) or the next year with a 49-year-old Ray Milland in *Dial M for Murder* (US 1954) went virtually unremarked at the time. Of course such inequalities do not only belong to Hollywood. French cinema has a long tradition (or bad habit) of the 'thank heaven for little girls' syndrome.

Audiences and fans

A key move since the 1970s across film and TV studies has been away from an often elitist scholasticism centred on textual readings. This assumes that it can say what audiences are making of texts, by its own textual analysis, and has often located reception as merely the absorption of dominant ideologies. Such academic practices have been partly replaced by more interest in the very different uses which actual audiences might be making of such 'texts'. The move has been made possible partly by

- the expansion of video and then DVD and Internet distribution, making textual analysis more widely practised and accessible
- the growth of Internet use, for 'eavesdropping' on fans, an academic practice which is often argued to be a kind of ethnography
- the expansion of higher education, opening to different voices, experiences and demands, some of them those of fans (see Jenkins 1992[2000]).

However, a few points need to be made before moving to discuss some of this work on cinema stars and audiences: first, close, systematic, theoretically curious and sustained work on audiences is still rare, methodologically difficult and expensive to conduct – except via the free provision of the Internet to most academics. Many of the most cited academic audience studies have been necessarily based on very small samples: see Barker and Brooks (1998) on the difficulties of such research in cinemas and Geraghty (1998) for methodological difficulties in TV work.

Second, fandom, a related phenomenon (see Chapter 6) is mostly confined to TV serials, such as *X-Files* or *Xena: Warrior Princess*, for reasons of accessibility and immediacy, though it is not confined to TV, especially since TV serials such as *Star Trek* tend to 'make it' to 'the big screen'.

Third, the Internet, while presenting a wealth of resources for all kinds of research, is far from a transparent window on to the inner worlds of fans and other audience members:

- There is a high element of 'performance' on the Net, often involving its relationship to anonymity and to the potential identities which can be played in or on it.
- Despite its undoubted democratizing potential, it is by no means a 'free access' medium. Literacy, access to a computer and to 'free time' (often of unemployment or of kinds of privilege) are needed for fandom or audience activity on the Internet.
- Such problems of method are not solved by some academics claiming not to be ethnographers but to be 'really' fans themselves, while never letting slip a too-revealing or embarrassing enthusiasm.

Fourth, as Slater (1997) points out (see also Chapter 7) on celebrations of audience and consumer power more generally:

> In addition to the problem of sociologically framing the activity and freedom of the consumer, there is the . . . problem [of] the political

nature of struggles over meaning . . . whatever freedoms the consumer may have they do not constitute *power* in the sense that manufacturers and media conglomerates have power over things and meanings.

(Slater 1997: 171)

Nevertheless, work on audiences for stars has gone some way to democratize film study. Lofty pronouncements on presumed textual effect on passive audiences will never be the same again. Though textual and indeed ideological discussion will always be a major pleasure for many film enthusiasts, the assumption that audience positions can simply be read off a text, or a star image, has gone. This has often been achieved by the attentions of writers with alliances outside higher education, such as gays, or feminists, with more of a commitment to using accessible language (see Mckee 1998).

Other historical evidence, read loosely in conjunction with fan and audience literature, suggests that long before such work audiences can be seen to have *negotiated* rather than being totally *determined* by the doubled structures of star publicity and performance. This goes against the desire of some postmodern accounts to suggest that it is only contemporary audiences, weaned on intertextuality, who can manage this. In Chapter 6 I summarize some of Hansen's (1991) work on the, then scandalous, uses to which female audiences put the image of the silent film star Valentino. A later, famous example would be the shocking early demise of Janet Leigh's character in *Psycho* (US 1960). This seems to have been striking partly *because* it activated audience knowledge of the star system itself. Its shock was not in relation to Leigh's 'nice wife of Tony Curtis' star narrative outside the film, though this was part of the casting decision, but of audience awareness that the only expensive star in a movie was not usually dispatched so soon. That audiences registered such surprise may be partly testament to their simultaneous performance-awareness and immersion in the narrative, a 'double' reading (or kind of involved reflectiveness).

Stacey (1994) studied, via a selection of letters, the memories of fandom of female audiences in 1940s Britain in relation to Hollywood female stars. She suggested several areas of pleasurable escape for such audiences, both cinematic and 'extra-cinematic', such as

- devotion to the star which emphasizes her difference from the fan
- the star as role model
- pretending to be the star while fully aware that this is not the case
- selectively emphasizing an actual similarity of star to fan in order to associate with a star image and so on.

All of these are heavily bound up with pleasure in the consumerist role of stars as introducing new kinds of hairstyle, make-up, costume and ways of being in the world. Jenkins (2000[1992]) summarizes more generally (see also Barker and Brooks 1998): 'Fan viewers watch . . . texts with close and undivided attention, with a mixture of emotional proximity and critical distance' (p. 791) and suggests that the 'community' of fans (again, mostly for TV forms) produces its own little 'utopian' spaces – the fans' gatherings, out of the 'playful, speculative, subjective' (p. 792) readings which they produce. They can even make up a base for consumer activism, lobbying the producers of their favourite texts for alterations, to save a series and so on.

Performance, presence, acting

Screen star acting is performed by a person with a parallel and powerful off-screen presence. Because of the sheer cost of employing stars, they are given privileged access to screen and narrative space, lighting, and so on, as well as to audience interest through previews and publicity.

Further, under the studio system, and to some extent today, because stars have often been cast as part of the film/genre/studio's 'branding' or promise of certain kinds of narrative and production values, the whole construction of the star image off-screen tries to add to the sense of *authenticity* in a performance. Gay studio system actors such as Rock Hudson or bisexuals such as Barbara Stanwyck, for example, had to publicly perform heterosexual relationships off-screen as well as on – though there was always the chance that publicity material could float free of such anchorings, along with the pleasures, and pain, of subcultural groups 'in the know' (see Russo 1981; Medhurst and Munt 1998).

The key area of star 'authenticity', as debated for acting, has usually centred on the difference between 'impersonation' and 'personification' (see Maltby and Craven 1995: ch. 6). Under 'personification' actors are assumed to find themselves in a role by virtue of a physical presence (and offstage life-narrative) which conforms to the 'type' of that role, whether 'dumb blonde' or 'boxer'. John Wayne 'just is' a cowboy type. This categorization usually signals low status for the performance, since physical presence (usually of conventional attractiveness) is assumed as a 'given' and therefore 'unearned'. There is of course a further gendered dimension, in that acting itself ('all about emotions', 'about showing yourself off', 'not real work') is seen as not proper work for 'real men'.

When 'impersonating', however, actors are assumed to create a role from the range of skill and imagination they possess. Often there will be praise for a role seen as being very different from the star's real being. Actors are said to 'disappear' into the role, leaving behind the 'real' self, including the body which, in the end, is so distrusted or disavowed in high art or theatrical discourses. Such actors/stars (such as Meryl Streep, Robert De Niro, Dustin Hoffman) are valued in relation to the range of roles they have successfully taken on and the degree to which those are perceived as *psychologically* realistic – in fact an extraordinarily difficult quality to measure.

At the far edge of discussions of acting now is the so-called Kuleshov effect of early Soviet cinema (Maltby 1996: 234) where it was said that an actor's face was edited together with three other shots: ones of a bowl of soup, a child playing with a toy bear and a woman lying in a coffin. The actor's expressionless face was the same in all three shots, but it is said that audiences raved about his acting: deep sorrow when looking at the dead woman, joy when looking at the child playing and so on. The final shot of an impassive Garbo at the prow of the vessel taking her away from her kingdom and her lover in *Queen Christina* (US 1933) has been likewise praised as great acting, even though Garbo was responding to advice that she 'think of nothing' when performing the scene. Perhaps Bruce Willis was told the same for the long take of his first, mostly silent appearance in *Pulp Fiction*.

Casting is equally important, though rarely discussed in work on stars, perhaps because it is seen to detract from the star's performance and intentionality (see Lovell and Kramer 2000). A materialist understanding of stars might estimate precisely such career decisions as their choice of casting agency, or the choices made by a particular film's casting director.

---

a good director . . . doesn't direct you, he casts you properly in a film. If he casts you right in the part, then you're going to be great in the part.
(Tony Curtis interviewed in Boorman and Donohoe 1996: 11)

I was told point blank [by the casting agency] that I had no fuckability quotient.
(Ally Sheedy in Mike Figgis's *Hollywood Conversations*, Film Four, 1999)

The different experience of men and women actors in this area is also under-explored, as is the potential for casting unknown non-actors, in films by Loach or Sayles, or, differently, in *The Crying Game* (UK 1992) where casting an unknown, with no acting experience, and an androgynous name, meant that the real gender of a key character was a surprise to audiences. Certainly the effect of casting choices on the resonance of certain roles is underestimated in much writing on film. Because we are so used to the pleasures of contemplating certain faces and bodies as part of the moving screen's entertainment, it comes as something of a shock when that 'contract' is mentioned, as in David Thomson's (1995: 174) incredulity that someone 'so smart, funny, gorgeous and full-mouthed' as Thelma, played by Geena Davis, should still be hanging around in 'that part of the humdrum Southwest' and 'stewing in that marriage'. Or in Jonathan Rosenbaum's (1999) criticism of the glamour which the casting of (even the unknown) De Niro brings to the role of the psychopathic eponymous *Taxi Driver* (US 1976).

Stars are no longer publicized, by the studios, as being identical with the roles they play. Instead, for a prestige role, the effort involved in a performance is emphasized, and thereby perhaps the star's versatility, necessary to survive in a 'package unit' system. Since the 1960s it is 'the Method' approach to acting that has shaped most people's sense of star performance. It was developed by Lee Strasberg at the Group Theatre, and then the Actors' Workshop in New York in the 1930s. It began to dominate the New York stage in the 1950s, and then Hollywood. Unlike Stanislavski, who encouraged actors to work from their imagination, developing a range of skills, Method actors were asked to draw on their own personalities, conflicts and experiences.

> I remember Laurence Olivier asking Dustin Hoffman why he stayed up all night. Dustin, looking really beat, said it was to get into a scene being filmed that day, in which he was supposed to have been up all night. Olivier said, 'My boy, if you'd learn to act you wouldn't have to stay up all night'.
> (Robert Mitchum quoted in Maltby and Craven 1995: 247)

Oddly enough, though, valuations of screen 'authenticity' anchor the still high prestige of the Method. As Maltby and Craven (1995) suggest, Method acting can now be seen as a more intense kind of personification: the actor now has to 'become' the role psychologically as well as bodily. They cite Brando as a key example with his publicized painful self-exposure in *Last Tango in Paris* (US 1972). De Niro, Hopper and contemporary actors such as Edward Norton are clearly in the same tradition.

The Method involves highly gendered hierarchies of esteem, focused often on bodily display. Just as the early authorship/director emphases of the 1950s celebrated particularly male kinds of angst and forcefulness, so the kinds of major roles available for women in 1950s and 1960s do not allow chances for a display of prestigious Method skills (or of the bodies on show) by male stars such as Brando. Eve Marie Saint can be convincingly argued to give a wonderful performance in *On the Waterfront* (US 1955) but she is not at the narrative centre of the film, or its time on screen. Indeed it is hard to think of a 'serious drama' at the time which could have centred on a woman character with the kind of inarticulate angst, sexuality and bodily display which Brando performs there. It was only much later, with Jane Fonda's Method-influenced, Oscar-rewarded performance as a prostitute in *Klute* (US 1972) that publicity was given to, for example, her research among New York prostitutes, her work for the role, in ways which down-played the bodily display involved, let alone the parallels between prostitution and Hollywood screen acting for women.

Part of the success of the Method in 1950s Hollywood, with echoes in the gender status of stars today, was that it enabled the display of the troubles of a macho, usually 'inarticulate', working-class masculinity. It has been argued that the fondness of the Method school for such verbal inarticulacy is both Romantic (in the sense of the early nineteenth century position that language was to be distrusted: hence such types are more 'real' than other people) and highly gendered in a further sense: women are usually brought up to be more comfortable with language, and articulacy, especially 'emotional articulacy'. Equivalent female graduates of the New York Actors Studio, including Julie Harris, Kim Hunter and Marilyn Monroe, could not have had access to the same roles in the high prestige dramas. In the case of Monroe this was because of the pre-existence of a powerfully 'dumb blonde' star image, though the 'dumb' here has very different resonances. Access to cultural respectability through such performance has remained largely the domain of male stars in male genres such as the gangster film or thriller. White male stars, I should have written. The whole question of colour, and the lag in technological developments in the expressive lighting and filming of black skins via appropriate film stock, also helps to determine the unequal allocation of high status roles, often dependent on close up and clearly perceptible facial gesture (see Dyer 1997).

This is part of the core of stars' value to the studios: their physical presence, as cast and visually constructed in huge screen narratives. Of course this is highly gendered. That crucial term 'presence' can move us away from the deeper scepticisms of postmodernism about any kind of evidence, and can be made to invoke a sense of an irreducibility, after all the work of construction, in a star performance, in its physical commitment to a role. It may draw attention to a sense of human limits, of 'stopping points' to theory, and to material human bodies. This seems important at a moment, like that of the arguably 'overdeveloped' western world now, so bound up with celebrating virtualities and weightless transformations, 'knowledge economies' and 'information orders' in which the body, time, habit and the material weight of things can be ignored.

So, though plastic surgery is, and has been, widespread in Hollywood, bone surgery to alter height, and certain major aspects of the face, is not. Sylvester Stallone, as the result of a childhood illness, has a partially para-lysed face which means he finds it hard to give a sincere looking grin; Christo-pher Reeves, Rock Hudson and Michael J. Fox are sites for the discussion of disease and, potentially, the spectrum of disability which we all share, or will most likely share in, through illness, accident or old age.

Of course this 'raw' is 'played' in different ways: Jodie Foster's height and slight build in *The Accused* (US 1988) or in *The Silence of the Lambs* (US 1991) is clearly part of her signifying potential in those films' constructions: of the FBI in *The Silence of the Lambs* as a patriarchal institution within which she eventually 'wins out'. But this physical 'given' is further con-structed by framing, costume and casting, for example in the autopsy scene where she has to clear the room of tall, be-hatted, uniformed police officers who literally look down on her as an oddity within such a routinely male dominated organization. Her face, described by several of my students as 'elfin', is hard to pin down in relation to conventional codes of glamour, or of 'harshness' – the mouth seems to be often remembered as less full than it is, partly because of the assertive way that Foster shapes and performs her speech, both in interview and in role.

Foster's voice is felt by many fans to be a key part of her presence, 'strong but husky', with a 'country' accent in many roles. She also has a capacity for forceful emotional whisper which can 'break' between the chords of huskiness – in many of the scenes with Hannibal Lecter, or at the key moment of *Som-mersby* (US 1993), for example, when she confesses her love for the Richard Gere character. In fact a key part of star presence across a range of media involves voices and sound workers. Audience enjoyment of voices seem still bound up with the ways that a voice is understood as less constructed, more authentic than visible appearance, as a 'trace' off the body: its size, its gender to an extent (though this is highly open to negotiation on both sides of the screen), its smoking habits even (see Gaines 1992a; Branston 1993). The irri-tation of many British audiences with the upper class voices in British films from the 1930s to the 1950s, for example, took the form of questions such as 'Why are there only two types of people in our films – the Cockney and the Oxford accent type?' (Porter and Harper 1998). A little later, the Scottish accent and brusque delivery of lines by Sean Connery as James Bond in 1962 were crucial signifiers of the more classless 'modern' social world of Bond-as-scripted-and-performed-in-the-Broccoli-films, compared to the upper class John-Buchan-hero-in-the-Cold-War agent of Fleming's novels (see Chapter 3; see also Blake 1992 on Bennett and Woollacott 1987). The voice is arguably as important to this early reinvention of Bond as is Connery's working class star image and rugged rather than suave, Pierce Brosnan style beauty. (Brosnan's oddly multinational, possibly light Irish-American accent does not seem to perform the same kind of work, at a later moment in the Bond cycle, possibly because it is not articulated to such a working class image as that of Connery's early life. Brosnan's is arguably both a softer and a steelier image of Bond.) The most extraordinary contemporary use of star voices is in big animations features, where they can evoke a star presence without any visual (more expensive) appearance by the star, apart from, at most, an evocation of their facial features in the drawing of the character. Woody Allen, Sharon Stone and Sylvester Stallone are all recognizable in *Antz* (US 1998), as is Tom Hanks in *Toy Story 2* (2000), all at a fraction of their usual hiring fee.

Of course such discussion of unique physical presence could apply to any actor (Figure 5.1). Stars are special because a presence on screen is heavily constructed for them. After all, if you have paid $20 million for Nicholas Cage, your budget usually demands that he be framed, lit, scripted and sound-designed for prominence. In addition they bring the (expensively constructed) resonance, the ghostly presence of their star image, whether off-screen or from celebrated previous roles.

Foster's real-life well-publicized absent childhood father plays into and alongside the role of Clarice Starling, otherwise hardly a star vehicle, in the

> Jodie was never traditional looking. And I think that has a lot to do with her success. It was just at the beginning of women's liberation, and she kind of personified that in a child. She had a strength and uncoquettishness. Maybe it comes from being raised without a father to say, 'Turn around and show Daddy how pretty you look.'
> (Evelyn Foster, Jodie's mother, interviewed by Linda Miller, *American Film*, 1988)

sense that it is not written specially for Foster, who has to stay true to an existing best-selling novel. Sigourney Weaver is inconceivable in the role not only because of height, class and cultural signifiers in her life story as well as her face and demeanour, which are at odds with the character, but also

Figure 5.1 The details and differences which make up the uniqueness of a star presence are here evoked for the claims of another 'brand'
Reproduced with permission of United Distillers and Vinters

because the audience 'knows' she kills aliens: why would Lecter pose a problem?

Such discussion of the specific signifying potential of a voice, eyes, a quality of demeanour is fraught with methodological problems. The drift is easily towards

- enjoyable but impressionistic textual description
- failing to separate the character as scripted from the star's performance/ image, indeed the temptation to invert the two: 'Jodie Foster' instead of, say, the naming convention of character and star: Clarice Starling/Jodie Foster
- failing to disentangle performance and acting from the director's instructions and style, and the contributions of other film workers in areas such as costume, make-up and cinematography (see Lovell and Kramer 2000).

Post-studio stars

As early as the 1950s the studios feared 'that the actor would enter into competition with them for his or her own image revenues' (Gaines 1992a: 164). The mid-1970s saw a rise in the importance of agencies such as ICM and CAA as film stars, no longer under seven-year contracts, became increasingly responsible for their own images. As the biggest cinema stars were seen to be crucial to the big studio's hugely financially risky projects, their costs to the studios rose. Barker and Brooks (1998: 180) suggest that the turning point in such individual contracts was Stallone's US$15 million for *Rocky IV* in 1983. Contracts now also often include large proportions of box-office take.

The fascinations of stars as embodying ideological debate or 'play' now compete with a range of other visual cultural forms, which can in turn feed back into films:

- Popular music, especially music videos: Tasker (1998: 14) points to the ways that 'Music video, like advertising on which it draws, has lent itself to the development of visual images of powerful women that imply a narrative context while not exactly "needing" to explain away their presence'. She applies this, for example, to *The Body Guard,* where Kevin Costner's character is perpetually juxtaposed with, framed by, or contemplating *images* of Whitney Houston's character (Tasker 1994: 183), a classic extension of the 'high concept' film type.
- The short films of advertising.
- Sport: this makes an interesting comparison to cinema, publicly airing key

questions around gender difference, or national identity, or overlapping science fiction in its construction of debates around 'appropriate bodies' for men and women, or the limits of competitiveness (as figured in drug debates) and how far human bodies should be pushed within such performance.

- Even the academy (which has its highly paid 'stars' and media celebrities: Jacques Derrida, Camille Paglia, Edward Said, Judith Butler).

> Judith Butler's [book] *Gender Trouble* [1990] . . . has a status in Queer Theory circles comparable to that of Judy Garland's Carnegie Hall album in pre-Stonewall camp subcultures.
>
> (Medhurst 1998a: 282)

- And politics (the 'B' film star turned president Ronald Reagan is not the only recent politician to have understood the need to 'perform' politics, or to have misjudged the 'management of visibility' in intimately mediated political systems (see J.T. Thompson 1995: 140–8).

We could speculate further, that stars in cinema now are more likely to figure in discussions which are both closer to their own work of performance, and which relate to aspects of the post-Fordist work and leisure patterns of their audiences, at least in the industrialized west. There have always been films which use disguise as a plot function, or are to some extent self-reflexive and interested in performance as subject matter, such as musicals, theatre and showbiz films like *All About Eve* or *A Star is Born*. But increasingly, and in more fine-grained ways, recent films have seemed attentive to the nuances and anxieties of performing identity (see for example *Six Degrees of Separation*, *Working Girl*, *Sommersby*, *Martin Guerre*, *Kiss of the Spider Woman*, *Network*, *Broadcast News* and *Face/Off*). The questions raised by the visibility of stars' bodies and performances perhaps echo many people's awareness of the visual reception of their own bodies and 'performances' in highly gendered, age-d and race-d presentational cultures, in both work and leisure spheres.

> In such writing, and the work of Erving Goffman is pre-eminent, social life is seen as a matter of impression management . . . We know about performance, instinctively as it were, because we do it all the time.
>
> (Silverstone 1999: 69, 71)

'Performance' (and 'performance-related') is now a term with unignorable presence in many working lives, certainly in the media, public relations, the 'caring' professions, administration and management, and education. Hochschild (1983, 1997) has theorized 'emotional labour' in many jobs, paid and unpaid, often highly gendered, which itself requires to be performed, whether through the smile at the supermarket checkout or in the nursing ward, the toughness of expression of debt collectors or (see Cameron 2000) the 'smiley' voices of telephone helplines. Cinema audiences have always been interested in learning, through cinema and its offer of images of successful performance, how to 'perform the everyday self', whether in the playground, the workplace or the bedroom. They now seem to be invited to take quite specific kinds of interest in aspects of film performances such as the bodies of Brad Pitt in *Fight Club* (US 1999), or Linda Hamilton in *Terminator-2* (US 1991) or Demi Moore in *GI Jane* (US 1998) as evidence of self-transformation in workout. 'The look' of 'the spectator' may often now be one of comparison against the ideals of 'body fascism', as some would call the unprecedentedly public and discussable surveillance of bodies, cellulite, penis and breast size in the tabloid discourses of contemporary western culture.

> unlike most bodies formed in the . . . entanglement of heredity, lifeways, and work, Schwarzenegger's body is more alien than natural, the product of a rigorous regime of self-government as well as . . . steroids . . . More specifically, training embodies certain relations that are also embedded in screen spectatorship . . . training requires constant self-inspection – touching, looking, imagining – centred on mirrors.
>
> (During 1997: 2)

Finally, the display of an evidentially transformed body in the examples above, the desire of audiences to hang on to some notion of authenticity, works in tension with stars' digital 'cloning' (which the 'multi-roling' in some of the films above seems to comment on). This is not the utterly new of postmodern announcements. It extends long-standing practices of body modification and construction within the studio system and later (plastic surgery, hair implants for men, workouts, 'touching up' of the visual image, anorexia, use of body doubles: see Clark 1995). But it has been hugely accelerated with digitality. Scott Billups, key worker on *Jurassic Park,* was recently reported to be working on a fully convincing version of Marilyn Monroe, scanning characteristic gestures, musculature and movements. He has already made a TV programme where Marlon Brando interviews a virtual version of his younger self (Kane 1997).

Hoarier tales abound: of the male star with a heavy drug problem who was so out of it for the action sequences that a digital version had to complete the film; of a female star of a certain age, whose body-surface was scanned in its prime for copyright use in future years . . . 'once we have that, her synthespian image can theoretically be playing 35-year-olds until she's 85. She could be an eternal franchise of herself.'

(Kane 1997: 3)

Stars, like the rest of us, have always had to perform within the biological and historical limits of particular bodies, and the dominant discourses shaping valuation of those – black or white? Male or female? Old or young? Diseased or healthy? Powerful contemporary 'postmodern' discourses and celebrations of an imagined entry into silicon or genetic utopias, are much more fascinated by infinite changeability and a (highly privileged) refusal of natural limitations, such as age or disability. The contemporary star system with its apparently open discussion of implants, training routines and digitality seems to go along with these infinitely transforming discourses, in the body of Cher, or that of Demi Moore, or in masquerades such as those of Schwarzenegger, Stallone or Van Damme. Yet despite the constructions at work in filming a star, it is still true that the extra-textual body/image continues to matter for the fascinations of star appearances. Digital alteration, for example, poses problems later for the 'proof' of the interview close-up, the premiere.

The visibility of the most intimate details of stars' (and other actors') bodies make them particularly available for the imaging of powerful discourses around virtuality, the instability and constant mutating of the authentic in digital and genetically modifiable cultures. Jonathan Romney suggests:

It's plausible to imagine that, over the next few years, the inflation of hyper-real illusion will result in audiences so jaded that there will be a massive backlash against digital fantasy; viewers will want guarantees that they are seeing reality itself, with a minimum of mediation . . . the more extreme the better.

(Romney 1997: 222–3)

He cites Jackie Chan, advertised in his hit *Rumble in the Bronx* (US 1996) as 'the action star who does all his own stunts'; De Niro putting on 60 lbs in weight and taking real punches in *Raging Bull* as possible performance precedents.

Some Hollywood stars have recently sought, through high status theatrical performance or in film performances involving nudity or other 'risks', to bring together the two sides of the opposition 'star bodies' and 'star performance'. At one and the same time such performances also seem to demonstrate authenticity, bodily guaranteed authorship at a time when this is under threat. This is of course highly gendered, full nudity being highly unequally distributed between men and women on screen. The reception of Harvey Keitel's nudity in both *The Piano* and *The Bad Lieutenant* was fraught with anxiety, and had little of the openly lascivious or evaluative tone which greeted Nicole Kidman's stage performance. This was one of several in 1998–9, involving figures such as Kevin Spacey, Al Pacino, Ewan McGregor (even Charlton Heston and his wife), in small theatres, often at 'ordinary' rates of pay, in London's West End. Mark Lawson (1998) commented: 'Skilled in a style of acting which rewards fragmentation and revision, [such stars] are asked [on stage] to reproduce power in a medium favouring durability and instancy'. Lawson went on to speculate that the small size of the venues guaranteed disappointed fans, perhaps as if the stars need the experience to be the exact opposite of the distance and absence central to cinematic acting. He suggested a parallel with certain pop music performers, such as Portishead and Bjork, dependent on highly sophisticated electronic techniques, but making a point of appearing live before fans. A feminist journalist, Decca Aitkenhead (1998), pointed out that the critics reviewing *The Blue Room*, a legitimized 'serious' play, involving nudity for Kidman (followed in similar London appearances in *The Graduate* by Kathleen Turner and then Jerry Hall), operated the crudest kind of body-checking discourse:

> the man from the *Express* [considered] Ms Kidman . . . 'eye-sockingly, jaw-droppingly, head-swimmingly gorgeous' and the female reporter from the *Evening Standard* is quoted: 'We knew she wasn't fat, we knew she'd look pretty good, but this!' and describes craning to see if the actress had any cellulite, reporting 'None'.

Such discourses replicate in some ways the reception of Kidman's performance in Stanley Kubrick's last film, *Eyes Wide Shut* (US 1999), which so dazzlingly revealed the double standards of many film critics, the huge weight of authorship discourses around Kubrick's celebrity as well as the unequal gender division of the kinds of bodily display necessary for male and female stars/actors. Many fans were promised, by implication, that they could at last see the body so tantalizingly described in London theatre publicity. Hers became a 'body that matters', to adopt Judith Butler's (1993) phrase in the contemporary politics of body size, age and appearance which have always been so vividly dramatized by stars.

Further reading

Dyer, R. (1986) *Heavenly Bodies: Film Stars and Society*. New York: St Martin's Press.

Geraghty, C. (2000) Understanding stars: questions of texts, bodies and perform-ance, in C. Gledhill and L. Williams (eds) *Reinventing Film Studies*. London: Arnold.

Stacey, J. (1994) *Star-Gazing: Hollywood Cinema and Female Spectatorship*. London: Routledge.

MOVIES MOVE AUDIENCES

Most of us, as audience members, have experienced the movements which a film can produce, indeed which we may seek out when we decide to watch them – pupils widening at a performance, the signs of sexual arousal, hearts beating faster with recognitions – or, if we are unlucky, the seat shiftings of boredom and disappointment. We pay, one way or another, to be moved, we anticipate thrills, laughter, tears and cheers.

This chapter will explore:

- the ways that this 'textiness' of films has been thought, including the specific 'movements' of films, especially their different 'looks'
- the ways that movies have been asserted to move audiences, focusing in particular on two contradictory accounts: (a) debates around the term **identification** (audiences are helplessly 'sucked into' texts) and (b) debates around 'escapism' (audiences use them to simply 'bliss out')
- the powerful sets of pleasures at the level of exhibition which should not be seen separately from the pleasures (or disappointments) which films can produce.

The limits of textiness

Textual study of film, though still immensely pleasurable, at both 'ordinary' and academic levels, now faces several qualifications.

- The term 'cinema' is often used now to insist on the difference between the single 'film' or 'text' and the institutions which produce it and circulate it, tied into other cultural forms ('intertextuality'), commodities and pleasures. This clearly undermines confident (or pontificating) statements on what a film can be said to 'mean'.

- The 1970s 'apparatus' and 'screen' theory, developing the structuralist and psychoanalytic methods of much contemporary film study, is now often characterized as 'grand theory' (see Bordwell and Carroll 1996). It is said to have relied on the narrowest kinds of textual analysis for the grandest, most sweeping conclusions about the ideological effects of cinema.
- Such theory's lack of interest in actual audiences now seems particularly blatant, given its ambition to release them from ideological bondage. Indeed the limit position of its arguments was that 'spectators' were no more than 'effects of the film text' – unless of course they were academic spectators.
- There is now an awareness that if we want to ask how films might be representing our worlds, allowing us to imagine those, we need first to take account of complex 'refractions' of the aesthetics of films' processes and pleasures, as well as the relatively unexplored area of the mechanisms of interpretation, or how meanings are produced (see Durant 2000).

> Most of us watch movies, or go to the pictures. Film theory studies 'texts'.
>
> (Anon)

Let us consider a central paradox of textual study: the simultaneous need for and impossibility of authoritative textual interpretation. Of course this is one of the pleasures of friendly talk after seeing a film. And most entertainment cinema is designed to be instantly accessible to non-specialist audiences, so discovering meaning in a broad sense is not a problem.

Film study of its texts has mostly been interested in questions of representation: how do films come to have certain meanings? And how are these related to broader, cultural ones? For this it has needed a close attention to what is 'on screen', to formal detail (how *exactly* is the scene edited, lit or sound-recorded?). Such interest matters, partly in order to counteract the tendencies of 'purely' theoretical (or crudely populist) approaches. These treat texts as simply illustrations for their points, as simply having easily readable 'meanings' which can be assumed for all audiences, if the voice insisting on the reading is loud enough.

Yet textual analysis in a pure form is unimaginable. For purists, different screening conditions change films for audiences. Even in theatrical screenings, 'the size, proportion and resolution of the film image are no longer

Videos . . . , *I have very little doubt from the synopses*, served to fuel your fantasies and isolated you from conventional counterbalancing. They carried a potency that could not be readily predicted, and served to desensitise you.
(Judge Justice Newman, sentencing two students active in a militaristic survival gang, for killing and dismembering their best friend, *Guardian*, 8 May 1999, emphasis added)

The dark in Western culture is oppressive, dangerous and a sign of wickedness. The rigour and remorselessness of *Seven*'s darkness serve not only to make it frightening and sinister, but are also redolent of the film's vision of the encroachment and profundity of sin. Seen in ideal conditions (a silver print in a properly darkened auditorium), it should be impossible to discern the contours of the screen, the film's darkness reaching out to embrace us.
(Dyer 1998b: 64–5)

under the control of the film makers . . . They are controlled by the physical circumstances, resources and commitment of the exhibitor' (Kolker 1998: 12).

No director has final cut; projectionists have final cut.
(Paul Thomas Anderson, director of *Boogie Nights*, in Mike Figgis's *Hollywood Conversations*, Film Four, 1999)

More centrally, even if we agree that a film text can be defined as 'a coherent, delimited, comprehensible structure' (Kolker 1998: 12) the claims made in discussion of a film or a scene from it will usually, simultaneously need to extend further than a description of its contents. They will reach into interpretation and therefore into (often unacknowledged) assumptions about audiences.

Where do text-centred approaches come from? The theoretical models for discussion of 'texts', such as films, reach back to pre-modern, Christian religious views of the creation and the naming of the world. Language, literature and gradually photography, and then film, were, at the extreme, assumed to work as a kind of disembodied 'naming' of an already existing material world. If a sufficiently talented or inspired writer or painter was in question, then this naming would allow access to universal truths about 'a human condition'. These truths were rarely seen as challenged by divisions such as gender, class or race.

> Some [male] audience members in Ghana in the 1960s couldn't afford to go to the cinema but paid the best storyteller to go in order to learn about the fights, bits of pithy dialogue, the walk, which were then all used as a source of 'urban cool'.
>
> (Anecdote related at the *Hollywood and its Audiences* conference, UCL, 1998)

Indeed, audiences were hardly visible in such accounts. The assumption was that meaning is already fixed and lies there, in events, people, objects, waiting for language or film to 'get at' or 'express' it, and thereby do the audience some good.

For the study of popular cinema to be taken seriously, one of the first moves of 1960s British film and nascent cultural studies was to ask ungentlemanly questions, which eventually led in the direction of: 'good' or 'convincing' or 'beautiful' according to what criteria? For whom? Who has the power (culturally, institutionally) to pronounce on such matters? Who says what was a realistic film or photo of certain kinds of life? *Whose* mirror is being held up? These were then merged with 1960s and 1970s approaches, deploying semiotics, structuralist and psychoanalytic models of meaning making, and much less interested in maintaining earlier notions of the human-socially 'shared', which was seen usually to work in the interests not of the majority but of those controlling the means of meaning making.

Those deploying these newer models of meanings in their relation to ideology hoped to act as theoretical/textual/scientific liberators, in what were times of radical political protest and change. Echoes of such an ambition, and its rhetorical forms, are still present in the much more politically cynical postmodern and post-structuralist theory. As Kate Soper (1991) among others has pointed out:

> Why challenge truth if not in the interests of revealing the potentially manipulative powers of the discourses that have attained the status of knowledge?
>
> (Soper 1991)

However, the model developed in much 1970s film study was often one of heavily determined 'spectators' in the grip of patriarchal or otherwise ideologically malign texts. Paradoxically, unlike the connoisseur rankings of Sir

Kenneth Clark's BBC television *Civilisation* series, or John Berger's (1972) challenge to that approach (in *Ways of Seeing*), the chosen method, semiotics, was said to be trying to 'hold off' questions of the value of different stories or images in order to explore the ways meanings are constructed through signs. Film theorists, trying to get film studied seriously in schools, colleges and universities, made huge claims for textual study, usually in terms of 'meaning' and of 'codes'. The question became not so much what universal and edifying *truth* was being expressed in a film, but how were certain *codes* being deployed – of editing, or of dark–light relations, of what constitutes a 'happy ending'? In whose interests? According to what assumptions?

The questions are still good ones. But it now seems, at least for the promised radical political project of semiotics and structuralism, that the moment for the release of that brake, that 'holding off' of debates on value, was one which never came. An emphasis on endless deconstructing took its place. This is bound up with the fundamental scepticism not only about aesthetic value, but also about the value of the social, of history, within semiotic and structuralist approaches as they got taken up in film studies. Even where a focus on the structuring power of 'language' or 'the unconscious' was oriented towards political change, the claims made for such structures were so abstract and sweeping as to isolate them from ordinary social processes (such as study of the distribution or exhibition of films) as well as from the conscious experience of ordinary viewers. If 'language' and 'the unconscious' determine us all so hugely, as 'spectators' whose responses can be simply read off from textual analysis, what is the point of analysing 'merely' empirical and historical audience engagements, or exhibition practices? And what is the point of trying to talk about political agency?

The key problems for textual study now include questions which emerged partly as a response to the dominance of the 'decoding' model, which entered media analysis out of telecommunications theory and then semiotics (see Corner 1998: 48). For all its usefulness, it now needs to be rethought, or at least resituated in relation to other media processes. Too many, too good questions have been raised around the following:

- Its stern focus on 'meaning', to be neatly 'decoded', as though discovering the plans of some master coder with diabolic powers over audiences (see Nowell-Smith 2000).
- The related question: how can we balance sophisticated 'readings' with an awareness of the pleasurable, aesthetic elements of movies?
- The incapacity of simple 'decoding' models to handle the heterogeneity and activity of audiences and especially fans. In particular, the jump from

a textual point ('this off angled close-up . . .') to confident conclusions ('*forces* the audience to . . .'), often through the concept of 'identification', is being valuably rethought.

- Yet, in all this rethinking, how to combine the valuable emphasis of certain structuralist and semiotic approaches (that audiences produce meanings) with historical interest in the unequal distribution of the power to hierarchize those meanings? This involves the structures of the texts they get to see, though also the widespread aesthetic and cultural conventions, or codes, which encourage certain responses and marginalize others.

These points have been made and developed since the late 1970s. Movies move partly because they involve formal systems which are specific to cinema, such as the looks of the camera, lighting, editing, framing and production. They also involve aesthetic processes not solely specific to cinema, such as conventions around beauty, narrative structuring (which seems to some extent cross-cultural) and verbal play. These, as social semiotics emphasizes, do not float free of the broader social contexts in which the film is produced and circulates. What kinds of stories are the most told ones within a culture, or subculture (happy ever after or not? How is 'happiness' defined?).

It is now probably worth reiterating that semiotics' emphasis on the ways that texts *signify*, that the form of a text is inseparable from its *meanings* remains central to modern media study. I want however to focus on two approaches to textual *pleasures*: theories of 'the look', and of 'identification'. Both of these, despite their potential, can be used to simply repeat the movement from 'text' to 'effect' of pre-semiotic 'effects' models. As a result they have been fruitfully rethought in recent years.

Mulvey and moving 'looks'

> Together AOL and TW (Time Warner) give rise to a formidable combination of internet 'eyeballs' and content.
>
> (Miles Saltiel, *Guardian*, 11 January 2000)

Probably the most anthologized article in the field of feminist media theory (if not all of film theory) is Laura Mulvey's (1989) piece 'Visual pleasure and narrative cinema'. The article is often cited as though it were the only thing Mulvey ever wrote, and as though it were still the only piece on the area of 'looking' in cinema. Let us consider its assumptions, and the way its groundbreaking case has been subsequently qualified.

Much film study at the time, partly following work on photographic imagery, looked to art historians (see Berger 1972) to account for how the illusion of space was constructed in films – the use of perspective, positioning, deep-space cinematography and so on. But *unlike* paintings or photos, film, as a time based medium, delicately balances stillness and action, offering ceaselessly shifting positions for its viewers. We can never keep to a fixed vantage point in cinema; the cutting constantly shifts us from one position to another, albeit easing the potential jolts of this via the norms of the continuity system.

Mulvey's writing was only one part of post-1968 'second wave' feminism (see Thornham 1997: ch. 1), interested in trying to change women's positions in the world of unequally paid work, of unpaid housework, of unequal reproductive labour. Intertwined with this was an attempt to change how those experiences were understood through media imagery, both in critical/theoretical writing, and in production, especially avant-garde film-making (Mulvey was active in both areas, as well as in demonstrations such as that against the Miss World contest in 1970).

> The Miss World competition is not an erotic exhibition; it is a public celebration of the traditional female road to success ... We were dominated while preparing for the demonstration by terror at what we were about to do.
>
> (Mulvey and Jimenez 1989: 3–5)

A key contrast for them was that between the near absence of actual women in cultural and other areas of production, and the proliferation of particular kinds of images of women in the mass media.

The other context for Mulvey's intervention was the work of 'forerunner' theorists, post-1968 American feminist writers on film such as Marjorie Rosen (1973), Mollie Haskell (1975) and Joan Mellen (1974) who wrote out of assumptions that cinema, an apparently realistic medium, bearing traces of reality in its visual and sound images, works ideologically to 'reflect', or rather distort, a social reality whose nature can be taken for granted. This social reality is then assumed to be the real and only site of meaningful social conflict. Mulvey's (1975) most celebrated article, also interested in female stars, bears the traces of using the very different theoretical tools to hand from European theory in 1972–3 (when it was actually written). These include

- the 'cinema as ideological apparatus' theories of Christian Metz and Jean-Louis Baudry, both drawing on

- Louis Althusser's version of Marxism interlocked with the psychoanalytic theories of Jacques Lacan and Sigmund Freud.

Such theories (necessarily, given their ambitious sweep) were often sustained by a suspicion of empirical research, such as observed experience of 'real life data', sociological interviews, or quantitative methods. This 'empiricism' was seen as hostile to any kind of theorizing and as deeply conservative.

Mulvey (1975) explored the uneasy relationship between the forward drive of a Hollywood film narrative and the potential of the static images within it to resist that drive. She speculates on how unconscious processes might contribute to the voyeuristic fascinations of films. The 'rule' of the continuity editing system that the actor never look at the camera is said to give the sense that we are watching events on screen without the knowledge of their participants, and to pleasure unconscious and voyeuristic drives in such a positioning. Then, how might these systems of looking, and films' audiences, be gendered, or divided unequally between the sexes?

This paper intends to use **psychoanalysis** to discover where and how the fascination of film is reinforced by pre-existing patterns of fascination already at work within the individual subject and the social formations that have moulded *him*.

(Opening sentence of Mulvey's 'Visual pleasure and narrative cinema', 1975, emphasis added)

The broad lines of the argument, with some of Mulvey's own later revisions, are as follows. At the level of narrative, the active role of making things happen and controlling events in (studio) Hollywood films usually belonged to a male character; the female lead was often virtually peripheral to fictional events. So much is familiar from the literary narrative theories of the Russian formalist Vladimir Propp (1975) on the 'princess' function often occupied (as a kind of reward for the hero) by female characters in classic tales.

Mulvey in her rethink of the 1975 article (Mulvey 1981) suggests that this 'princess' function is rarely fully carried out in contemporary narratives, whether of advertising of movies. It has become more true that involvement with expectations of public activity, as well as enjoyment of such figures as *Xena: Warrior Princess*, is now far from confined to males.

However this narrative structure (shared by literature, radio and others) interweaves in film with three different 'looks':

- looks between characters
- the 'look' of the camera at the action
- the look of 'the spectator' at the screen.

The next step is to relate these to highly speculative structures of **voyeurism** and fetishism, argued as formative, unconscious drives.

> Women are simultaneously looked at and displayed, with their appearance coded for looked-at-ness . . . [the woman's] visual presence tends to . . . freeze the flow of action in moments of erotic contemplation.
>
> (Mulvey 1989[1975]: 190)

Mulvey then suggested that these can be fed back into a rethought model of ideology, involving adequate and inadequate recognitions of the real. Her conclusion was that 'the woman', usually played by a star (she cites Lauren Bacall, Marlene Dietrich), remained passively decorative, rarely having the camera aligned with her look in the film's narrative. She is often fetishized, or fixated upon, constructed over and over as 'to be looked at' by both male characters and the film's spectators.

Finally, these 'spectators' were theorized, on the evidence of the texts on screen, as being 'male', not literally, of course, but in the systems of looking at women which they were 'forced' to operate (see quote on p. 138).

Cine-psychoanalysis

This early work on the specifics of how cinema might be moving its audiences seized partly on the ways that film differs from theatre, or even TV. Until fairly recently film was watched in the dark, on a large screen, with the viewer occupying a space both partly public and partly private, hoping not to have intimate reactions overseen by others, yet enjoying relating to the screen as part of an audience. It has seemed to many to be a scenario particularly suited to the pleasuring of fantasies. One of the key emphases of psychoanalysis, the importance of dream or near-dream fantasy and unconscious states, seemed an alluring way beyond the empirical emphases of existing sociological accounts of effect.

As a result some film theory has assumed a high status for psychoanalysis, as a 'master' discipline for the study of cinema (which there is no space to go into here, nor is my main interest in it, but see Thornham 1997; Hill and

Church-Gibson 1998; Cook and Bernink 1999 for helpful accounts). A few, very broad points are now worth making: first, one problem is that by definition the unconscious is not directly amenable to analysis or conscious questioning – that is why it is called 'the unconscious'! This is not to write it off. There seems to be evidence that deeply unconscious forces are at play in all of us, approached through dreams, slips of the tongue, compulsively repeated patterns of behaviour. But film studies has to hang on to a sense that this evidence is hotly contested, especially the extent to which it is either fully repressed, or easily retrievable in analysis (see the late 1990s debates on 'false memory syndrome': Kitzinger 1998).

Second, there then follow questions of mediation, such as how does this transfer to film? Is the film amenable to a reading as 'symptom', like the patient on the psychoanalyst's couch? Is film a 'symptom' of the embedding culture ('giving away' its patriarchal nature, for example)? If so the transfer through from culture to screen is remarkably direct, given all the processes of film-making, cultural histories, accidents, censorship and so on. Is it a 'symptom' of the director – of Kubrick's or Hitchcock's obsessions for example? In which case the same questions, basically ones of exactly how texts mediate the social, apply (see Buscombe *et al.* 1992).

Third, whether Freudian or Lacanian, such approaches are, as Murray Smith (1995) points out, nightmarishly determinist, with real difficulties conceptualizing agency and change:

> For Lacan, social experience irrevocably alienates us from our 'true' beings; as we learn language we become permanently enmeshed in a social system ('the Symbolic') which alienates us from 'the Real'.
>
> (M. Smith 1995: 236)

Freud, too, can be said to have an essentially tragic view of human existence, which he sees as determined from early traumas, necessarily repressed desires and so on, one which fits uneasily with the radical political and therefore more conscious aims of, for example, Mulvey's feminist project.

Fourth, it has also been objected, for 'feminist cine-psychoanalysis', that Mulvey and others, in drawing so heavily on the theories of male psychoanalysts such as Freud and Lacan, were using theories which had no interest in women's experience. It was not just that such theorists were male (that would not necessarily prevent them from producing useful insights) but that their theories were almost exclusively interested in 'the male' and his passage to an adult, repressed identity, in Freud through the Oedipus conflict, in Lacan via the 'mirror phase' (see Andermahr *et al.* 1997). The result for film study was that women viewers seemed to have two choices:

- either identify in a masochistic way with women constructed solely according to their narrative passivity and visual 'looked-at-ness'
- or take up the male viewing position, and with it a kind of 'transvestism' of identification (Mulvey 1981).

Fifth, writers on Freud have admitted to problems with much of his work, including the ways he seems to have interpreted the evidence of female patients. It is often suggested now that his writing should be treated as literature, as providing elusive but occasionally fruitful metaphors for exploring the unconscious; the same has been said for Lacan.

For some, psychoanalytic terms, in their very metaphoric-ness, can be alluring. The language of Freudian-Lacanianism is full of visual metaphors, available for obscure or playful or suggestive punning, such as 'the mirror phase', 'castration', 'lack'. Compared to number-crunching figures from content analysis, discussing the mysteries and metaphors of the mirror phase or the castration complex ('I love it when you talk post-structuralist') can still be as seductive as Mulvey suggested it was in 1975:

> I sometimes feel the excitement, novelty and sheer difficulty of semiotic and psychoanalytic theory overwhelmed other political concerns and commitments. The priority was to establish the psyche's political reality and its manifestation in image and representation. Looking back . . . it seems as though deeply important changes were engulfing society while I was looking elsewhere.
>
> (Mulvey 1989[1975]: xii)

For some students, even now, this language can be hugely intimidating. Coming to such theories for the first time (even where they are used only as one part of an analysis) they have to grapple with unfamiliar and also metaphorical terms, at whatever levels they are being used, in academic courses where often no time can be allocated to adequately explore the connections of film studies to theories from 'outside' it.

Finally (like the recurring use of the confusing visual metaphor of the Lacanian mirror phase) it is now part of an overemphasis of the visual within cinema study (see Jay 1992 for fascinating linkages around this) as opposed, for example, to the aural, or to the many systems which cinema shares with other cultural forms such as literature.

You do not have to be a Woody Allen fan to realize that psychoanalysis and (something slightly different) psychology has had a broad effect on Hollywood cinema. Murray Smith (1995: 211–12), for example, suggests that between the late 1930s and the 1940s there was a wave of popularizations of Freudian theory (in the form of a broad sense of unconscious and repressed drives, the 'ego' and the 'id') in the USA which began to relate to the Production Codes as well as the proliferation of psychotherapy as a practice and a discourse. This affected the 'moral gradations' of melodrama. While the censorship codes demanded a return to the harsh moral landscape of good versus evil and retributive endings (gangster lying dead in the street, 'bad woman' not allowed to survive the film's ending) popularized notions of psychoanalysis seem to have softened such severity. The language of 'good' and 'evil' was replaced by that of 'health' and 'adjustment' in films like *Nightmare Alley* (1947), *The Snake Pit* (1948), *Spellbound* (1945), *Cat People* (1942), *Possessed* (1947) and *Whirlpool* (1949).

But it is the textual application of psychoanalysis which has so decisively entered film and cultural theory. Linda Williams (1990) argued, from a position sympathetic to psychoanalysis, that 'despite the many reservations that can be levelled against it, psychoanalytic theory has proved an unavoidable partial explanation of the desires that drive sexual fantasy and pornography' (p. 270). Elsewhere (1998: 270) she tries to combine both psychoanalytic and Marxist approaches to fetishism (as in commodity fetishism, see Bruzzi 1998 for further discussion).

Meanwhile, in the mid-1990s, enormously influential film theory from the 'Wisconsin School' (see Chapter 1; Bordwell and Carroll 1996; Bordwell and Thompson 1997) has turned to cognitive psychology, in conjunction with Russian formalist narrative theory, as a way to think about spectators' shifting engagements with film. These reject the idea that an individual's 'readings' or 'identification' are locked into early, commonly shared 'moments', such as the 'mirror phase' said to enable 'entry into language' from Lacanian theory, or Oedipal conflicts around the separation from the mother figure from Freudian. Instead the individual is conceived as a rational being. During a film the individual is involved in decoding cues and organizing sensory data, such as the relationship between 'plot' and 'story', conceptualized as 'information' (see Nowell-Smith 2000). The emphasis is on the viewer working to trace cause–effect in the narrative. The film 'triggers' the viewer's cognitive mental responses and formal patterning through various cues – lighting, tone of voice and so on. Such a model, however, raises its own problems:

- It could be said to assume 'empty' yet fully formed, rational viewers, waiting for the 'cues' and 'triggerings' of 'the text', without any already existing response.
- The aesthetic aspect of films becomes very hard to discuss in such a model (see Smith 1995; Nowell-Smith 2000).
- The 'already existing', which is excluded from the cognitive model, would

encompass not only preconscious drives and the whole realm of emotional affect, but also other formations, such as race, class, gender, sexuality, as having effects on viewing. The cognitive model has been said instead to posit: a 'viewer as a sexless, genderless, classless, stateless "hypothetical entity" ' (Nichols 1992, quoted in Kaplan 1998: 276).

- It works most convincingly, and is most often used, with only a few genres, such as detective thrillers, where the piecing together of plot and story is needed for the pleasures of solving the mystery.
- An odd similarity has also been noted to precisely the models of the cinema 'spectator' which cognitive approaches seek to challenge. Both 'cine-psychoanalysis' and 'the cinematic apparatus' deploy a 'highly condensed and somewhat mechanical theory' (Kaplan 1998: 276) of ahistorical viewers.
- It also, finally, resembles the 'ideal consumer' of economic theory, here efficiently optimizing choices in the marketplace of meanings.

Murray Smith (1995) however, also working with cognitive and Russian formalist frameworks, suggests that it is possible to skew such investigation towards political and historical processes: see p. 145.

Identification and narratives

'Identification' is another key term through which our engagements with films have been discussed. It is often used to suggest an utter absorption (often implied as passive) into the narrative (and even documentary) forms which film usually takes. The term implies a further, related one: **identity**. This is often then used to suggest that the 'identification' of a 'spectator' into a film, or character, or scene, produces a particular, often single, social identity, often assumed to be negative or oppressive (though the same model is often at work in hopes for propaganda forms, such as early Eisensteinian montage: see Staiger 1992).

The issues that its use raises are complicated. They include a suspicion of emotion, and involvement in the still dominant models of much film study, emerging from various currents:

- Post-structuralist and postmodernist scepticisms tend to be sarcastic about involvement of any kind, valuing supremely an emphasis on 'difference' over what is 'shared' or 'same'. This comes from early structuralist models of language and their acceleration into post-structuralist abandonments of sharable meaning or the possibility of meaningful recognitions (see Andermahr *et al.* 1997 for incisive discussions).

- Film Studies also inherits a distrust of the 'illusion of reality' said to be produced in photographic derived artworks, especially film and TV, which are assumed to produce identification via 'mere' emotional response to the real seeming images on screen. This also surfaces as a legacy from the particular ways that Brechtian-Marxist emphases were taken up in the 1970s. (Oddly, for recent cinema, the ways that 'high concept' Hollywood movies produce moments which are openly in excess of any realist ambitions, in the interest of trailer moments, might be said to pose problems for this 'distanciating' project and its assumed-to-be-duped viewers. But these come from way inside the industry.)
- The term 'identification' has a specifically psychoanalytic charge in referring to key stages in the formation of the personality (especially Lacan's theory of the mirror phase, with its deep distrust of recognition and 'identifying' moments, couched in visual terms: see Cook and Bernink 1999: 346–7).

As several writers (Maltby and Craven 1995; M. Smith 1995; Andermahr *et al.* 1997; Barker and Brooks 1998 among others) have pointed out, the term is not helpful in the way it suggests a total, *unthinking* absorption of 'the spectator' into moments which are asserted to have 'compelled' identification by various means. Maltby and Craven (1995: 212) make a useful distinction between point of view, which they use to mean a position of knowledge offered by the narrative, and viewpoint, which refers to the position in space of the film, the angle, height, etc. of a shot. Other terms, such as *involvement, engagement* or *investment* in a text, may offer more flexible models for the various movements of both film and of the viewer's attention and emotions, as well as for the *conscious* part of the viewer's side of the encounter. Some researchers have suggested that fan viewing operates with a mixture of intense emotional involvement and critical distance (Barker and Brooks 1998; Jenkins 2000[1992]).

Murray Smith (1995) proposes replacing the blanket use of terms such as 'identification', in tandem with 'point of view', by a systematic attempt to categorize several distinct levels of engagement with characters, which together make up the structure of sympathy offered by a particular film and entered into by, rather than swallowing up, its viewers. His terms for these different levels of *engagement* include:

- *alignment*: referring to the way a film gives us access to the actions, thoughts and feelings of characters (for example *The Silence of the Lambs* or *Fight Club* may 'align' us with a character without inviting 'allegiance' to him and his values)
- *allegiance*: the way a film attempts to marshal our sympathies for or against the various characters in the world of the fiction

- *keying*: the stressing of one character's experience, tuning a sequence to that 'key', while not making it impossible to view other perspectives.

These different levels offer a way out of thinking via a single '*identification*', especially if that is understood as a 'self-oblivion' of spectator into text. The audience is not 'dragged along/by the scruff of the text' (Mulvey 1989: 29) into sympathetic involvement with any character whose point of view is filmed, in this more differentiated model.

> identification can only be made through recognition, and all recognition is itself an implicit confirmation of an existing form.
>
> (Friedberg 1993, writing from within a Lacanian approach)

Smith takes his optimism about viewers' imaginative engagement with fiction further. He argues for higher valuation not only of involvement, recognition and even emotion in the understanding of viewing processes. He also argues for the continued importance of the notion of human agency or 'personhood', a fundamental element of both our social interactions and of our imaginative activities. Post-structuralists argue there is nothing to reflect in narratives, that they bestow an ideologically suspect order on what is in fact the absolute randomness of existence. This is a paradoxical claim for post-structuralism, which often claims to be politically liberating, and which implicitly claims the status of truth for its otherwise absolute scepticisms.

Smith (1995) suggests that such approaches overlook the fact that what narratives represent – human social life – already has an implicit narrative structure: that of human action, which is intrinsically time-centred, moving between past experiences, present states, and anticipations and intentions directed towards the future. He deploys what he calls cognitive anthropology to give historical dimensions to his suggestions, including the use of the concept of an active and multiple 'imagination' rather than other models for mental process, whether the deep determinism of Freudian-Lacanian models, or the empty reactive processing of many cognitive accounts. Barker and Brooks (1998: 287–9) also argue for use of this concept.

> The topography of imagination as I will develop it is not that of untrammelled, virgin territory; it is criss-crossed by culturally established routes.
>
> (M. Smith 1995: 47)

Similarly work by John Corner (1998: 103–6) opens out models of the 'effects' of violent films, by implication on 'vulnerable' (or 'over-identifying') audiences. He distinguishes between 'turn on' and 'turn off' violence in films. 'Turn off' violence aims, by editing, camera point of view, and so on, to produce feelings like those which might accompany witnessing violence in real life. Audiences might be expected to respond by drawing on systems of ethics they use in assessing reality. 'Turn on' violence aims to produce feelings of a distinctly aesthetic kind. It might be designed to produce pleasure in (certain) viewers, appealing to other than ethical norms, perhaps aesthetic ones, seeking to produce pleasurable excitement (though see Schlesinger *et al.* 1992). Such work complicates the most widespread ways of talking about our various engagements with movies, and invites the theoretical move from 'spectator' to 'audiences'.

From spectators to audiences

> The persistent question 'what about the women in the audience?' and my own love of Hollywood melodrama . . . combined to convince me that, however ironically it had been intended originally, the male third person closed off avenues of enquiry that should be followed up.
>
> (Mulvey 1989[1981]: 29)

Much has changed, both in films and in their embedding cultures. They circulate now in more intensely visual-commercial and also surveillance contexts, and many audiences have a correspondingly increased awareness of their workings. *The Piano* (New Zealand 1993) for example, is a celebrated 'cross-over hit', having moved from 'art film' status to commercial success. It puts into confusion many aspects of the systems of looks, nudity, costume fetishization and narrative in studio films. Yet it seems to exert kinds of fascination which suggest that the codes of looking argued by Mulvey (1975) are still sufficiently strongly operated (for example around the display of the nude male body) as to produce elation on the one hand, or discomfort and even disgust when broken. The system still seems somehow in place because this film is felt to violate it.

Mulvey's (1975) position has been taken in many directions, sometimes by herself. Hansen's (1991) work on the silent star Valentino's extraordinary appeal to his fans, is a kind of bridge between text centred psychoanalytic informed work and audience research. She considers socio-economic factors, studio publicity, fan literature, and non-visual aspects of film-making, but also speculates thus on the 'looks' of Valentino:

> whenever Valentino lays eyes on a woman first, we can be sure she will turn out to be the woman of his dreams, the legitimate partner in the romantic relationship; whenever a woman initiates the look, she is inevitably marked as a vamp, to be condemned and defeated in the course of the narrative.
>
> (Hansen 1991: 262)

She suggests that the 'spectator position' offered to audiences is structurally analogous to that of the 'vamp' within the story. All of these movements (and not simply 'the look'), she argues, produces what his fan literature suggests is the transgressive cultural figure of a man who beckons the female spectator (and here she radically revises Mulvey) 'beyond the devil of phallic identification into the deep blue sea of polymorphus perversity . . . a threat not merely of sexual difference but of a different kind of sexuality' (Hansen 1991: 274).

Over the course of the 1980s, other groups interested in questions of representation, around gender, race, sexuality, produced vivid theoretical disagreements with Mulvey's ahistorical model. Nevertheless the celebrated argument, however psychoanalytically couched, opened the way for more fully social questions. Black writers for example, pointed to gaps in her position:

- The fetishistic value argued for the female star has simply not been available to black women absent from star systems (Young 1996: 15–18).
- Other kinds of oppressive looking have been operated by 'groups [which] have historically had the license to "look" openly while other groups have "looked" illicitly' (Gaines 1988, quoted in Young 1996: 18). Terms such as 'class tourism' or the exploration of the look at the exotic 'other' in travel discourses are examples.
- Very different positions might be offered, for example, by psychoanalysis based in non-European family structures or other theories than Freud's – those of Winnicott for example. Freud's metaphor of 'the dark continent' for female sexuality embodies the Euro-centric, nineteenth century flavour of his theories.
- Lesbian and gay writers have pointed to the monolithic nature of the 'male = active' position as the only one offered the viewer by Mulvey's formulation. What happens in this model to the active (lesbian) female

gaze (Mulvey's 'transvestism' in her 1981 revision) or the desiring gay male gaze at the male body?

Mulvey's 'spectator' was to some extent displaced towards theorization of actual audience members, using interviews, study of fan literature, appeals for letters about past cinema-going, questionnaires.

Stacey (1994) working partly from the evidence of letters and question-naires from over 300 keen cinema-goers of the 1940s about women's view-ing, sent to her as a result of an advertisement, made the key arguments that:

- the pleasures of spectatorship work on conscious as well as unconscious levels
- the experience of actual spectators in actual cinemas needs to be addressed
- 'identifications' between women in the audience and women constructed on screen contain forms of homoerotic pleasures which have yet to be explored (see also Chapter 5).

'Escape', utopias and cinemas

> the flight into a fictional fantasy world is not so much a denial of reality as playing with it.
>
> (Ien Ang, *Watching Dallas*, 1985)

When I go to my local multiplex, as I begin to enjoy my expensive 'ancillary product' (usually Ben and Jerry ice-cream) a huge slogan comes up on screen: 'The Great Escape'. Then we're straight into the adverts.

The obvious meaning of 'escapism' involves an 'escape, especially from reality'. Implying totally uncritical viewers, it is used to disparage film and TV fictions as irresponsible mass forms – as opposed to the 'seriousness' of art or documentaries. Escapism often equals 'genre' entertainment forms, and within them, in a very gendered move, the musical and romance. This is taken for granted, even though the more 'male genres' of the war film or courtroom drama (higher status because signifying a connection to 'public' issues) equally provide an entertaining escape from the everyday, and stage their conflicts via equally polarized melodramatic oppositions and scenarios of confession.

What sorts of 'escape' have different audiences made, and do they make, into movies? How have these been theorized? Richard Dyer (1973, 1993) made an early move to defend the pleasures of film entertainment forms. He took over the derogatory use of the term 'escapist' and argued that what was enjoyable about entertainment or genre forms was *precisely* the kinds of fantasy escape they allow from everyday realities. 'Utopian' he suggested could, surprisingly, be a way of thinking the cultural and even political 'reach' of movies which might not seem to be political in the accepted/realist/'public sphere' sense of the term (the inclusion of explicit political themes, and so on).

The origins of the term 'utopia' are themselves fruitfully ambiguous in this context, deriving from the Greek for both 'no place' (*ou topos*) and 'good place' (*eu topos*), seeming both to evoke and to deny the possibility of a connection to conventional politics. Its history, for film and cultural theory (see Brooker 1999), now has to include:

- Engels' (1969[1880]) contrast of 'utopian' with 'scientific' socialism, in art works and political thinking. This has been melded with Marxist emphases themselves to produce a discourse that 'utopian' refers to a vague and ill-thought-out social optimism: the example usually given is the failure of the high rise housing blocks of modernist architects. Often, too, it is now seen as over-prescriptive and rationalist rather than dreamy and escapist.

- Two different strands of the Marxist Frankfurt School: (a) Marcuse's (1978) argument that true art both critiqued, made strange its surrounding social order, and was also oriented towards a utopian impulse or vision, and (b) Bloch's argument – later developed by Enzenberger (1974) and also Jameson (1990) – that popular forms included moments of utopian aspirations, the 'image of something better' than the realm of the everyday, in Dyer's (1973) words.

- Dyer and others also drew on the Russian cultural theorist Mikhail Bakhtin (1984) in his work on sixteenth century carnival as an expression of desires 'to turn the world upside down' in moments of utopian celebration and play. This was transferred to entertainment cinema. It was argued that even in such dismissed forms as the musical, or comedy, could be found pleasures which could transform the everyday, could teach us 'what utopia would feel like'. Writing in the early 1970s on the American film musical Dyer contrasts popular entertainment with real world problems. The musical sensuously evokes, especially in its dance 'numbers', abundance in place of scarcity, community in place of alienation, energy instead of exhaustion, intensity instead of dreariness.

> Our dreamscapes have become domesticated – we now look for fantasy and escape in our back gardens and on our dinner tables.
> (Andy Medhurst, Day for night, *Sight and Sound*, June 1999)

These are important steps in connecting audiences' delight in 'escaping' into movie-going. But as Medhurst's quote indicates, it may have to be rethought in contemporary contexts of film viewing, and of the spread of 'utopian' imagery into most consumer advertising.

Stacey's (1994: 59) work began such a rethink. She suggested that Dyer's model needed to be more specified since:

- Different audiences might bring different needs to the cinema depending on their cultural and historical circumstances. Dyer's terms (scarcity, exhaustion) need to be explored around different social divisions such as gender, class, ethnicity, age, sexuality.
- They also need to be taken beyond the encounter, still textually conceived, with 'the screen' out towards the larger social area of exhibition: 'cinema-going', the role of 'dream palaces' in her chosen period, the 1950s. Such cinemas themselves are both partial escape and provide pleasurable rituals. They are materially pleasurable, luxurious places. Is their function today, within contemporary shopping malls, the same?
- The opportunities for self-transformation promised by tie-in products during the studio era (Stacey 1994: ch. 5), and certainly now, need to be addressed. As she put it 'escapism involves a multi-dimensional set of processes, rather than one single mechanism' (Stacey 1994: 122).

One could [argue] that, contrary to the claim made by much film theory that 'the cinematic institution' works to endorse and sustain dominant ideology, popular cinema problematises all social categories – class, race and ethnicity, national identity, gender, sexuality, age and so forth. The invitation to the cinema is based on the promise that spectators may experience the thrill of reinventing themselves rather than simply having their social identities or positions bolstered.

(Pam Cook 1998: 234)

Research by Joanna Lacey (1999) further fine-tunes notions of utopian escapism. Her work suggests that the consumption of Hollywood film musicals by white working class women in Liverpool in the 1950s needs to be understood, not so much as a pure blissing out into the full 'escape' of movies, but as a much more conscious kind of 'coping' (see Steedman 1986). This is 'rooted in the materiality of lives, within the daily negotiation of structures of deprivation, hardship and poverty' (Lacey 1999: 54) especially in the women's daily domestic labour.

More than this, 'America' functioned in Liverpool as a negotiated fantasy space, not only through experience of GI (US soldiers) settlements nearby, but also in relation to British postwar discourses of affluence and consumer goodies (see Chapter 2). Movies, especially American musicals, are movingly spoken of as a 'magical world': 'Who can despise it? Only them that's got a lot more can despise it', says Barbara, one of Lacey's interviewees (Lacey 1994: 55). (Movies may have also represented fantasies of America even for Americans – of New York's urban sophistication, or of a sweeter, more communally cohesive small town past.)

Importantly too, such movies focus the very local connections which Liverpool had with America in two ways:

- As a key trading port, it occasionally offered these women fabrics, nylons, magazines and shoes from the United States: Maria recalls giving relatives pictures of stars from magazines and asking them to bring back the fabrics shown.
- At an imaginary level, the ethnicity of many Liverpudlians themselves, as second or third generation Irish immigrants, who had imagined America as the land of hope and ultimate destination, may clearly be part of the enthusiasm for US cinema.

One interviewee, Maria, says: 'we saw Americans through happiness, that's how we saw Americans'.

(Lacey 1999: 55)

Lacey (1999) offers a rich account of *Calamity Jane* (US 1953). She emphasizes, for example, its setting in the mythical Midwest of the western genre. This is usually closely associated with the American Dream that 'anyone can make it from log cabin to White House', though here the emphasis is on the achievement of building a homestead. Such a generic setting allowed Liverpool 1950s audiences, not many years away from the 1941 blitz bombing of the city, to make warm imaginative engagements with hopes of building a better life.

Gomery (1992) has emphasized the extent to which, in the USA itself, studio Hollywood consisted not only of the East coast financiers or West Coast production of movies but crucially also exhibition practices, especially in the 1920s 'picture palace' years (Figure 6.1). These 'palaces' have been seen as a frippery, as the 'excesses of the moguls'. But he argues convincingly that they are key to how the majors became the majors. The account is worth summarizing (and comparing to the different but related appeal of contemporary mall multiplexes):

Figure 6.1 A palace of dreams?
BFI Films: Stills, Posters and Designs

- The picture palaces were located in cities of 100,000 or more population; designed to accommodate 1500 people in ornately decorated deluxe buildings; had orchestras of more than a hundred players in the larger ones and sometimes thousands of light bulbs, often in three primary colours so that silent films with live music could use changing light motifs.
- Movie-goers could use splendid restrooms with paintings and mirrors; free child care was often provided, as were smoking rooms and a huge corps of ushers (often male college students working through their summer break). Air conditioning was also provided, a near-utopian modern consumer luxury, especially in cities like Chicago and New York in summer months.
- The dark itself offered privacy to groups with no other legitimate access to comfortable, unchaperoned space.

- The dream palaces were often sustained by the profits from ancillary product. Audience indulgence in convenience food – candy at first, then popcorn, which was cheap – was so popular during the 1930s Depression that it often formed the exhibitors' main source of profit. Cinemas made popcorn an important US harvest between 1934 and 1940. Coca Cola was introduced after the Second World War (when most of its product had been sent to Americans fighting the war) along with Morton's salt (sprinkled on the popcorn to create thirst) and an intermission break to ritualize and push the sales of confectionery.

There is a crucial class as well as gender aspect to these pleasures. Cinema was then one of very few institutions offering such comfort, safety and respect to working class and lower middle class people. There is also, of course, an ethnic dimension: black audiences were routinely segregated (Figure 6.2),

Figure 6.2 'Princess (picture theatre) audience in the thirties (coloured balcony in upper left)'. Utopia for black audiences?
Copyright by Jonathan Rosenbaum. Reproduced from *Moving Places* by Jonathan Rosenbaum, Berkeley/Los Angeles/London: University of California Press, 1995.

either into separate cinemas, or special accommodation in mostly white cinemas (see Gomery 1992: ch. 8).

Such research is a powerful corrective to the excesses of text based readings – whether distrustful or celebratory. It suggests that audiences are not so much 'moved' by 'texts' as disposed to enjoy entertainment films as part of their use of a whole set of cinema's embedding pleasures and irritations, usually linked to other modern commodities, activities and cultural structures.

Further reading

Corner, J. (1998) Codes and cultural analysis, in J. Corner, *Studying Media: Problems of Theory and Method*. Edinburgh: Edinburgh University Press.

Gomery, D. (1992) *Shared Pleasures: A History of Movie Presentation in the United States*. London: British Film Institute.

Smith, M. (1995) *Engaging Characters: Fiction, Emotion and the Cinema*. Oxford: Clarendon.

Thornham, S. (1997) *Passionate Detachments: An Introduction to Feminist Film Theory*. London and New York: Arnold.

IDENTIFYING A CRITICAL POLITICS
OF REPRESENTATION

Among the richest terms in study of the media is 'representation'. Very broadly, it offers ways of thinking through the connections between media imagery, the rest of the real, and cultural-political change. I am using 'politics' here in the sense of 'a mode of activity which aims to effect a change in the social order, and the distribution of power and resources within that order' (Perkins 2000: 81) but it also needs to be seen, as she continues, as 'a mode of activity or inactivity, which aims to maintain an established order'.

This is a connection which has often been given up on as irrelevant since the late 1970s. This chapter tries to handle the tensions between such broadly political emphases, and the extent to which films will always 'escape' such representational demands. You may choose, of course, simply not to be interested in such questions.

Two contradictory emphases are now often made. One is on the sheer difficulty of using the term 'representation' here. This is partly because thinking about media influence has become more complicated since the 1970s, and also because any simple sense of the groups being represented has fragmented. The other emphasis, however, suggests that any such effort of representation is ludicrous or pointless. It laments 1970s cultural, and then identity politics, not openly, but by reference to a nebulous phantom of 'political correctness' (see Dunant 1994; Frith 1994), often along with celebrations of pleasures and audience powers over texts. By such accounts the battles of representation have all been won and are now being kept alive only by a humourless, pleasureless, tightly organized movement. This powerful discourse has helped produce one of the main problems facing contemporary study of media: a huge hesitation and anxiety about making *any*

social interpretation of texts, settling instead for the pleasures of play, bricolage and the assertion that audiences are free to interpret and appropriate
anyway.

This chapter will explore:

- the theoretical changes which have occurred since the 1970s' discovery of
  the political usefulness of the term 'representation'. These include the rise
  of identity politics; the emphasis on 'difference'; and a growing sensitivity
  to the ways that the formal and aesthetic pleasures of texts might complicate a sense of their 'meanings'.
- what has been unmade, as well as gained in these shifts, in particular the
  marginalization of class and of other types of inequality. The title of this
  chapter is used by Tessa Perkins (2000) to argue for both an incorporation
  of the theoretical achievements of the 1980s and 1990s (part of 'reflexive
  modernity', in Giddens' phrase) and a new commitment to 'a politics
  of representation . . . more thoroughly grounded within particular socio-
  cultural contexts'.

From representation to identities

The concept of 'representation' is rich with several related meanings. It signals that filmed images, like all kinds of language work, are constructions,
're-presentations' of an apparently 'real' world, not simple presentations or
transparent windows on to it. It also draws attention to the ways that certain kinds of character, events, stories seem to be *re-presented* over and over
again, while other ways of imaging/imagining those are excluded, or even
rendered invisible.

The questioning of why certain images and signifying structures should
persist, while other imaginings should be invisible, has enabled a third,
political resonance for 'representation'. This is its connection with political
or other 'representatives', or lack of them, and the argument that the repetition or naturalization of certain images and plot lines might affect organized politics, as well as dominant cultural perceptions, for certain groups.
They are argued to have results on the street, or in the job centre, or the
home. Though cinema forms only one of the factors shaping such inequalities, the linkage of the 'public' and the 'private' in these debates has been a
powerful achievement.

Other terms have tried to express this sense of a doubleness in cinema's
imagery: the loaded meaning of 'image', as both 'picture' and as the broader
way in which particular groups or sets of activities are imagined. Richard
Dyer (1993, 1998c) writes of 'the matter of images', both their material

being (arrangements within light projected through celluloid, in classic 'film') and the ways they often 'matter' ideologically, have material effects in the rest of the real world, including how people are able to imagine themselves and their possibilities.

> It is . . . not just a matter of a different disposition of light on women and men, but the way the light constructs the relationship between them. The sense of the man being illuminated by the women is a widespread convention . . . The woman is more fully in the light, the man posed so that he seems to intrude, yearn towards it.
>
> (Dyer 1993: 134; see Figure 7.1)

This belief that certain kinds of images are oppressive, and can be changed, seems now to possess an enviable confidence. This confidence has itself been a political force. Indeed it seems ironic that this sort of power is viewed nostalgically. It is now so familiar in endless news discussions of the importance of the confidence of stockbrokers or investors for the sustaining of economic life as we know it. How has confidence in the usefulness of 'representation' been eroded?

The debates focus partly, again, around the legacy of 'the Enlightenment'. This is now seen as shaping a modern western scholarship which is marked by attempts to reveal general, all-encompassing principles which can lay bare the basic features of natural and social reality. 'Enlightenment thought' is emphasized as rooted in an 'objectivity', in fact originating in earlier religious practices and producing a role for the secluded scholar in making evident the word of God as revealed in 'His' creations. This helped to produce a 'God's eye view' for western theory, which of course can only *pretend* to come from an impossible 'outside' free of social conflict and process. Many of the social movements of modernity, whether the 1950s and 1960s US Civil Rights movement, or the 1960s waves of feminism and class struggle, have insisted on the impossibility of such 'objectivity'. Arguing that they have been made invisible, or misrepresented by it, they sought to represent, or make visible their experiences and political positions in a range of ways, including media images.

However, in the 1980s there emerged even more radical, less directly political scepticisms, by post-structuralist and postmodernist theorists, about what were alleged to be the failings of Enlightenment thought and ideas of progress. These are summarized well elsewhere (see Strinati 1995; Morley 1996; McGuigan 1999) but four relevant points are discussed here.

Figure 7.1 Clark Gable and Jean Harlow in a highly gendered pose and lighting set-up repeated in many 1930s and 1940s publicity shots of male and female stars. (See Dyer quote on page 157.)
Picture: MPTVA/LFI

First, 'Enlightenment' derived thought is said to deploy an inadequate sense of history as being simply linear and evolutionary. Post-structuralism and postmodernism hold that the concepts of progress, scientific knowledge, emancipation of various kinds, on which debates for more adequate representation ultimately rest, are no more than 'grand narratives', wishfully shaping history to a happy ending.

Second, 'enlightened' thought is said to overemphasize the extent to which we can think of coherent selves. Instead the power of unconscious processes is asserted, in particular of language (including media imagery) as itself producing rather than reflecting (or representing) our sense of self and the world. This affects the possibility of making realist images of groups, experiences, since, for one thing, in structuralist theory nothing can be directly named, or made visible. It always has to be defined by its difference from something else: man–woman, East–West; gay–straight, and so on.

Third, it is also said (this is part of the legacy of Foucault's work) to fail to understand that the very criteria or discourses by which claims to objective knowledge and truth are legitimized are humanly constructed. This was a valuable emphasis, especially for those who wanted to argue that representation within such systems could be changed. It raises huge problems, though, for political movements. Not least is the problem: once religious authority for political positions disappears, by what 'master discourse' do you justify claims that certain set-ups are unjust since all is discourse? Such scepticism runs deep through theorists such as Foucault, with his emphasis on the ways that powerful discourses produce the objects of study which they 'name'.

Fourth, identity politics, that final splintering of the assumptions of many Enlightenment thinkers that they spoke for 'mankind', began from about the 1970s to emphasize the ways 'we all' inhabit and perform several identities. Such positions now often question the existence of the very groups which excite their analyses.

Terms such as 'identity' and 'identification' have usually been 'constructed on the back of a recognition of some common origin or shared characteristic with another person or group, or with an ideal, and with the natural closure of solidarity and allegiance based on this foundation' (Hall 1996: 2–3). Yet key tensions persist between universalizing, truth-claiming tendencies which are necessary for political action, once a group conceives of itself and tries to act as having interests in common and more sceptical awareness of the problems and fractures in any such attempts at 'speaking for' or representing what is never, in fact, a wholly unified grouping. This has been augmented by the drive of consumer capitalism, especially advertising, to offer 'not the older pleasures of "self-understanding", of knowing and accepting our place, but the new delights of ever-shifting bricolage and blur' (Pfeil 1988: 73).

> Far from having been no more than an 'essentialist error' the emergence of lesbian and gay identity politics around the world has been one of the most remarkable social advances in the post-war period.
> (Simon Watney 1998: 381)

Representation, stereotyping, politics

Within cinema study the specific implication of this has been that the use of the term 'representation' is now often questioned and equated with the simplest kinds of stereotyping theory, which I now want to sketch.

Theories of stereotyping have argued that the media, in the imaginings they circulate about certain characters and situations, may keep suggesting to large audiences that x or y character is typical of a particular social group, and then that the whole group should be viewed in certain, usually negative ways. Some easily grasped features (of hair, voice or gesture for example) which are suggested always to belong to a group, are put at the centre of the representation. They may seem to have 'a grain of truth'. But this judgement is usually made from outside the group in question, by white people about blacks, for example, or about the poor by the well off. Even if evidence apparently exists ('but surely in the 1950s many women *were* housewives?') the stereotype then repeats, across a whole range of media and informal exchanges, and in its own terms, that this characteristic is *always* the *central* truth about that group. Stereotypes may also take a feature which is an *effect* of a group's situation and encourage audiences to feel it is the *cause* of that group's low status – the 1950s housewife's preoccupation with the domestic, or the black slave's lack of education, for example.

> In twenty-two of the twenty-eight films dealing with gay subjects from 1962 to 1978, major gay characters onscreen ended in suicide or violent death.
> (Russo 1981, quoted in Medhurst and Munt 1998: 69)

Finally, questions of who controls distribution of such images mean that, even if there is often a grain of truth in particular stereotypes at some moments in history, they keep being circulated long after the end of the situations that gave rise to them. Stereotypes are simultaneously categorizations and evaluations of groups. The emphasis, for the groups in question, has often been that the valuations are 'negative': the dumb blonde 'demeans' all women; gay men are 'never taken seriously'. Efforts are then made to replace them by 'positive' ones. The method often used for such argument is content analysis, an approach assuming a relationship between the frequency with which a certain item appears in media texts and the responses of its audiences to the group or activity involved in it.

The engagement with such positions has involves, firstly, a reconsideration of 'meaning' in cinema:

> Much film study has revolved around questions of 'what films mean' . . . firstly a study of forms whose workings seem unfamiliar or difficult . . . often circulating as 'art cinema'. Then, since entertainment films are deliberately made so as to be easy to understand . . . the other arena of such study has been exploration of either the meanings (broadly ideological ones) which might be hidden from popular audiences, or the processes by which such ordinary meanings are activated . . . The questions raised by arguments that film offers broadly political 'representations' of the rest of the world often invoke these two areas.
>
> (Nowell-Smith 2000: 9)

This connection is now seen to ignore questions of aesthetics: the forms and pleasures which films offer, or indeed their formal needs, which may overwhelm or render meaningless an exclusive focus on meaning.

Second, it has been argued, that stereotypes, definable as widely circulated ways of categorizing particular groups, are unavoidable. Even for individual sense making, broad categorizations (including the way the brain processes raw experience) seem essential to simplify the world for the purposes of everyday understanding and action. For costly media forms, distributed on a mass scale, needing to spread their meanings broadly, they may be essential. Early cinema, aimed at large, unknown, illiterate audiences, certainly soon learnt how to communicate via quickly established visual, and then *audio*-visual stereotypes and discourses, often adopted from theatre melodrama, with its frozen tableaux and polarized virtue/vice characterizations. Film costumes, make-up, sets and later voices and music condensed stereotypical recognitions such as: 'academic/intellectual' (lots of putting on and taking off glasses); Mexican (moustache or unshaven; excitable; 'Latin' music); 'homosexual' (limp-wristed-ness, luxurious dressing-gown worn during the day) and so on.

Third, one of the questions which arises is how many members of the groups in question, with knowledge of such debates, and the desire to change them, are employed in such industries? Yet these quantitative or numerical claims from the other side of the screen ('x or y group forms x per cent of the population and should therefore have x per cent of film roles') have also been attacked, not only as inadequate to the complexities of films' narrative needs, but also as 'mere political correctness' or 'quota politics' (often when a telling point has been made about the social size of the group in question). Disabled people, for example, are the largest 'minority' group in the UK (estimated at 10–12 per cent). As Jessica Evans (1998) points out, most of us will at some point in our lives be disabled – whether congenitally, or through old age, illness, or accident and so on.

Fourth, also questioned has been the assumption, in arguing for more 'positive' rather than 'negative' representations, that we can demonstrate the 'effect', on 'the audience', of certain repeated sets of images, plot lines and character positions.

Fifth, many of the assumptions about representation which had to be argued hard for in the 1960s and 1970s are now quite widespread. In conditions of hugely massified further and higher education, let alone a popular culture saturated with entertainment imagery, commented upon by writers and presenters schooled in these debates, eager for 'edgy' copy, it is no surprise that 'inside' cinema, many 'ordinary' audience members are now alert to the major objections that groups have raised about their representation on screen. At the same time, 'outside' cinema, there has been an erosion of traditional political forms of debate, that 'public sphere' where political representation was supposed to be rehearsed and where arguments on image 'representation' could therefore take effect. Unprecedented levels of cynicism exist (especially in the USA) at ever more expenditure on spectacular and remote official politics.

---

it comes as quite thrill when, midway through *Bulworth*, Beatty's campaigning senator throws down an unfashionable gauntlet: 'Lemme hear that dirty word – socialism' . . . In the film's linchpin scene, Bulworth publicly rebukes his insurance paymasters, calling for a single payer, socialised national health system.

(Richard Kelly, *Sight and Sound*, February 1999)

Though there is some evidence of an appetite for critical engagement with conventional political issues even in the USA (perhaps in the cult status of Oliver Stone's films or of movies like *Erin Brockovitch*, *Wag the Dog*, *Bulworth*, *The Insider*) more obviously popular have been 'political-as-personal' questions, of 'micro-politics', as they are made debatable in highly publicized celebrity stories and forms, and TV fictions. The popular series *Ally McBeal*, for example, regularly stylizes and takes to comic and fantastic extremes some of the most intimate and quirky aspects of cultural-political issues around (privileged metropolitan) experiences of work, gender and sexuality.

Finally, a powerful manifestation of the hostility to any interest in how sets of images might still be said to relate to the rest of the social world has been the creation of the stereotype of a movement called 'political correctness' or PC. This stereotyping discourse (not without its 'grain of truth' in the real) has been an invaluable resource to tabloid entertainment journalism, with its tyrannical insistence on 'fun' and no more than 'fun' for its readers (see Holland 1998). Even the leading film scholar Noel Carroll rather casually cites something vaguely called 'political correctness' as one of his five major impediments to film theory (see Bordwell and Carroll 1996).

The term emerged in the 1980s in the USA and then Britain (see Dunant 1994; Frith 1994), mostly as a response to the rise of 'identity' or 'cultural' politics and, indeed, cultural studies, which, broadly, replaced the emphasis of 1960s politics on class with questions of race, gender, sexuality and other kinds of cultural differences. These have contributed to such changes as the transformation of the gender and ethnic composition of the modern university, especially in the USA, since the late 1950s.

But such political and academicized movements took place in the highly conservative administrations of Thatcher and Reagan. Within the still often racist and homophobic context of much American and British culture, it has been easy to caricature the inexperienced and prescriptive ways such changes were sometimes implemented: 'changing the word instead of changing the world' (Sivanandan 1990). The necessary kick start given to inequalities by systems of affirmative action, or the attempt to call attention to the words and phrases through which political perceptions are constructed and sustained have often had to work in the absence of any other kinds of liberatory politics: 'shut up and shop'. As such they can indeed sometimes operate in too narrowly focused ways. But the lazy set of caricatures of 'PC' commissars, which often wants to avoid the complexities of fuller debate of inequalities, has created fantasies, which are powerfully available for comedy, of a narrow, bigoted movement insisting on nothing more than commissar, letter-of-the-law 'correctness'. It can easily seem a kind of imaginary resurrection of the Eastern bloc by other means, after the end of state socialism from 1989 and one which of course ignores the actual sparkiness and diversity of debates within groups seeking to shift the conditions of their representation.

Realisms

Some sense of the real is always at stake in any politics, and certainly in the claims of 'a politics of representation'. Yet realist forms and connections are under pressure, from theoretical approaches announcing the end of any certainty about what texts, or the rest of the real, consist of. There have been several key changes, including:

- The development of digital forms (anything can be simulated on screen; nothing is necessarily 'true') which de-secure claims on the part of photography, films or documentaries to the status of evidence for political debate.
- An accompanying awareness that many of realism's 'codes' (hand-held unsteady camera, black and white film stock as 'historical') can be, and have been simulated and therefore cannot act as certain 'evidence' – the camera shake is no longer clear evidence of filming under difficult or uncertain conditions, for example.
- An excitement, in film study, at exploring other, lower status film forms and genres, such as fantasy, comedy, melodrama, which were lampooned for years, often in highly gendered terms, for being 'unrealistic' but which now look set to take over the whole agenda of attention.
- An increasing awareness of the ways that cinema does not only 'mean', just as it is not only a realist 'mirror'. Aesthetic and formal operations have to be understood, and may often run counter to a desire to declare the work of fictions to be realistic.
- The claims of realism to access 'truth'. This term is now more likely to be replaced by 'truths', moving targets rather than 'a thing' which will stay still while a fully realistic image is drawn. Truths are seen as re-presented and even constructed through *discourses* and *discursive regimes*, a term which replaces 'stereotypes' in many accounts. This last is part of a broad shift towards Foucauldian models of discourse rather than the less plurally conceived 'ideology' of earlier Marxist models. What is often lost, however, is a sense of the unequal distribution of discursive power: some discourses, such as that of consumer advertising, are emphatically more powerful than others.

However, attempts to theoretically 'undo' the supposed vice like grip of the 'classic realist text' (see Corner 1998a: 68–75) raised as many problems as they sought to address, and too easily sought to dismiss the longing for 'realistic images', especially of marginalized groups or experiences. John Corner argues a valuable distinction between these two:

- 'thematic realisms', which propose a relation between what a text is about and reality

- 'formal realisms', or the ways that texts achieve real-seemingness in their representation of the world, especially in the way they 'look'.

Take *Life is Beautiful* (*La Vita è Bella*: Italy 1998) for example, the Oscar-winning box-office success about an Italian Jew, deported to a concentration camp with his son, who convinces the child that the camp is part of an elaborate game in order to hide from the child the horror of what is happening. He saves the son's life, though at the cost of his own.

Though part slapstick comedy, of a particularly Italian kind – *bufo* – it is played out in a semi-realistic setting and style, with Roberto Benigni making much of his historical research on costume, camp settings and so on. Admirers of the film operated assumptions from both thematic and aesthetic realisms. It was said that though children never survived the death camps (thematic), it was a fable (aesthetic) about 'human resilience', 'the survival of the human spirit' (an apolitical stance, jumping out of the accountabilities of the thematic position). More critical sympathetic positions argued that its feel-good relation to the historical real of the Nazi death camps is partly won by avoiding scenes of violence in Italy and by projecting anti-Semitism on to the Germans (thematic/historical). Its Oscar triumph, and its $38 million release in Italy at a time when that country was beginning an uncomfortable revaluation of its wartime past, including the 7500 Jews deported to Nazi death camps, raises huge questions of thematic realism in their relation to aesthetics.

As does the huge success of the big budget ciné-vérité style of the opening sequence of *Saving Private Ryan* (US 1998). As Corner pointed out (1998b) for many viewers the Omaha beach sequence successfully merged potentially diverse kinds of realist illusion: 'documentary realism', imitating the original Capa photographs of the Normandy landings, 'produces the sense of contemporary actuality footage (certified at one point by a blood-splashed lens)'; subjective realism puts the viewer into a disorientated field of vision of a soldier advancing under heavy fire, with heavy breathing on the soundtrack and so on. This was enough either to 'guarantee' the accuracy of the rest of the film's representation of modern war, or to render it 'a disappointing fictional coda'. Either way it raises important questions for representations of war in entertainment forms, of how 'seeing' relates to knowing and feeling, and the need to understand the tension between aesthetic and thematic realisms.

Another area of emphasis, 'extremed' in surrealism, has been kinds of film-making which have wanted to draw on the power of cinema to take audiences' imaginations into 'other places' of possibility or recognition. This focuses the problem, for 'representation' that the imaginative power of fiction films depends partly on a kind of suspension not only of disbelief, but also of the need always to be understood as referring to the known social world. The problem, as Gledhill (1995) puts it for gender politics, is

> How can one think of the sensationalising and personalising dynamic of popular culture in relation to a critique of gender relations? [in which] the mythic functions of representational art . . . steals, as it were, the bodies of historically and socially constituted figures for the symbolising functions of fantasy.
>
> (Gledhill 1993: 77)

An example of such dilemmas in cinema might be 'period pieces', where for the sake of eliciting audience involvement, the norms of hairstyle, or costume, or sexual encounter are 'modernized' in ways that can be convincingly argued as ahistorical (see Bruzzi 1998; see also L. Williams 1988 on *Mildred Pierce* and historical questions of women, labour and the Second World War). Performances too, can often be in tension with the stereotypes or dominant discourses which are still in play in the resonance of certain stories. Elizabeth Shue's performance as a prostitute in *Leaving Las Vegas* (US 1994) may well overwhelm the extent to which the film can, nevertheless, be said to recirculate and reanimate discourses of 'the prostitute with a heart of gold'. Or when the Welsh actor Rhys Ifans in *Notting Hill* (US 1999) performs the stereotypical lustful working class Welsh dork lost in the sophistication of a metropolis, the skill of his performance, as well as the (over) familiarity of the fictional type as type, works to undercut the role's referential quality, that is as referring and confirming certain images of Welshness. Some audience members, even within the groups said to be maligned, may choose to disavow their awareness of such broader connections for the sake of the pleasures offered by going along with a film's 'textiness'. Or they may decide to appropriate a skilful performance by a Welsh actor as itself denying the stereotype being played on.

Audiences

Does all this mean we should just learn to stop worrying and love the flux? Gledhill (1988), in an earlier piece on *Coma*, suggested the point of interventionist (here feminist) analysis is to 'pull the symbolic enactments of popular fictions into frameworks which interpret the psychic, emotional and social forces at work in women's lives' (Gledhill 1988: 87) (and by extension those of other cultural-political groups). Part of this might locate fictions in relation to 'thematic realism', though with a sense of how tricky this 'correspondence' of a 'real' and an 'imaged' now is.

Another part would be to argue that the 'aesthetic' and formal aspects and needs of cinema do indeed complicate an *easy* recourse to 'representation'. John Corner (1998a) for example has argued that violence (like stereotyping) is hard to dispense with, is possibly even essential to narratives. It provides action, intensifies characterization, serves to make vivid the resolution of certain plots, and is a chance to display special FX in film.

But it is a mistake to see the next step as a necessary and complete severance of connections to the rest of the real – for example what kinds of violence, how necessary are they, and to which narratives and audiences, and when, where? Formal and aesthetic aspects of film never float, culture free, within some eternal realm. They operate in relation to audiences, their different levels of cultural power and 'taste', and also to the historically established, and therefore changeable, formal characteristics of 'texts'.

This thing 'taste' is usually treated as a universal, natural, disinterested quality which you either have or don't have, and which marks you out as distinct, or distinguished. Pierre Bourdieu (1984), using a mass of elaborate survey material in France, argued that this supposedly natural, universal quality is actually formed along the lines of class. Just as access to financial capital is unequally distributed and gives a person economic security and status, so the media/art forms we feel easy with will be related to our social and class position via what he calls 'cultural competences' (knowledge of a particular genre) deriving from our accumulation of 'cultural capital' (from the investment of time and other resources in watching, reading, discussing). Some give more status than others in certain contexts: how easy does a person show themselves to be with Shakespeare, or the vocabulary of modernist poems, at the opera, or with a soap opera?

Others, in the related field of 'historical poetics' (see Bordwell 1989; Jenkins 1995; M. Smith 1995), have argued for the social and historical embeddedness of formal, textual structures and audiences' responses to them. A current example might be the impact on narrative structure of contemporary blockbusters' status as the centres of huge, global computer games franchises (see Chapter 3). Or, take the ways that racist structures outside and inside the film industry meant that colour stock sensitive to dark skin tones were not invented for many years, impacting on estimates of performance by black actors (see Dyer 1997). This emphasis opens the possibility of *acknowledging but not simply celebrating* the role of the formal, the aesthetic, the affective on both sides of the aesthetic encounter, and putting it into contact with other historical processes.

Take the 'unhappy' ending, and 'unrealistic images of women' in the controversial film *Thelma and Louise* (US 1990) as a focus for arguments so far. First, its commercial nature involves complex ideological calculations. This was a $17.5 million movie falling into Schatz's second category of contemporary Hollywood production: a 'mainstream' film, involving stars (though at the time of its making not involving major stars) but not a calculated blockbuster hit. It had 'sleeper hit potential', the capacity to bring in revenues through 'word of mouth', perhaps via controversy. The film scored best, in test screenings, with young males (*Sight and Sound*, July 1991) partly because of its innovative use of traditionally male genres such as the western, the road and buddy movie. But its liberal/commercial attempt to invoke such audience involvement 'across from' their own gender identities meant that its script took care to construct key male characters as non-threateningly over the top, slightly comic sexists, like the lorry driver, or Thelma's husband, along with a painstakingly sympathetic construction of Louise's partner and the detective, played by Harvey Keitel.

Second, the film's (profitable) controversy included questions such as whether the ending is a defeat for the two female heroes and as such a moral 'lesson' for women in the audience. But such questions involve genre frames,

What has this film to do with feminism? [It] is little more than a masculine revenge fantasy in which the gender of the leading characters has been switched . . . unlike Stallone and Eastwood, who routinely get away with murder and mayhem, Thelma and Louise are backed into a corner from which death is the only escape . . . its effect is to reinforce the message that women cannot win.

(Joan Smith, review of the film, *Guardian*, 9 July 1991)

rather than realism or some kind of unmediated politics. Should the ending be understood as falling into a tradition of unhappy endings in the so-called 'woman's film'? Might this not allow women's desires, voiced in its story, to persist more vividly in the imaginations of the audience than happens with 'happy endings'? What on earth would a happy ending consist of?

Should the ending be seen as inseparable from other generic contexts, such as the road movie? This has traditionally celebrated the wild male existential trip, involving fast cars, a wide open landscape, whisky, 'babes', a few, last, soiled dollars, hip outsider status, a journey without aim or end. *Thelma and Louise* remakes this, with moments of angst and decision posed very differently for the two female heroes, who are outlaws, yes, but outside a law which operates in grossly gendered ways in that part of the USA where they happen to journey. Other details produce pleasurable difference from the male-centred road movie: the tiny bottles of spirits;

the turquoise Thunderbird, the male sex object, emphatically reversing Mulvey's (1975) gendering of to-be-looked-at-ness, and so on. In such contexts the ending can work as a moment of decision ('Somethin's crossed over in me, and I can't go back. I mean I just couldn't live') along with, arguably, a celebratory montage of postcards from the outlaw trip, signifying, to some viewers 'they are dead but will live on'.

Pam Cook puts the film into a broader cultural-historical context (but one which still sees a correspondence to the cultural 'real' of women's lives). She argues for more ambiguous interpretation:

> The interesting thing about *Thelma and Louise* . . . is that suddenly women have reached an impasse . . . Whereas during the '70s it was possible to see women taking to the road and this . . . was the end of the movie, they had everywhere to go, in *Thelma and Louise* . . . women have nowhere to go, they have to take the choice to leap over the edge rather than go back and . . . that . . . can be as liberating as it is pessimistic.
>
> (Pam Cook, in *Reel Women*, Channel 4 television, 1994)

Willis (1993) and others have asserted the pleasures, for female audiences, of a kind of take-over of this male genre by the lead characters:

> the process by which the film parades the take-over of these cliches fore-grounds 'the posturing involved' and the 'theft/take-over' mobilises for women the pleasures of . . . identification with embodied agents of travel, speed, force and aggression . . . at the same time the spectacle of women acting like men works to disrupt the apparent naturalness of certain postures when performed by a male body.
>
> (cited in Tasker 1998: 143)

This is very different from objections to the film as an oppressive gender switch, making the women into honorary men, as has been objected to films with strong women protagonists, especially if they wield guns or embody what Yvonne Tasker (1993) calls 'musculinity' (see *GI Jane* [US 1999] as test case for such controversy). Further to the edge of such cultural/textual speculation are the seizures of such moments by groups with an interest in shifting images of themselves – gays calling themselves queens or queers; the celebration of deadly 'lipstick lesbians' in films such as *Basic Instinct* (US 1996) or *Bound* (US 1996).

Sigourney Weaver called her role in *Aliens* 'Rambolina'.

> I like the sissy [stereotype of gay men]. Is it used in 'negative' ways?
> Yeah. But my view has always been: visibility at any cost. Negative is
> better than nothing.
>
> (Harvey Feirstein, in *The Celluloid Closet*, TV, 1996)

> because the dominant culture offers lesbians so few images to identify
> themselves with, the rare surfacing of these images has come to hold a
> special place within the lesbian subculture. Although such images
> were constructed within the contours of the dominant heterosexual
> culture and its reliance on models of pathology, the meanings attached
> to the images have been frequently transformed, either through
> women's involvement in production . . . or, more frequently, within
> the lesbian spectator's imagination.
>
> (Weiss 1992: 28)

These show an impatience with traditional textual discussion, which often
claimed to judiciously 'weigh' a 'whole film' with the authority of a judge.
Instead, to return to *Thelma and Louise*, some fans choose to celebrate or
take off from 'moments' in a text, or to reverse the meaning of images often
taken to be 'negative'. Henry Jenkins (2000: 165), for example, quotes a
fan's short story taking off from the end of the film, imagining two vampire
bats fluttering from the wrecked Thunderbird as lesbian vampire lovers. The
appeal of such fan fiction, and its current prominence in Film Studies, is
partly due to the sheer cheek of its appropriation of otherwise threatening
or unsympathetic texts, or moments from texts.

It also shifts the 'mirror' model of representation, where groups marginalized by the media are seen to agree on shared values (as in the 1960s
slogan 'black is beautiful' or the 1980s 'We're here, we're queer') which
they then demand of the films which 'represent' them. In a striking reversal
of the usual case against media power to inculcate behaviours, members of
some denigrated groups have described learning to 'be' part of the group
through media images. Gay and 'queer' cultural politics have explored the
often extraordinarily oblique ways in which films, and the subcultural discourses around them, have helped their viewers to recognize themselves as
existing at all (see Dyer (1986) for example on the ways the image of Judy
Garland or gossip around 'closeted' stars has been used). This has been particularly important for gay identities, not usually as visually identifiable as
those of gender, age, race or certain kinds of disability. But such learning
works both ways. The oppressive ('know your place') powers of media to

offer mostly self-hatred and to internalize 'deviant' status are less often stressed now. But there is ample evidence that they still operate for some groups, often those (recently around issues of disability) who will have to take them on, and learn from the different 'stages' of other groups in their own struggle for adequate and diverse representations (see Evans 1998).

The burden of representation

Such responses come partly out of challenges to what has been called the 'burden of representation', seen as arising for directors who feel their images must 'stand in for' or represent a single group's reality. This is often because such directors are involved, either via liberal identification with, or as a member of, groups or subcultures becoming aware of the inadequacy of their representation in the media. The early stages of such groups becoming visible in films, in more than derisory or painful ways, is often when the political weight of 'representing', 'standing in for' the invisible truths of a group's experiences is felt most keenly.

> I'm the only one . . . the only Negro actor who works with any degree of regularity. I represent ten million people . . . and millions more in Africa . . . on the screen . . . and I'm not going to do anything they can't be proud of. Wait 'til there are six of us; then one of us can play villains all the time.
>
> (Sidney Poitier, 1950s–1990s black star, quoted in Griffith and Mayer 1971: 478)

Despite the importance of these moments, responding partly to activism by the groups in question, queries arise such as: supposing the group had good grounds for the surliness reprimanded as 'negative', or supposing they felt that the dominant set-up was screamingly absurd? They may well wonder if certain images are 'positive' only for those who want to be reassured that all is well with a ludicrous or unjust set-up?

On the other side of the screen, the burden which film makers experience in being held accountable for representations felt to be negative can lead to furious boycotts, demonstrations and controversy. *My Beautiful Laundrette* (UK 1986) for example was furiously attacked as some British Asians registered threats to their already denigrated image, experienced as attacks on the street, at work or in the press.

The results of fuller access to image-making can be films such as *East is East* (UK 1999) or *The Adventures of Priscilla, Queen of the Desert* (Australia

1994). The confidence of such films seems to be located in some ways 'inside' groups which (temporarily?) have more access to representational space, through long struggles for funding, fuller debates, TV slots, as well as a seizure of the right to be comic and complex. As a result the most telling and intimate criticisms of the group can be voiced, though this will always run the risk of allowing racist or homophobic response to feel legitimized: 'See, we always said they were like that. Now they're saying so too'. There is no such thing as the '100% right on positive image' which will guarantee to change audiences, or replace negative images all on its own. That does not mean textual debate is pointless but that it needs wider arenas in which to play out informed discussions.

'Positive' images cannot be prescribed as antidotes to 'negative' ones, as they once were. Cultural understandings of the problems of 'Other-ness' and how to represent it are now complicated. Silverstone (1999) writes generally of the problems of:

> representing the Other in texts and tales that somehow must pass the muster of translation from one culture to another. How do I represent the Other in what I write or film without, on the one hand exoticising him or her? How do I represent the Other in what I write or film without, on the other hand, absorbing him or her into my own sense of myself?
>
> (Silverstone 1999: 135)

Nevertheless questions of inequality remain, sometimes involving unequal distribution of cultural capital or competences. How might a wide range of audiences be made to feel comfortable with 'different' images? What do films represent in terms of employment opportunities for groups currently underemployed in the industry? Such questions are not currently as fashionable as those posed by studies which reverse the usual sense of production to assert the capacity of fans and other audience members to produce meanings. But as Slater (1997) points out:

> whatever freedoms the consumer may have they do not constitute *power* in the sense that manufacturers and media conglomerates have power over things and meanings. They have neither the same control over resources nor the power to structure objects and messages (and choose which are to be produced), nor do their 'readings' have the same public significance and consequence, *except* in the one instance that cultural studies focused on for so long, spectacular subcultures.
>
> (Slater 1997: 171)

The 'psychedlic trips upon a text' (Eco 1990: 52) of fans and their 'slash' fictions, do indeed now 'count' within Film Studies, but they need to be held in a tension with more traditional, political-economic 'countings'. For example, how many black actors can 'bank' a Hollywood movie on their presence alone? What is the proportion of older men to women starring in big movies? How many, and what kinds of people, fans or not, have access to the Internet? And finally, what is the power of the big studios to copyright-control fan fictions out of existence?

Such 'countings' relate to films in whose images certain groups or activities are made to feel they do not count, or are being rendered visible on other terms than many of its members would want (see Perkins 2000). To alter such relations there is a need not just for more 'women' or 'blacks' in an industry (though that is important), but for more people from such groups who are aware of the need for, and committed to change in the areas of representation.

The under-debated question of class identities may offer an edge to such debates, since class relates to power relations in the film as any other industry. 'Class' is too often taken to mean simply 'working class'. As a result a missing ingredient of much discussion of such recent hits as *Fight Club* (US 1999) or *American Beauty* (US 2000) has been the ways that these addressed, albeit fragmentarily, issues of executive and suburban middle class experience in the USA. At the other end of the spectrum, one of the most 'Other-ed' groups in contemporary Britain and elsewhere is the so-called 'underclass' or 'socially excluded'. This group is officially defined partly as composed of 'non-workers and long-term unemployed' (see Munt 2000: 55). But it is also, more loosely, used to describe single parenthood and criminality, often drug related, and is crossed by gendered 'otherings' ('single mums on council estates') and racial ones ('black drug dealers'). Though often exoticized, this group is no longer amenable to academic hero-ization of solidarity or discovery of working class worthiness. As Haylett (2000) suggests of the central character in Ken Loach's *Ladybird, Ladybird* (UK 1994), Maggie is 'not there to please an audience of social workers'. The issue is not so much that Maggie is 'not really like that' (that is, refuses to practise birth control, runs off with her children, selects bad partners) 'but that her behaviour is so . . . readily pathologised by middle class professionals'. Such characterizations, or those of the 'socially excluded' youths in *La Haine* (France 1995) or the young women in *The Dream Life of Angels* (France 1998) and the French agri-business workers in *Will It Snow for Christmas?* (France 1996) try to offer engagements with hugely marginalized groups *on the (uncomfortable) terms of their protagonists*. An interest in such debates is rare, even though they raise rich issues, as Bob Light suggests (in a letter to *Sight and Sound*, January 1999) on an article by John Hill (*Sight and Sound*, November 1998):

The working class has broadened, so 'white collar jobs [such as social workers] that were once seen as middle class have been proletarianised; it is now made up almost equally of women and men; it is now racially mixed; and it is increasingly located in the southern half of Britain . . . All too often the 'baddies' in Loach movies (*Ladybird, Ladybird* is the obvious example) are low-grade white collar workers rather than real figures of capitalist authority.

But then class, as Miller (2000) points out has been an uncomfortable topic in film studies, on both sides of the screen:

Class conflicts and solidarities make their mark as clearly in most people's lives as do those of religion, gender, nation, sexuality, race and age. But the concept of class is dogged by association with state socialism and totalitarian government.

(Miller 2000: 539)

Part of the contradictions for cinema are that 'film requires massive finance, always at the production stage, but especially now at the level of distribution and promotion – so it is the province of the wealthy. But also needs a mass audience to succeed, and must appeal across class tastes' (Miller 2000: 542). In contrast to the 'can do' 'feel good' emphases of other kinds of identity politics, moves to consider the 'silent injuries of class' in relation to films, industry structures, audiences' access to and ease with films can seem daunting. The 'post-feminist' celebration of class mobility, class 'cross-dressing' and make-over in a film such as *Working Girl* (US 1988) seems much more fun, part of the long tradition of rags to riches fantasy which has indeed flashed up often vivid images of class difference and struggle in popular films. *Rocky* (US 1976), *Flashdance* (US 1983) or *Saturday Night Fever* (US 1977) have addressed the desire to transcend the misery of class orders, though, as Miller (2000: 542) says, always in individualistic ways relying on personal traits and determination ('making dreams come true'), melting away class division, rather than explicitly evoking those terms whose terms whose name can hardly be spoken, whatever the evidence that they still exist: solidarity and collective political action.

You know what bugs me about human endeavour? I've never been the human in question, have you?
(Words used by cynical 'cyber-pixie' Fifi in ads to launch *PlayStation2*, September 1999)

Back to the future?

Endlessly debated or just implied, even in formalist discussion, questions of representation remain at the heart of much film study. They focus the sharpest pleasures and pitfalls of the theoretical and political changes of the 1970s, 1980s and 1990s, which are much broader than, but still implicated within film studies. They raise alluring questions:

- How to hold together the capacity of film to shape our sense of ourselves as socially situated agents along with the formal pleasures which they play with, and allow us to play in?
- How can we retain what is valuable, in political and social semiotic approaches – the sense of film codes as constructed within unequal structures of social power – without giving in to the position of some post-structuralist theorists that all such codes are equally just another set of 'language games'?
- How can an emerging sense that the socially shared, the *achievement* of being able to identify across differences, should be valued as highly as the role given to the pleasures of hybridity and difference? These have been central to structuralist and post-structuralist methods and to key changes in thinking race, gender and sexuality (see Hall 1996). How can such modern and liberalizing experiences be related to the need to address inequalities – whether of class division or of access to a wide range of films, both 'local' and 'global'?
- Representational-cultural politics still present challenges to the persistent inequalities they seek to point to and intervene in, embodied, for example, in the 1990s slogan 'I'll be a post-feminist in post-patriarchy'. How can these live alongside the exhilarating possibilities promised by more fluid networks of affiliation and response? How can we avoid discussing differences as though they are all 'relative' or equivalent?

Obviously some postmodern scepticism about the godlike, usually white, non-working class male 'voices' of modernity (defined as Enlightened thought) has had a strong appeal for movements such as feminism or ecological politics. But since these movements are political, they still have to try to mobilize action through words like 'we' and 'solidarity', 'false images' and 'injustice', and 'progress'. These are inherited from Enlightenment-modernity's language of political aspiration, however ironized or ignored by parts of 'the linguistic turn' of post-structuralism.

'Identity politics' has, valuably, moved analysis to think not so much of 'whole' single classed or gendered or raced subjects, slots to which we are totally assigned for ever, but instead of fluid sets of identities, which each of us inhabits in multiple and shifting ways, and which we can pleasure through acts of consumption. We are never only, say, a woman, black, a child, or disabled. 'Authenticity' does not even hang out in the (currently marginalized) area of social class but might be productively thought via the diasporic travelling of ethnic groups, with results for them which are both painful and pleasurable. Andy Medhurst (2000: 32) argues that it may be more productive to think of ways, painful and pleasurable, in which people inhabit the identity of 'once working class', a sort of temporal journey which could apply to many people's experience of now abandoned or complicated earlier identities.

Any political account of representation will need to be aware of how key identities are constructed, and can be changed, though it now knows such effort is always likely to be held in a tension with the formal workings and pleasures of films. It is arguable too that there has always been more aware-ness of the fractured nature of individuals and social movements, and the rhetorical and performative nature of collective politics, than the announce-ment of these by post-structuralist and postmodern scepticisms allow for. Difference and debate are neither new nor disabling for such movements. But it is certainly the case that politics, as well as film study, involves choices, votes, affiliations, groupings and also inequalities, which 'representation' still has the power to address. Such politics and explorations cannot stay with the pleasures of endless difference. They always have to involve a 'stop-ping point', however provisional and subject to history: the vote has to be taken, the sentence, the movie has to end – and so does the book.

Further reading

Dyer, R. (1993) *The Matter of Images: Essays on Representations*. London and New York: Routledge.

Gledhill, C. and Williams, L. (eds) (2000) *Reinventing Film Studies*. London and New York: Arnold.

Munt, S. (ed.) (2000) *Cultural Studies and the Working Class: Subject to Change*. London and New York: Cassell.

Stam, R. and Miller, T. (2000) *Film and Theory: An Anthology*. Oxford and Cam-bridge, MA: Blackwell.

GLOSSARY

Agency: (a) the role of the human 'actor' as individual or group in directing or effectively intervening in the course of history (after Brooker 1999: 3); (b) 'agencies' put together packages for films, promote and orchestrate the careers of actors and other workers.

Art films: defined in the USA as foreign language films, or English language films from outside the USA. More broadly the term often slips over to include films which might be called 'independent' or 'alternative' to the 'mainstream' – all more complex categories than they seem.

Avant-garde: any artistic movement which is 'ahead of the mainstream' ('guard' in original military usage) and usually experimental.

Blind booking and block booking: Hollywood studio business practices which forced an exhibitor to buy, sight unseen, or in blocks, a whole line of mediocre or unpopular films along with the few features which are of interest.

Capitalist: belonging to the social system known as capitalism, emerging roughly in the seventeenth century in Europe, characterized by and celebrating competition and the accumulation of capital; driving towards the **commodification** of all human products and the maximization of the profits of companies (now often conglomerate corporations).

Ciné-vérité: literally, 'cinema truth' (French), originally an approach to documentary film-making which emphasized the need to get as close to events as possible via unobtrusive equipment, high shooting ratio of footage shot to footage used. Now often used of a style (such as shaky hand-held camera) which seeks to resemble such 'spontaneous' filming.

Classical Hollywood Cinema: term developed by David Bordwell, Janet Staiger and Kristin Thompson to describe the aesthetic and industrial norms of the Hollywood studio system.

Cognitive psychology: a kind of psychology which (as opposed to psychoanalysis) stresses the rational processes of thought and behaviour, and sees them as changeable.

Commodified: a commodity is anything which can be bought or sold, usually within capitalist social relations. 'Commodified' as applied to culture, or other processes, normally implies an undue spread of values, services or items, which can be bought and sold.

Continuity system: the process of selecting, assembling and arranging motion picture shots in sequence (editing), usually also including shooting, for the purposes of continuity or easy 'legibility' in the telling of a story through filmed images.

Cultural capital: part of the work of Pierre Bourdieu on the ways that class structures are reproduced through not only economic capital but also cultural capital, that is 'culture that has been "sacralised" [or legitimized] through the recognition conferred by cultural power holders' (Andermahr *et al.* 1997: 38).

Discourse: a term from linguistics and from the work of Michel Foucault (1926–84). It refers to any regulated system of statements (such as 'film reviewing') or language use which has rules, assumptions and conventions – and therefore exclusions. Contemporary uses of the term often replace 'ideology', seen as not sufficiently plural. They also explore how discursive rules, and associated material practices, come to organize and regulate knowledge, and even to produce it, by the power to 'name' and categorize, for example discourses constructing the category 'underclass' in 1990s Britain.

Divorcement: the 1948 result of the anti-trust suit begun in 1938 by the US Supreme Court, against the **vertically intregrated** majors, decreeing that their trade practices constituted a monopoly. They were ordered to 'divorce' or separate their exhibition branches (in the USA) from their production and distribution activities.

Fans: usually characterized as potential fanatics, obsessed and hysterical. Recent work, part of that on audiences or 'consumers' more generally, tries to escape this gendered pathologization, and explores the many ways fans 'rework' the object of their enthusiasm whether those be the meanings of individual films or of stars.

Globalization: a process which renders activities global not national, often simultaneous or instantaneous, and which often involves interdependence. Global processes are often said to have an intimately linked opposite: 'local' ones.

High concept: films from about the 1980s (though *Jaws* is often cited as precursor) characterized by successful pitching at pre-production stage, especially via market research processes, cross-over, simply summarizable product ('*Alien* is *Jaws* in a spaceship') and successful saturation advertising, especially through TV, at the post-production, pre-first-weekend stages.

Hybridity: combination of differences, whether styles, or technologies, or cultural forms.

Identification: the capacity of a viewer to merge imaginatively at least some of another's identity into his or her own. Often implied to be total, unthinking and working only in terms of identities shared by viewer and character.

Identity: a sense of those qualities by virtue of which individuals come to feel that they belong to particular groups, usually according to the main social identities of age, ethnicity, class, disability, gender or sexuality. A hotly debated term in cultural studies as a sense of identity as 'given' and singular erodes under the impact of emphases on 'difference' and the multiple and often contradictory identities most people inhabit.

Ideological: ideologies are sets of ideas which (a) give some account of the social world, usually partial and selective; (b) come to seem 'natural'; (c) are systematically related to the unequal distribution of power in society.

IMAX: a wide-screen camera projection system, first exhibited in 1970. It projects 70 mm film onto a very large screen, whose image fills most of the spectator's field of vision.

Independent: usually defined as small firms with no corporate relationship to a distribution firm or a major studio.

Intertextuality: the many ways in which media and other texts interact with each other, rather than being unique, separate or distinct.

Media imperialism: the spread of media industries following the imperialist conquests of rich and powerful nations. The term points to the inequalities of this 'one-way flow'.

Melodrama: as opposed to its everyday usage (associated with exaggeration), film studies has explored this kind of drama, developing an elaborate language of gesture and spectacle, often heavily polarized, flowing into early cinema but visible in most genres. It is also sometimes used of domestic, especially women's drama films.

Mise-en-scène: literally 'having been put into the scene'; a rather slippery term, often taken to describe the sets, lighting, costume, actors' and camera's movements in a film. Argued here to collapse unhelpfully together the work of cinematographer, production design, actors, and others.

Modernism: innovative artistic movements which ran roughly from the 1920s to the 1970s.

Modernity: a historical phase, inseparable from capitalism, usually theorized as beginning around the eighteenth century, with the French Revolution and other breaks with a feudally hierarchized, deferential past. Some accounts equate it with 'late modernity' or the **post-Fordist** or computer technologized phase from about the 1960s.

MPAA/MPPDA: Motion Picture Association of America/Motion Picture Producers and Distributors of America: trade association or cartel of the major Hollywood studios to coordinate industrial practices and policies and represent the industry.

MPEAA: Motion Pictures Export Association of America: founded 1945 to promote the elimination of trade and other barriers to the 'free flow' of US films and protect US copyrights.

New Hollywood: term most often used of a brief period of film-making in Hollywood, from the 1960s to 1975 which was relatively adventurous in both form and content, alluding to both European art cinema and older Hollywood films.

Package unit films: post-studio films which, instead of being produced on a factory-type line, are each treated as a 'one-off', with a package of stars, crew, director and others brought together for a specific film.

Performance: concept which (along with 'masquerade') draws on study of theatre to emphasize the social constructedness of identity, which is not 'given' but has to be successfully 'performed'.

Post-Fordist: 'Fordism' was coined by the Italian Marxist Gramsci for the kinds of social relations that accompany mass production and assembly line techniques of manufacturing, pioneered by Henry Ford – as in the studio system of film-making. Post-Fordism, by contrast, is said to produce a range of products, to subcontract parts of the production process to a number of firms, and to use new technology for 'just-in-time' production, responsive to consumer demand – as in the package unit production of post-1960 Hollywood.

Postmodernism: a slippery term, often used to refer to cultural styles marked by pastiche, intertextuality, genre blurrings, 'raiding the image bank' of now widely available cultural media forms, and resulting from what postmodern philosophy asserts is the 'death of the grand narratives' of universal explanations of history in terms of progress, reason and so on.

Postmodernity: a way of characterizing late modernity that constructs it as a phase in which consumption, high technologies of simulation and global media results in postmodernist sensibilities.

Post-structuralist: a set of mostly French theories derived from the 'binary' emphases of structural linguistics but going further, both in an emphasis on the importance of broadly 'linguistic' processes (the so-called 'linguistic turn') and in abandoning any sense of verifiable truth, unified subjectivity or referentiality: no shared meanings are possible because everything is understood only through difference.

Product placement: the placing of branded products in a film, often for large sums of money, in such a way as to enhance the products' image.

Psychoanalysis: theory and practice of treating neuroses, founded in the work of Sigmund Freud (1856–1939), and the theories of how unconscious mental processes deemed 'normal' relate to its findings and procedures, especially a reliance on repressed memories.

Public sphere: term normally used of informational, journalistic, 'official-political' public arenas or forms of those arenas to be aimed at as an ideal, by public service broadcasting, for example. The idea of such a 'public sphere' is argued by many postmodernists to be dead, and anyway not worth reviving in its inevitably white, hyper-rationalist, male forms.

Star: a performer in a particular medium whose figure enters into subsidiary forms of circulation, such as fan magazines and TV appearances, the image thus produced feeding back into future performances (based on Ellis 1982).

Structuralist: an approach to critical analysis which emphasizes universal structures underlying the surface differences and apparent randomness of myths, stories, media texts and so on; these structures are often understood as structuring myths around oppositions, such as good/bad, black/white.

Studio system: Hollywood's factory-like method of making films from about 1920s to 1950s; involved with **vertical integration**.

Synergy: the process of combining two separate products so that they 'feed' each other, as in a film and computer game using the same animated characters.

Tie-ins: products which accompany and help publicize the release of a film in mutually beneficial ways.

Utopian: relating to theories of 'utopia' from the Greek *ou topos* = no place and *eu topos* = good place.

Vertical integration: the integration of the levels of production (of films), distribution (of prints) and exhibition or promotion (of movies in cinemas), usually identified with the studio system, though effectively still operating in Hollywood cinema.

Voyeurism (also called 'scopophilia'): term from Freudian psychoanalysis: the pleasure of looking while oneself being unseen. Used in thinking about male pleasure in the ways cinema has 'traditionally' constructed women stars as 'objects of the male gaze'. See Chapter 4 on 'the look'.

BIBLIOGRAPHY

Abel, R. (1999) *The Red Rooster Scare: Making Cinema American, 1900–1910*. Berkeley, CA: University of California Press.

Adorno, T. (1984) *Aesthetic Theory*. London and New York: Routledge and Kegan Paul.

Adorno, T. and Horkheimer, M. (1997[1944]) *Dialectic of Enlightenment*. New York: Verso.

Aitkenhead, D. (1998) Knowing me, knowing you, knowing Nicole Kidman in the nude. It's fame, *Guardian*, 25 September.

Allan, S. (1999) *News Culture*. Buckingham: Open University Press.

Allen, M. (1998) From Bwana devil to Batman Forever: technology in contemporary Hollywood cinema, in S. Neale and M. Smith (eds) *Contemporary Hollywood Cinema*. London: Routledge.

Allen, R. (1998) Home Alone together: Hollywood and the 'family film'. Paper presented to the Hollywood and its Spectators: the Reception of American Films, 1895–1995 Conference, University College, London.

Allen, R. and Gomery, D. (1985) *Film History Theory and Practice*. New York: Alfred A. Knopf.

Andermahr, S., Lovell, T. and Wolkowitz, C. (1997) *A Concise Glossary of Feminist Theory*. London and New York: Arnold.

Anderson, P. (1983) *In the Tracks of Historical Materialism*. London: Verso.

Ang, Ien (1985) *Watching Dallas: Soap Opera and the Melodramatic Imagination*, trans. D. Couling. London: Methuen.

Bakhtin, M. (1984) *Rabelais and his World*. Bloomington, IN: Indiana University Press.

Balio, T. (1993) *Grand Design: Hollywood as a Modern Business Enterprise 1930–1939*. New York: Scribner's.

Balio, T. (1998a) A major presence in all of the world's important markets: the globalisation of Hollywood in the 1990s, in S. Neale and M. Smith (eds) *Contemporary Hollywood Cinema*. London: Routledge.

Balio, T. (1998b) The art film market in the new Hollywood, in G. Nowell-Smith and S. Ricci (eds) *Hollywood and Europe: Economics, Culture, National Identity 1945–1995*. London: British Film Institute.

Barker, M. and Brooks, K. (1998) *Knowing Audiences: Judge Dredd, its Friends, Fans and Foes*. Luton: University of Luton Press.

Barker, M. and Petley, J. (eds) (1997) *Ill Effects: The Media/Violence Debate*. London and New York: Routledge.

Barnouw, E. *et al.* (eds) (1997) *Conglomerates and the Media*. New York: New Press.

Barthes, R. (1977[1968]) 'The death of the author', in R. Barthes *Image, Music, Text*, trans. S. Heath. New York: Hill and Wang.

Baudrillard, J. (1988) Consumer society, in M. Poster (ed.) *Jean Baudrillard: Selected Writings*. Stanford, CA: Stanford University Press.

Baudrillard, J. (1975) *The Mirror of Production*. St. Louis, MO: Telos Press.

Baudrillard, J. (1994[1981]) *Simulacra and Simulation*. Ann Arbor, MI: University of Michigan Press.

Baudry, J-L. (1970) Ideological effects of the basic cinematic apparatus, in P. Rosen (ed.) (1986) *Narrative, Apparatus, Ideology*. New York: Columbia Press.

Baxandall, M. (1972, 1988) *Painting and Experience in Fifteenth Century Italy: A Primer in the Social History of Pictorial Style*. New York: Oxford University Press.

Bazin, A. (1971) The western, or the American film *par excellence*; The evolution of the western, in H. Gray (ed.) *What is Cinema?* vol. 2. Berkeley, CA: University of California Press.

Bazin, A. (1997) *Bazin at Work* (ed. B. Cardullo). London: Routledge.

Beck, U. (1992 [1986]) *Risk Society: Towards New Modernity*. London: Sage.

Becker, H.S. (1982) *Art Worlds*. Berkeley, CA: University of California Press.

Belton, J. (1994) *American Cinema/American Culture*. New York: McGraw-Hill.

Belton, J. (1998a) American cinema and film history, in J. Hill and P. Church-Gibson (eds) *The Oxford Guide to Film Studies*. Oxford and New York: Oxford University Press.

Belton, J. (1998b) The star system and Hollywood, in J. Hill and P. Church-Gibson (eds) *The Oxford Guide to Film Studies*. Oxford and New York: Oxford University Press.

Bennett, T. (1998) *Culture: A Reformer's Science*. London: Sage.

Bennett, T. and Woollacott, J. (1987) *Bond and Beyond: The Political Career of a Popular Hero*. London: Macmillan.

Berger, J. (1972) *Ways of Seeing*. Harmondsworth: Penguin.

Biskind, P. (1998) *Easy Riders, Raging Bulls: How the Sex-Drugs-and-Rock and Roll Generation Saved Hollywood*. London: Bloomsbury.

Blake, A. (1992) Tony Bennett and Janet Woollacott, *Bond and Beyond*, in M. Barker and A. Beezer (eds) *Reading into Cultural Studies*. London and New York: Routledge.

Bloch, E. (1990 [1959]) *The Principle of Hope*. Oxford: Blackwell.

Bloch, E. *et al.* (1977) *Aesthetics and Politics*. London: Verso.

Bogle, D. (1994) *Toms, Coons, Mulattoes, Mammies and Bucks: An Interpretive History of Blacks in American Films*. Oxford: Roundhouse.

Boorman, J. and Donohoe, W. (eds) (1996) *Projections 5: Film-Makers on Film-Making*. London and Boston, MA: Faber and Faber.

Bordwell, D. (1989) *Making Meaning: Inference and Rhetoric in the Interpretation of Cinema*. Cambridge, MA: Harvard University Press.

Bordwell, D. (1996) La nouvelle mission de feuillade: or what was mise-en-scène?, *The Velvet Light Trap*, 37: 23.

Bordwell, D. and Carroll, N. (eds) (1996) *Post-Theory: Reconstructing Film Studies*. Madison, WI and London: University of Wisconsin Press.

Bordwell, D. and Thompson, K. (1997) *Film Art: An Introduction*, 5th edn. New York: McGraw-Hill.

Bordwell, D., Staiger, J. and Thompson, K. (1985) *The Classical Hollywood Cinema: Film Style and Mode of Production to 1960*. London: Routledge & Kegan Paul.

Bourdieu, P. (1984) *Distinction: A Social Critique of the Judgement of Taste*. London: Routledge.

Branston, G. (1995) Viewer, I listened to him . . . voices, masculinity, 'In the line of fire', in P. Kirkham and J. Thumim (eds) *Me Jane: Masculinity, Movies and Women*. London: Lawrence and Wishart.

Branston, G. (2000) Why theory?, in C. Gledhill and L. Williams (eds) *Reinventing Film Studies*. London and New York: Arnold.

Branston, G. and Stafford, R. (1999) *The Media Student's Book*, 2nd edn. London and New York: Routledge.

Briggs, A. and Cobley, P. (eds) (1998) *The Media: An Introduction*. London and New York: Longman.

British Film Institute (1980) *MGM* (Dossier no. 1). London: British Film Institute.

Brooker, P. (1999) *A Concise Glossary of Cultural Theory*. London and New York: Arnold.

Brooker, P. and Brooker, W. (1996) 'Pulpmodernism: Tarantino's affirmative action', in D. Cartmell, I.Q. Hunter, H. Kaye and I. Whelehan (eds) *Pulping Fictions*. London and Chicago: Pluto.

Brunsdon, C. (1997) *Screen Tastes*. London and New York: Routledge.

Bruzzi, S. (1998) *Undressing Cinema Clothing and Identity in the Movies*. London and New York: Routledge.

Buscombe, E. (ed.) (1998) *The BFI Companion to the Western*. London: British Film Institute.

Buscombe, E., Gledhill, C., Lovell, A. and Williams, C. (1992) Psychoanalysis and film, in M. Merck (ed.) *The Sexual Subject: Screen Reader in Sexuality*. London and New York: Routledge.

Butler, J. (1990) *Gender Trouble: Feminism and the Subversion of Identity*. London: Routledge.

Butler, J. (1993) *Bodies that Matter: On the Discursive Limits of Sex*. London: Routledge.

Cameron, D. (2000) *Good to Talk? Living and Working in a Communication Culture*. London: Sage.

Campbell, D. (2000) Trouble in Tinseltown, *Guardian*, 20 January.

Carroll, N. (1982) The future of allusion: Hollywood in the seventies and beyond, *October* 20: 51–78.

Carroll, R. (1999) Filmgoing can ruin your hearing, *Guardian*, 12 August.

Carter, C., Branston, G. and Allan, S. (eds) (1998) *News, Gender and Power*. London and New York: Routledge.

Carter, E. (1998) 'Desire' untamed: Hollywood stars in 1930s Germany. Talk given at Hollywood and its Spectators, Commonwealth Fund Conference, London, January.

Caughie, J. (ed.) (1981) *Theories of Authorship*. London: Routledge.

Chanan, M. (1983) The emergence of an industry, in J. Curran and V. Porter (eds) *British Cinema History*. London: Weidenfeld and Nicolson.

Chanan, M. (1996) *The Dream that Kicks*, 2nd edn. London: Routledge.

Charney, L. and Schwartz, V.R. (eds) (1995) *Cinema and the Invention of Modern Life*. Berkeley, CA: University of California Press.

Christie, I. (1994) *The Last Machine: Early Cinema and the Birth of the Modern World*. London: British Film Institute.

Clark, D. (1995) *Negotiating Hollywood: The Cultural Politics of Actors' Labor*. Minnesota, MN: University of Minneapolis Press.

Collins, J., Radner, H. and Collins, A.P. (eds) (1993) *Film Theory Goes to the Movies*. London and New York: Routledge.

Cook, J. and Lovell, A. (1981) (eds) *Coming to Terms with Hollywood: BFI* (Dossier no. 11). London: British Film Institute.

Cook, P. (1998) No fixed address: the women's picture from *Outrage* to *Blue Steel*, in S. Neale and M. Smith (eds) *Contemporary Hollywood Cinema*. London: Routledge.

Cook, P. and Bernink, M. (eds) (1999) *The Cinema Book*, 2nd edn. London: British Film Institute.

Corner, J. (1998a) *Studying Media: Problems of Theory and Method*. Edinburgh: Edinburgh University Press.

Corner, J. (1998b) 'Seeing is not feeling' letter to *Sight and Sound*. December.

Corrigan, T. (1991) *A Cinema without Walls: Movies and Culture after Vietnam*. New York: Routledge.

Crofts, S. (1998) Authorship and Hollywood, in J. Hill and P. Church-Gibson (eds) *The Oxford Guide to Film Studies*. Oxford and New York: Oxford University Press.

Curran, J. and Porter, V. (1983) (eds) *British Cinema History*. London: Weidenfeld and Nicolson.

Davis, M. (1990) *City of Quartz: Excavating the Future in Los Angeles*. London: Verso.

Di Cillo, T. (1995) *Living in Oblivion and Eating Crow: Notes From a Film Maker's Diary*. London: Faber and Faber.

Donald, J. and Donald, S.H. (2000) The publicness of cinema, in C. Gledhill and L. Williams (eds) *Reinventing Film Studies*. London: Arnold.

Dunant, S. (ed.) (1994) *The War of the Words: The Political Correctness Debate*. London: Virago.

Durant, A. (2000) What future for interpretive work in Film and Media Studies? *Screen*, 41(1): spring.

During, S. (1997) Popular culture on a global scale: a challenge for cultural studies?, in H. Mackay and T. O'Sullivan (eds) *The Media Reader: Continuity and Transformation*. London: Sage with The Open University.

Dyer, R. (1973) Entertainment and Utopia, in R. Dyer (1992) *Only Entertainment*. London: Routledge.

Dyer, R. (1979) *Stars*. London: British Film Institute.

Dyer, R. (1986) *Heavenly Bodies: Film Stars and Society*. New York: St Martin's Press.

Dyer, R. (1991) Appearance on *The Late Show* (March), cited in J. Nelmes (ed.) (1999) *An Introduction to Film Studies*. London and New York: Routledge.

Dyer, R. (1993) *The Matter of Images: Essays on Representations*. London and New York: Routledge.

Dyer, R. (1997) *White*. London and New York: Routledge.

Dyer, R. (1998a) *Stars*, 2nd edn. London: British Film Institute.

Dyer, R. (1998b) *Seven*. London: British Film Institute Film Classics.

Dyer, R. (1998c) Introduction to Film Studies, in J. Hill and P. Church-Gibson (eds) *The Oxford Guide to Film Studies*. Oxford and New York: Oxford University Press.

Eagleton, T. (1983) *Literary Theory: An Introduction*. Oxford: Basil Blackwell.

Eckert, C. (1991[1957]) The Carole Lombard in Macy's Window, in C. Gledhill (ed.) *Stardom: Industry of Desire*. London and New York: Routledge.

Eco, U. (1990) *The Limits of Interpretation*. Bloomington, IN: Indiana University Press.

Ellis, J. (1982, 1992) *Visible Fictions: Cinema, Television, Video*. London: Routledge.

Elsaesser, T. (1972) Tales of sound and fury: observations on the family melodrama, *Monogram*, 4.

Engels, F. (1969[1880]) Socialism: utopian and scientific, in K. Marx and F. Engels, *Selected Works*, vol. 3. Moscow: Progress Publishers.

Enzenberger, H.M. (1974) *The Consciousness Industry: On Literature, Politics and Media*. New York: Seabury Press.

Ettedgui, P. (ed.) (1998) *Cinematography Screencraft*. Crans, Switzerland: RotoVision.

Evans, J. (1998) Disability: feeble monsters: 'making up' disabled people, in A. Briggs and P. Cobley (eds) *The Media: An Introduction*. London and New York: Longman.

Ewen, S. and Ewen, E. (1982) *Channels of Desire*. New York: McGraw-Hill.

Fleming, C. (1998) *High Concept: Don Simpson and the Hollywood Culture of Excess*. London: Bloomsbury.

Foucault, M. (1969) What is an author?, *Screen* 20(1): 13–29.

Francke, L. (1994) *Script Girls: Women Screenwriting in Hollywood*. London: Routledge.

Friedberg, A. (1993) *Window Shopping: Cinema and the Postmodern*. Berkeley, CA: University of California Press.

Frith, S. (1994) Political correctness, *Critical Quarterly*, 35(4).

Frith, S. (1996) Music and identity, in S. Hall and P. du Gay (eds) *Questions of Identity*. London: Sage.

Gabler, N. (1988) *An Empire of their Own: How the Jews Invented Hollywood*. London: W.H. Allen.

Gaines, J. (1988) White privilege and looking relations: race and gender in feminist film theory, *Screen (The Last Special Issue on Race)*, 29(4): 12–27.

Gaines, J. (1992a) *Contested Culture: The Image, the Voice, and the Law*. London: British Film Institute.

Gaines, J. (ed.) (1992b) *Classical Hollywood Narrative: The Paradigm Wars*. Durham, NC: Duke University Press.

Gaines, J. (2000) Dream/factory, in C. Gledhill and L. Williams (eds) *Reinventing Film Studies*. London and New York: Arnold.

Gaines, J. and Herzog, C. (eds) (1990) *Fabrications Costume and the Female Body*. London and New York: Routledge.

Gamman, L. and Makinen, M. (1994) *Female Fetishism: A New Look*. London: Lawrence and Wishart.

Gamman, L. and Marshment, M. (eds) (1988) *The Female Gaze: Women as Viewers of Popular Culture*. London: The Women's Press.

Gandhy, B. and Thomas, R. (1991) Three Indian film stars, in C. Gledhill (ed.) *Stardom: Industry of Desire*. London and New York: Routledge.

Garnham, N. (1987) Concepts of culture: public policy and the cultural industries, *Cultural Studies* 1(1): 23–37.

Garnham, N. (1990) *Capitalism and Communication: Global Culture and the Economics of Information*. London: Sage.

Geraghty, C. (1998) 'Audience' and 'ethnography': questions of practice, in C. Geraghty and D. Lusted (eds) (1998) *The Television Studies Book*. London and New York: Arnold.

Geraghty, C. (2000) Understanding stars: questions of texts, bodies and performance, in C. Gledhill and L. Williams (eds) *Reinventing Film Studies*. London: Arnold.

Giddens, A. (1991) *Modernity and Self-Identity: Self and Society in the Late Modern Age*. Cambridge: Polity.

Gledhill, C. (ed.) (1987) *Home is Where the Heart is*. London: British Film Institute.

Gledhill, C. (1988) Pleasurable negotiations, in E.D. Pribram (ed.) *Female Spectators: Looking at Film and Television*. London and New York: Verso.

Gledhill, C. (ed.) (1991) *Stardom: Industry of Desire*. London and New York: Routledge.

Gledhill, C. (1992) Between melodrama and realism: Anthony Asquith's *Underground* and Charles Vidor's *The Crowd*, in J. Gaines (ed.) *Classical Hollywood Narrative: The Paradigm Wars*. Durham, NC: Duke University Press.

Gledhill, C. (1995) Women reading men, in P. Kirkham and J. Thumim (eds) *Me Jane: Masculinity, Movies and Women*. London: Lawrence and Wishart.

Gledhill, C. and Williams, L. (eds) (2000) *Reinventing Film Studies*. London: Arnold.

Goffmann, E. (1959) *The Performance of Self in Everyday Life*. New York: Anchor.

Gomery, D. (1991) Methods for the study of the history of broadcasting and mass communication, *Film and History*, 21(2–3): 55–63.

Gomery, D. (1992) *Shared Pleasures: A History of Movie Presentation in the United States*. London: British Film Institute.

Gomery, D. (1996a) Transformation of the Hollywood system, in G. Nowell-Smith (ed.) *The Oxford Encyclopaedia of Film History*. Oxford: Oxford University Press.

Gomery, D. (1996b) 'Towards a new media economics', in D. Bordwell and N. Carroll (eds) *Post-Theory: Reconstructing Film Studies*. Madison, WI and London: University of Wisconsin Press.

Gomery, D. (1998a) Hollywood as industry, in J. Hill and P. Church-Gibson (eds) *The Oxford Guide to Film Studies*. Oxford and New York: Oxford University Press.

Gomery, D. (1998b) Hollywood corporate business practice and periodizing contemporary film history, in S. Neale and M. Smith (eds) *Contemporary Hollywood Cinema*. London: Routledge.

Goodridge, M. (1998) International star chart, *Screen International*, 5–10 September.

Goodridge, M. (1999) Power 2000, *Screen International*, 10 December.

Goodwin, C. (1998) On target for equality? *Independent*, 5 July.

Gorbman, C. (1987) *Unheard Melodies: Narrative Film Music*. Bloomingdale, IN: Indiana University Press.

Gordon, B. (1999) *Hollywood Exile: Or How I Learned to Love the Blacklist*. Austin, TX: University of Texas Press.

Grant, C. (2000) www.auteur.com? *Screen*, 41(1): spring.

Grant, L. (1998) Boys only in the big picture, *Guardian*, 21 April.

Grantham, B. (2000) *'Some Big Bourgeois Brothel': Contexts for France's Culture Wars with Hollywood*. Luton: University of Luton Press.

Griffith, R. and Mayer, A. (1971) *The Movies*. London and New York: Spring Books.

Gripsrud, J. (1998) Film audiences, in J. Hill and P. Church-Gibson (eds) *The Oxford Guide to Film Studies*. Oxford and New York: Oxford University Press.

Gunning, T. (1990) The cinema of attractions: early film, its spectator and the avant-garde, in T. Elsaesser with A. Barker (eds) *Early Cinema: Space, Frame, Narrative*. London: British Film Institute.

Gunning, T. (1995) Tracing the individual body: photography and early cinema, in L. Charney and V.R. Schwartz (eds) *Cinema and the Invention of Modern Life*. Berkeley, CA: University of California Press.

Habermas, J. (1985 [1981]) Modernity – an incomplete project, in H. Foster (ed.) *Postmodern Culture*. London: Pluto.

Habermas, J. (1989) *The Structural Transformation of the Public Sphere: An Enquiry into a Category of Bourgeois Society*. Cambridge: Polity.

Hall, S. (1996) Introduction: who needs identity?, in S. Hall and P. du Gay (eds) *Questions of Cultural Identity*. London: Sage.

Hall, S. (ed.) (1997) *Representation: Cultural Representation and Signifying Practices*. London: Sage.

Hansen, M.B. (1991) Pleasure, ambivalence, identification: Valentino and female spectatorship, in C. Gledhill (ed.) *Stardom: Industry of Desire*. London and New York: Routledge.

Hansen, M.B. (1995) America, Paris, the Alps: Kracauer (and Benjamin) on Cinema and Modernity, in L. Charney and V.R. Schwartz (eds) *Cinema and the Invention of Modern Life*. Berkeley, CA: University of California Press.

Hansen, M.B. (2000) The mass production of the senses: classical cinema as vernacular modernism, in C. Gledhill and L. Williams (eds) *Reinventing Film Studies*. London and New York: Arnold.

Haskell, M. (1975) *From Reverence to Rape: The Treatment of Women in the Movies*. London: New English Library.

Hattenstone, S. (1999) Master of the mouse: profile of Michael Eisner, *Guardian*, 10 April.

Haylett, A. (2000) 'This is about us, this is our film!' Personal and popular discourses of 'underclass', in S. Munt (ed.) *Cultural Studies and the Working Class: Subject to Change*. London and New York: Cassell.

Hill, J. (1998) Film and postmodernism, in J. Hill and P. Church-Gibson (eds) *The Oxford Guide to Film Studies*. Oxford and New York: Oxford University Press.

Hill, J. (1999) *British Cinema in the 1980s*. Oxford: Oxford University Press.

Hill, J. and Church-Gibson, P. (eds) (1998) *The Oxford Guide to Film Studies*. Oxford and New York: Oxford University Press.

Hillier, J. (1992) *The New Hollywood*. London: Studio Vista.

Hochschild, A. (1983) *The Managed Heart: The Commercialisation of Human Feeling*. Berkeley, CA: University of California Press.

Hochschild, A. (1997) *The Time Bind: When Work becomes Home and Home Becomes Work*. New York: Metropolitan Books/Henry Holt.

Holland, P. (1998) The politics of the smile: 'soft news' and the sexualisation of the popular press, in C. Carter, G. Branston and S. Allan (eds) *News, Gender and Power*. London and New York: Routledge.

Hollows, J. (1995) Mass culture theory and political economy, in J. Hollows and M. Jancovitch (eds) *Approaches to Popular Film*. Manchester and New York: Manchester University Press.

Hollows, J. and Jancovich, M. (eds) (1995) *Approaches to Popular Film*. Manchester and New York: Manchester University Press.

Jameson, F. (1990) *Signatures of the Visible*. London: Routledge.

Jameson, F. (1991) *Postmodernism, or, The Cultural Logic of Late Capitalism*. London and New York: Verso.

Jay, M. (1992) Scopic regimes of modernity, in S. Lash and P. Friedman (eds) *Modernity and Identity*. London: Institute of Contemporary Arts.

Jeancolas, J-P. (1998) From the Blum-Bymes Agreement to the GATT affair, in G. Nowell-Smith and S. Ricci (eds) *Hollywood and Europe: Economics Culture, National Identity 1945–1995*. London: British Film Institute.

Jeffords, S. (1994) *Hard Bodies: Hollywood Masculinity in the Reagan Era.* New Brunswick, NJ: Rutgers University Press.

Jenkins, H. (1995) *Historical Poetics*, in J. Hollows and M. Jancovich (eds) *Approaches to Popular Film.* Manchester and New York: Manchester University Press.

Jenkins, H. (2000[1992]) 'In my weekend-only world . . .': reconsidering fandom, in R. Stam and T. Miller (eds) *Film and Theory: An Anthology.* Oxford and Cambridge, MA: Blackwell.

Kael, P. (1970) Trash, art and the movies, in P. Kael, *Going Steady.* Boston, MA: Little, Brown.

Kane, P. (1997) Half of Hollywood has fallen in love with this sweet little thing. The other half is terrified of her, *Guardian*, 17 January.

Kaplan, E.A. (ed.) (1988) *Postmodernism and its Discontents: Theories, Practices.* London: Verso.

Kaplan, E.A. (1998) Classical Hollywood film and melodrama, in J. Hill and P. Church-Gibson (eds) *The Oxford Guide to Film Studies.* Oxford and New York: Oxford University Press.

Kapsis, R.E. (1992) *Hitchcock: The Making of a Reputation.* London and Chicago: University of Chicago Press.

Kellner, D., Liebowitz, F. and Ryan, M. (1984) *Bladerunner*: a diagnostic critique, *Jump Cut*, 29.

Kerr, P. (ed.) (1986) *The Hollywood Film Industry.* London and New York: Routledge and Kegan Paul and the British Film Institute.

Kinder, M. (1996) Spain after Franco, in G. Nowell-Smith (ed.) *The Oxford Encyclopaedia of Film History.* Oxford: Oxford University Press.

King, B. (1985) Articulating stardom, *Screen*, 26(5): 27–50.

King, J. (1990) *Magic Reels: A History of Cinema in Latin America.* London: Verso.

King, N. and Miller, T. (1999) Authorship and Cinema, in P. Cook and M. Bernink (eds) *The Cinema Book*, 2nd edn. London: British Film Institute.

Kipnis, L. (1998a) Pornography, in J. Hill and P. Church-Gibson (eds) *The Oxford Guide to Film Studies.* Oxford and New York: Oxford University Press.

Kipnis, L. (1998b) Film and changing technologies, in J. Hill and P. Church-Gibson (eds) *The Oxford Guide to Film Studies.* Oxford and New York: Oxford University Press.

Kitzinger, J. (1998) The gender-politics of news production: silenced voices and false memories, in C. Carter, G. Branston and S. Allan (eds) *News, Gender and Power.* London and New York: Routledge.

Kolker, R. (1998) The film text and film form, in J. Hill and P. Church-Gibson (eds) *The Oxford Guide to Film Studies.* Oxford and New York: Oxford University Press.

Kramer, P. (1998a) Post-classical Hollywood, in J. Hill and P. Church-Gibson (eds) *The Oxford Guide to Film Studies.* Oxford and New York: Oxford University Press.

Kramer, P. (1998b) Would you take your child to see this film? The cultural and social work of the family-adventure movie, in S. Neale and M. Smith (eds) *Contemporary Hollywood Cinema*. London: Routledge.

Kuhn, A. and Street, S. (eds) (1999) *Journal of Popular British Cinema vol. 2: Audiences and Reception in Britain*. Trowbridge: Flicks Books.

Lacey, J. (1999) Seeing through happiness: Hollywood musicals and the construction of the American Dream in Liverpool in the 1950s, in A. Kuhn and S. Street (eds) *Journal of Popular British Cinema vol. 2: Audiences and Reception in Britain*. Trowbridge: Flicks Books.

LaPlace, M. (1987) Producing and consuming the woman's film, in C. Gledhill (ed.) *Home is Where the Heart is*. London: British Film Institute.

Lawson, M. (1998) As star-struck as ever, *Guardian*, 21 November.

Lovell, A. and Kramer, P. (eds) (2000) *Screenacting*. London: Routledge.

Lovell, T. (1980) *Pictures of Reality: Aesthetics, Politics and Pleasure*. London: British Film Institute.

Macdonald, M. (1995) *Representing Women: Myths of Femininity in the Popular Media*. London and New York: Arnold.

MacCabe, C. (1999) Bayonets in paradise, *Sight and Sound*, February.

McGuigan, J. (1999) *Modernity and Postmodern Culture*. Buckingham: Open University Press.

Mackay, H. and O'Sullivan, T. (eds) (1999) *The Media Reader: Continuity and Transformation*. London: Sage with The Open University.

Mckee, A. (1998) Identity crisis, *International Journal of Cultural Studies*, 1(3): 425–31.

McLaughlin, L. (1998) Gender, privacy and publicity in 'media event space', in C. Carter, G. Branston and S. Allan (eds) *News, Gender and Power*. London and New York: Routledge.

Maltby, R. (1996) 'A brief romantic interlude': Dick and Jane go to $3^{1}/_{2}$ seconds of the classical hollywood cinema, in D. Bordwell and N. Carroll (eds) *Post-Theory: Reconstructing Film Studies*. Madison, WI and London: University of Wisconsin Press.

Maltby, R. and Craven, I. (1995) *Hollywood Cinema*. Oxford: Blackwell.

Marcuse, H. (1978) *The Aesthetic Dimension*. Boston, MA: Beacon Press.

Mathews, T.D. (1998) See the movie. Ogle the star, *Guardian*, 27 November.

Mattelart, A., Delcourt, X. and Mattelart, M. (1984) *International Image Markets: In Search of an Alternative Perspective*. London: Comedia.

Medhurst, A. (1991) On *Brief Encounter*, *Screen*, 32(2): 196–205.

Medhurst, A. (1998a) Mapping this book, in A. Medhurst and S.R. Munt (eds) *Lesbian and Gay Studies: A Critical Introduction*. London: Cassell.

Medhurst, A. (1998b) Camp, in A. Medhurst and S.R. Munt (eds) *Lesbian and Gay Studies: A Critical Introduction*. London: Cassell.

Medhurst, A. (1998c) The big tease, *Sight and Sound*, July.

Medhurst, A. (1999) Day for Night, *Sight and Sound*, June.

Medhurst, A. (2000) If anywhere: class identifications and cultural studies academics, in S. Munt (ed.) *Cultural Studies and the Working Class: Subject to Change*. London and New York: Cassell.

Medhurst, A. and Munt, S.R. (eds) (1998) *Lesbian and Gay Studies: A Critical Introduction*. London: Cassell.

Medved, M. (1993) *Hollywood vs. America*. London: HarperCollins.

Mellen, J. (1974) *Women and their Sexuality in the New Film*. New York: Dell.

Merck, M. (ed.) (1992) *The Sexual Subject: Screen Reader in Sexuality*. London and New York: Routledge.

Metz, C. (1982) *The Imaginary Signifier: Psychoanalysis and the Cinema*. Bloomington, IN: Indiana University Press.

Miller, T. (1998) Hollywood and the world, in J. Hill and P. Church-Gibson (eds) *The Oxford Guide to Film Studies*, Oxford and New York: Oxford University Press.

Miller, T. (2000) Class and the culture industries, in R. Stam and T. Miller (eds) *Film and Theory: An Anthology*. Oxford and Cambridge, MA: Blackwell.

Modleski, T. (1988) *The Women Who Knew Too Much*. New York: Methuen.

Morley, D. (1996) Postmodernism: the rough guide, in J. Curran, D. Morley and V. Walkerdine (eds) *Cultural Studies and Communications*. London: Arnold.

Mulvey, L. (1981) Afterthoughts on 'Visual pleasure and narrative cinema' inspired by *Duel in the Sun, Framework*, 15/16/17, summer.

Mulvey, L. (1975/1989) Visual pleasure and narrative cinema, *Screen* 1975, reprinted in L. Mulvey (ed.) (1989) *Visual and Other Pleasures*. London: Macmillan.

Mulvey, L. and Jimenez, M. (1989) The spectacle is vulnerable: Miss World 1970, in L. Mulvey (ed.) *Visual and Other Pleasures*. London: Macmillan.

Munt, S. (ed.) (2000) *Cultural Studies and the Working Class: Subject to Change*. London and New York: Cassell.

Neale, S. (1976) New Hollywood cinema, *Screen*, 17(2): 117–22.

Neale, S. (1985) *Cinema and Technology: Image, Sound, Colour*. London: British Film Institute/Macmillan.

Neale, S. (1990a) You've got to be fucking kidding!, in A. Kuhn (ed.) *Alien Zone*. London: Verso.

Neale, S. (1990b) Questions of genre, *Screen*, 31(1).

Neale, S. (2000) *Genre and Hollywood*. London: Routledge.

Neale, S. and Smith, M. (eds) (1998) *Contemporary Hollywood Cinema*. London: Routledge.

Nelmes, J. (ed.) (1999) *An Introduction to Film Studies*. London and New York: Routledge.

Nichols, B. (1992) Form wars: the political unconscious of formalist theory', in J. Gaines (ed.) *Hollywood Narrative: The Paradigm Wars*. Durham, NC: Duke University Press.

Nielsen, M. (1990[1983]) Towards a workers' history of the US film industry, in M. Alvarado and J.O. Thompson (eds) *The Media Reader*. London: British Film Institute.

Nowell-Smith, G. (ed.) (1996) *The Oxford Encyclopaedia of Film History*. Oxford: Oxford University Press.

Nowell-Smith, G. (2000) How films mean, or from aesthetics to semiotics and halfway back again, in C. Gledhill and L. Williams (eds) *Reinventing Film Studies*. London and New York: Arnold.

Nowell-Smith, G. and Ricci, S. (eds) (1998) *Hollywood and Europe: Economics, Culture, National Identity 1945–1995*. London: British Film Institute.

O'Sullivan, T. and Jewkes, Y. (eds) (1997) *The Media Studies Reader*. London: Arnold.

Paterson, P. and Farber, M. (1976) The power and the glory, *Film Comment*, May–June.

Perkins, T. (2000) Who (and what) is it for?, in C. Gledhill and L. Williams (eds) *Reinventing Film Studies*. London and New York: Arnold.

Petro, P. (2000) Mass culture and the feminine: the 'place' of television in Film Studies, in R. Stam and T. Miller (eds) *Film and Theory: An Anthology*. Oxford: Blackwell.

Pfeil, F. (1988) Potholders and subincisions, in E.A. Kaplan (ed.) *Postmodernism and its Discontents: Theories and Practices*. London: Verso.

Phillips, J. (1984) *You'll Never Eat Lunch in This Town Again*. London: Mandarin.

Pierson, M. (1999) CGI effects in Hollywood science fiction cinema 1989–95: the wonder years, *Screen*, 40(2): 158–72.

Pines, J. (ed.) (1992) *Black and White in Colour*. London: British Film Institute.

Porter, V. and Harper, S. (1998) The reception of American films in Great Britain during the 1950s. Paper presented to Hollywood and its Spectators Conference, London.

Pribram, E.D. (ed.) (1988) *Female Spectators: Looking at Film and Television*. London and New York: Verso.

Propp, V. (1975) *The Morphology of the Folk Tale*. Austin, TX: University of Texas Press.

Pumphrey, M. (1984) The flapper, the housewife and the making of modernity, *Cultural Studies*, 1(2).

Rebello, S. (1990) *Alfred Hitchcock and the Making of 'Psycho'*. New York: Dembner Books.

Rich, B.R. (2000) Days of reckoning: review of Bernard Gordon, *Hollywood Exile or How I Learned to Love the Blacklist*, *Sight and Sound*, February.

Riding, A. (1998) Titanic: the rough guide, *Guardian*, 27 April.

Romney, J. (1997) Million-dollar graffiti: notes from the digital domain, in J. Romney, *Short Orders: Film Writing*. London: Serpent's Tail.

Rosen, M. (1973) *Popcorn Venus: Women, Movies and the American Dream*. New York: Coward McCann and Geoghegan.

Rosenbaum, J. (1980) *Moving Places: A Life at the Movies*. New York: Harper and Row.

Rosenbaum, J. (1991) Guilty by omission, *Film Comment*, 27(5).

Rosenbaum, J. (1999) *Hell on Wheels: Taxi Driver* http: //www.chireader.com/movies/archives/.html

Rushdie, S. (1992[1983]) Attenborough's *Gandhi*, in S. Rushdie, *Imaginary Homelands: Essays and Criticism 1981–1991*. London: Granta/Penguin.

Russo, V. (1981) *The Celluloid Closet: Homosexuality in the Movies*. New York: Harper and Row.

Salamon, J. (1992) *The Devil's Candy: The Bonfire of the Vanities Goes to Hollywood*. London: Jonathan Cape.

Sartelle, J. (1996) Dreams and nightmare in the Hollywood blockbuster', in G. Nowell-Smith (ed.) *The Oxford Encyclopaedia of Film History*. Oxford: Oxford University Press.

Schatz, T. (1981) *Hollywood Genres: Formulas, Filmmaking, and the Studio System*. Philadelphia, PA: Temple University Press.

Schatz, T. (1993) The new Hollywood, in J. Collins, H. Radner and A.P. Collins (eds) *Film Theory Goes to the Movies*. London and New York: Routledge.

Schatz, T. (1997) The return of the Hollywood studio system, in E. Barnouw *et al. Conglomerates and the Media*. New York: New Press.

Schiller, H. (1997) Not yet the post-imperialist era, in H. O'Sullivan and Y. Jewkes (eds) *The Media Studies Reader*. London: Arnold.

Schlesinger, P., Dobash, R.E., Dobash, R.P. and Weaver, C.K. (1992) *Women Viewing Violence*. London: British Film Institute.

Sconce, J. (1995) 'Trashing' the academy: taste, excess and an emerging politics of cinematic style, *Screen* 36(4): 371–93.

Sergi, G. (1998) A cry in the dark: the role of post-classical film sound, in S. Neale and M. Smith (eds) *Contemporary Hollywood Cinema*. London: Routledge.

Shohat, E. and Stam, R. (1994) *Unthinking Eurocentrism: Multiculturalism and the Media*. London: Routledge.

Silverstone, R. (1999) *Why Study the Media?* London and Thousand Oaks, CA: Sage.

Singer, B. (1995) Manhattan nickelodeons: new data on audiences and exhibitors, *Cinema Journal*, 34(5): 5–35.

Sivanandan, A. (1990) *Communities of Resistance: Writings on Black Struggles for Socialism*. London: Verso.

Sklar, R. (1975) *Movie-Made America: A Cultural History of American Movies*. New York: Random House.

Slater, D. (1997) *Consumer Culture and Modernity*. Cambridge: Polity.

Smith, A. (2000) Marketing mouse and duck: review of *Hollywood Cartoons: American Animation in its Golden Age*, by M. Barrier, Oxford University Press, Times Higher Educational Supplement, 14 January.

Smith, M. (1995) *Engaging Characters: Fiction, Emotion and the Cinema*. Oxford: Clarendon.

Smith, M. (1998) Theses on the philosophy of Hollywood history, in S. Neale and M. Smith (eds) *An Introduction to Film Studies*. London and New York: Routledge.

Soper, K. (1991) Postmodernism, subjectivity and the question of value, *New Left Review*, summer.

Spoto, D. (1983) *The Dark Side of Genius: The Life of Alfred Hitchcock*. Boston, MA: Little, Brown and Company.

Stacey, J. (1994) *Star-Gazing: Hollywood Cinema and Female Spectatorship*. London: Routledge.

Staiger, J. (1986) Mass-produced photo plays: economic and signifying practices in the first years of Hollywood, in P. Kerr (ed.) *The Hollywood Film Industry*. London and New York: Routledge and Kegan Paul and the British Film Institute.

Staiger, J. (1992) *Interpreting Films: Studies in the Historical Reception of American Cinema*. Princeton, NJ: Princeton University Press.

Stam, R. (2000) Introduction to 'the author', in R. Stam and T. Miller (eds) *Film and Theory: An Anthology*. Oxford and Cambridge, MA: Blackwell.

Stam, R. and Miller, T. (eds) (2000) *Film and Theory: An Anthology*. Oxford and Cambridge, MA: Blackwell.

Steedman, C. (1986) *Landscape for a Good Woman*. London: Virago.

Strinati, D. (1995) *An Introduction to Theories of Popular Culture*. London: Routledge.

Tasker, Y. (1993) *Spectacular Bodies: Gender, Genre and the Action Cinema*. New York: Routledge.

Tasker, Y. (1998) *Working Girls: Gender and Sexuality in Popular Cinema*. London and New York: Routledge.

Tasker, Y. (1999) Bigger than life, *Sight and Sound*, May.

Taylor, H. (1989) *Scarlett's Women: Gone with the Wind and its Female Fans*. London: Virago.

Taylor, J.R. (1978) *Hitch: The Life and Work of Alfred Hitchcock*. London: Faber and Faber.

Thompson, J.B. (1995) *The Media and Modernity: A Social Theory of the Media*. Cambridge: Polity.

Thompson, K. (1985) *Exporting Entertainment: America in the World Film Market 1907–1934*. London: British Film Institute.

Thomson, D. (1995) *A Biographical Dictionary of Film*. London: André Deutsch.

Thornham, S. (1997) *Passionate Detachments: An Introduction to Feminist Film Theory*. London and New York: Arnold.

Tudor, A. (1999) *Decoding Culture: Theory and Methods in Cultural Studies*. London and Thousand Oaks, CA: Sage.

Uricchio, W. (1996) The First World War and the crisis in Europe, in G. Nowell-Smith (ed.) *The Oxford Encyclopaedia of Film History*. Oxford: Oxford University Press.

Vasey, R. (1996) The world-wide spread of cinema, in G. Nowell-Smith (ed.) *The Oxford Encyclopaedia of Film History*. Oxford: Oxford University Press.

Vincendeau, G. (ed.) (1995) *Encyclopaedia of European Cinema*. London: Cassell.

Vincendeau, G. (1998) 'Brigitte Bardot', in J. Hill and P. Church-Gibson (eds) *The Oxford Guide to Film Studies*. Oxford and New York: Oxford University Press.

Wallace, N.T., Seigerman, A. and Holbrook, M.B. (1993) The role of actors and actresses in the success of films: how much is a movie star worth? *Journal of Cultural Economics*, 17(1): 1–27.

Wasko, J. (1994) *Hollywood in the Information Age: Beyond the Silver Screen*. London: Polity.

Wasko, J. (forthcoming) *Understanding Disney*. London: Polity.

Watney, S. (1998) Lesbian and gay studies in the age of AIDS, in A. Medhurst and S.R. Munt (eds) *Lesbian and Gay Studies: A Critical Introduction*. London: Cassell.

Weiss, A. (1992) *Vampires and Violets: Lesbians in the Cinema*. London: Jonathan Cape.

Willemen, P. (1971) Distanciation and Douglas Sirk, *Screen*, 12(2): 63–7.

Willemen, P. and Pines, J. (eds) (1998) *The Essential Framework: Classic Film and TV Essays*. London: Epigraph.

Williams, C. (1994) Debate: after the classic, the classical and ideology: the differences of realism, *Screen*, 35(3).

Williams, L. (1988) Feminist film theory: *Mildred Pierce* and the Second World War, in E.D. Pribram (ed.) *Female Spectators: Looking at Film and Television*. London and New York: Verso.

Williams, L. (1990) *Hard Core: Power, Pleasure and the 'Frenzy of the Visible'*. London: Pandora Press.

Williams, L. (1994) 'Learning to scream', *Sight and Sound*, 15–17 December.

Williams, L. (1996) Sex and sensation, in G. Nowell-Smith (ed.) *The Oxford Encyclopaedia of Film History*. Oxford: Oxford University Press.

Williams, L. (2000) Discipline and fun: *Psycho* and postmodern cinema, in C. Gledhill and L. Williams (eds) *Reinventing Film Studies*. London and New York: Arnold.

Williams R. (1965) *The Long Revolution*. London: Chatto and Windus.

Williams, R. (1983) British film history: new perspectives, in J. Curran and V. Porter (eds) *British Cinema History*. London: Weidenfeld and Nicolson.

Williamson, J. (1993) *Deadline at Dawn*. London: Marion Boyars.

Willis, S. (1993) Hardware and hard bodies: what do women want? A reading of 'Thelma and Louise', in J. Collins, H. Radner and A. Preacher-Collins (eds) *Film Theory Goes to the Movies*. London: Routledge.

Wollen, P. (1998) Tinsel and realism, in G. Nowell-Smith and S. Ricci (eds) *Hollywood and Europe: Economics, Culture, National Identity 1945–1995*. London: British Film Institute.

Wollen, T. and Hayward, P. (eds) (1993) *Future Visions: New Technologies of the Screen*. London: British Film Institute.

Wyatt, J. (1994) *High Concept: Movies and Marketing in Hollywood*. Austin, TX: University of Texas Press.

Wyatt, J. (1996) Economic constraints/economic opportunities: Robert Altman as *auteur*, *Velvet Light Trap*, 38: 51–67.

Young, L. (1996) *Fear of the Dark*. London and New York: Routledge.

INDEX

ETHNIC MINORITIES AND THE MEDIA

Simon Cottle (Ed.)

- What are the latest developments in the production, representation and reception of media output produced by, for or about ethnic minorities?
- What informs the questions which media researchers ask and pursue when examining the mass media and ethnic minorities?
- What are the principal forces of change currently shaping the field?

There are few media issues more pressing, or potentially more consequential, than the representation of ethnic minorities. This authoritative text presents some of the latest findings of leading international researchers in an accessible and well-structured way. *Ethnic Minorities and the Media* opens with an introductory essay that maps recent approaches to the field. The book is then divided into three main sections covering:

- changing media representations
- changing contexts of production
- changing cultures of identity.

Each chapter is written by a leading international researcher who has contributed new findings or ways of thinking about media and 'race'. The authors present their work in an accessible way for undergraduate students, making explicit where it differs from or takes forward the findings of the previous studies in the field. Throughout the book, theoretical approaches are contextualized with reference to actual media institutions, professional practices, media representations and/or audiences.

For undergraduates, postgraduates or professionals studying the media or taking courses in mass communications, cultural studies, or sociology of 'race' and ethnicity, this book offers an up-to-date and accessible overview of the latest thinking in this fast-moving field.

Contents

264pp   0 335 20270 5 (paperback)   0 335 20271 3 (hardback)

MODERNITY AND POSTMODERN CULTURE

Jim McGuigan

- What is postmodern culture?
- Do modern values still matter?
- Why is everyday life now apparently more liberated than in the past yet, at the same time, strangely disconcerting?

Modernity and Postmodern Culture is a critical introduction to claims concerning the postmodernization of culture and society. Contemporary culture may be 'postmodern' in the sense of fluidity of meaning, changing power relations and commodification in art, entertainment and everyday life, but modernity persists in the dynamics of capitalist civilization, albeit in an increasingly reflexive mode characterized by widespread uncertainty about social existence, progress and rationality.

The theories of Baudrillard, Beck, Castells, Giddens, Habermas, Haraway, Jameson, Lyotard and others on the contemporary scene are discussed, and specific issues concerning architecture, theme parks, screen culture, science, technology and the environment are examined. Jim McGuigan argues that there have been tensions between instrumental and critical reason throughout the history of modernity that are still being played out. He questions the irrationalist tendencies and the accommodative attitude to prevailing conditions of much postmodern thought, and insists upon the enduring relevance of the Enlightenment tradition to social and cultural analysis.

Contents

192pp   0 335 19915 1 (paperback)   0 335 19916 X (hardback)

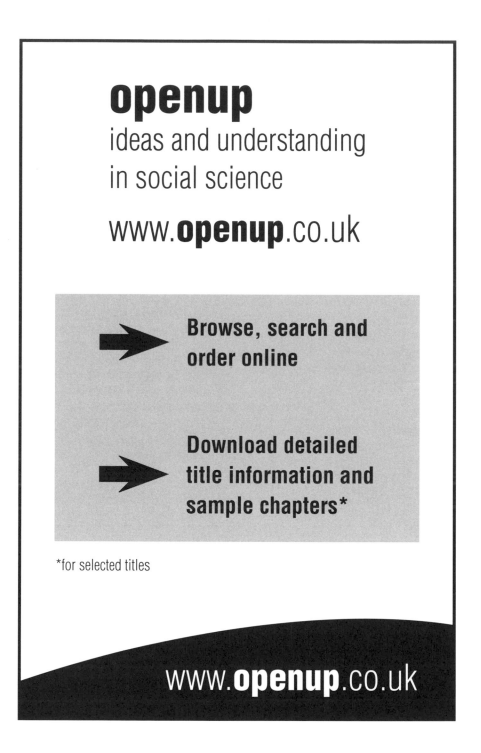